The Handbook of African American Literature

Florida A&M University, Tallahassee
Florida Atlantic University, Boca Raton
Florida Gulf Coast University, Ft. Myers
Florida International University, Miami
Florida State University, Tallahassee
University of Central Florida, Orlando
University of Florida, Gainesville
University of North Florida, Jacksonville
University of South Florida, Tampa
University of West Florida, Pensacola

The Handbook
of African American
Literature

Hazel Arnett Ervin

University Press of Florida

Gainesville · Tallahassee · Tampa · Boca Raton

Pensacola · Orlando · Miami · Jacksonville · Ft. Myers

Copyright 2004 by Hazel Arnett Ervin
Printed in Canada on acid-free paper

09 08 07 06 05 04   6 5 4 3 2 1

Library of Congress Cataloging-in-Publication Data
Ervin, Hazel Arnett.
The handbook of African American literature / Hazel Arnett Ervin.
p. cm
Includes bibliographical references (p.).
ISBN 0-8130-2750-0 (cloth : alk. paper)
  1. American literature—African American authors—Encyclopedias.
2. African Americans—Intellectual life—Encyclopedias. 3. African
Americans in literature—Encyclopedias. I. Title.
PS153.N5E78 2004
810.9'896073—DC22   2004049332

The University Press of Florida is the scholarly publishing agency
for the State University System of Florida, comprising Florida A&M
University, Florida Atlantic University, Florida Gulf Coast University,
Florida International University, Florida State University, University
of Central Florida, University of Florida, University of North Florida,
University of South Florida, and University of West Florida.

University Press of Florida
15 Northwest 15th Street
Gainesville, FL 32611-2079
http://www.upf.com

For
Mother, Gladys A. Arnett

Jerry W. Ward Jr.
Eminent scholar and professor of English
and African world studies, Dillard University

the late Claudia Tate
Professor of English and American studies, Princeton University

Contents

Preface

It is not to be expected that we shall reinvent literature, nor shall
we reinvent criticism. We shall, however, have to name the discrete
seemingly disparate elements that compose the structure of which
our vernacular literary tradition consists.
Henry Louis Gates Jr., introduction to *The Signifying Monkey*

Culture, the epic memory of practical tradition.
Amiri Baraka, "expressive language," in *Home*

We must insure that the people who made it possible for us are
properly remembered. Honored.
Alex Pate, "Making Home in the New Millennium,"
in *African American Literary Criticism, 1773 to 2000*

In the preface to *Cornerstones: An Anthology of African American Literature*
(1996), anthologist Melvin Donalson responds to the question "What is African American literature?"

> African American literature is a body of written and oral works, created
> by writers who share both a black African heritage and a unique Ameri
> can experience, that defines and celebrates black history and culture.
> ... [Furthermore,] [p]ossessing an extraordinary range of tones, topics
> and styles, African American literature, whether it speaks gently or
> screams passionately, challenges and provokes response and action.
> (xiii)

After defining African American literature, Donalson responds to the question "What is the function of African American literature?"

> African American literature is [the] celebration of black culture and
> history, thereby, helping to create a sense of racial cohesiveness and
> solidarity.... Together, the various literary forms of African American

literature give us a fuller appreciation of a body of work that honors the social, political, intellectual, and cultural history of African Americans. (xv)

Donaldson concludes:

> Perhaps most importantly, African American literature encompasses the breadth of the struggles, achievements, and roles of blacks in shaping American society.... Despite the difficult or perilous circumstances in which it was created [historical, social, and/or political], African American literature goes beyond apology and protest to include an array of works that display the writers' talent, imagination, mastery of black verbal forms and Eurocentric language, and concerns with themes both timely and timeless, personal and universal. (xiv)

Donalson's queries seemed significant in early 2000 when I began to consider the merits of a handbook of African American literature. In particular, his comments suggested that any substantial work of African American literary studies had to communicate the complexities of African American culture and of African American literature. Furthermore, it was suggested the work had to preserve the African heritage and to reflect the collective spirit and values of a people of color in the United States. Last, the work had to be of an African American poetics (literary, cultural, historical, intellectual, political, and social). I concurred with Donalson that, at a minimum, a handbook of African American literature had to meet these requirements.

Like most anthologists of African American literature, Donalson relies on chronology as the organizing principle of his collection. For a similar use of chronology, see, for instance, Arthur P. Davis, Sterling Brown, and Ulysses Lee, editors of *Negro Caravan* (1941) and Richard Barksdale and Keneth Kinnamon, editors of *Black Writers of America* (1972). For anthologists who come after Donalson, see, for instance, Henry Louis Gates Jr. and Nellie McKay, editors of *The Norton Anthology of African American Literature* (1997), and Patricia Liggins Hill, Trudier Harris, William J. Harris, R. Baxter Miller, and Sandra A. O'Neale, editors of *Call and Response: The Riverside Anthology of the African American Literary Tradition* (1997). In *Cornerstones*, Donalson begins the collection with African American oral literature from the early days of slavery (songs, speeches, sermons, folktales), and, then, he reveals written literature (poetry, fiction, drama) from the 1700s to the present. I accept chronology used by anthologists and editors in major collections of African American literature as an influential organizing principle when completing substantial works of African American literary studies. As a performative act, chronology communicates a consensus among anthologists, editors, and others of a definable canon in African American letters. More specifically, it communicates there is an African American literary history of genres, periods, movements, and major writers that are worth remembering. Chronology also confirms a continuity of rituals, verbal forms, tones, tropes, customs, and practices that reach back to Africa and, as stated by Gates in his epigraph, "compose the structure of which [an African American] vernacular tradition consists." Last, as once stated by Houston A. Baker, chronology reflects "a long black song," sung by male and female composers who were also slaves, teachers, librarians, doctors, nurses, activists, editors, journalists, anthropologists, students, and scholars. This continuity spawned by chronology must be preserved in print.

After making this decision, the question became, should chronology as a literal speech act influence the overall organization of my work? To answer this question, I had to turn to my own instinct and desires. I concluded that I preferred to see a handbook that went beyond the familiar genres, periods, and movements, that used major as well as minor writers and works as examples. I concluded that I even wanted a work that went beyond familiar terms, such as simile, metaphor, and personification, or familiar themes, such as journey and liberation, for these terms often lead to familiar discussions and/or conclusions about African American writers and works. Somehow, I would attempt to compile a handbook that engaged readers, beginning and returning, within and outside of the African American community, in extended and even abstract discussions about any of the following: What constitutes African American literature? What are its functions? What do African American writers regard as their roles? What are the artistic responsibilities of audiences? In other words, I wanted a handbook that provided general, specific, and abstract terms and information. I wanted terms that engaged readers in discussions about the familiar and the not so familiar whats, whys, and hows, or as Baraka states in his epigraph, about "the epic memory of a practical [African American literary] tradition."

To reach my goal, I decided to allow for queries by potential readers, beginning and returning, within and outside of the African American community. In many ways, these queries became the other organizing principles of my work. For example:

1. What defines African American culture?
2. What distinguishes an African American author's style?
3. What are the tones, topics, and tropes in African American literature?
4. Is there any significance (cultural, historical, aesthetic, etc.) to African American writers who speak gently? Who scream passionately?
5. What are black verbal forms?
6. How exactly does the literature honor the social, political, intellectual, and cultural history of African Americans?
7. What are the literary forms of African American literature? Do these forms function in traditional ways, or in other specific ways?
8. What are the important or recurring themes in African American literature?
9. When are themes in African American literature regarded as timely and timeless? Personal and universal?
10. When is language Eurocentric?
11. What constitutes African American English?
12. If, as Donalson states, African American literature goes beyond apology and protest, then what constitutes apology in African American literature? What is African American protest literature? And are there alternatives to apology or protest literature?

I am certain that eventually a handbook of African American literature will appear in print to fill the void for such a work in African American letters. Writing in the introduction to the work *The Oxford Companion to African American Literature* (1997), editors William Andrews, Frances Smith Foster, and Trudier Harris confirm as much when they reveal the ever-increasing celebratory and scholarly status of African American literature at the turn of the century:

> [In the twenty-first century] readership of African American writing expands and waxes increasingly multi-ethnic. [I]t is rare to find a library (particularly in schools and universities) that does not collect, or a general-purpose bookstore that does not market, literary works by African Americans.... [In the academy,] African American writers play increasingly prominent roles in newly reconstituted American literature and American studies, as well as women's studies and ethnic studies, curricula. (x)

Also in their introduction, the editors suggest an increase in African American literary scholarship. They write:

Appropriate recognition of African American writing *as* literature has been a long time coming in the United States. [But in] the last three decades general interest in and appreciation of African American literature, its history and aesthetics, have grown considerably. . . . [For example,] [s]ince 1970, Rita Dove, Yusef Komunyakaa, James Alan McPherson, Toni Morrison, Gloria Naylor, and Alice Walker have joined Gwendolyn Brooks and Ralph Ellison as winners of prestigious honors such as the Pulitzer Prize, the National and American Book Awards, and, in Morrison's case, the Nobel Prize for Literature. (x)

As an academician, an African American critic, and reader of African American literary art, I feel I have a vested interest in works of African American literary studies that are of an African American poetics (i.e., historical, cultural, political, social, and theoretical). Influenced by history, culture, philosophy, linguistics, and aesthetics (literary and theoretical), *The Handbook of African American Literature* is the first reference work of its kind to attempt to fill a poetic void in African American letters. In particular, this handbook is designed to assist readers, beginning and returning, within and outside of the African American community, in the classification, interpretation, analysis, and study of the literary history, culture, politics, and literary and theoretical aesthetics of African American literature. While this work includes terms that are common to the study of any literature (e.g., simile, metaphor, personification, and flashback), it also includes, as stated in Gates's epigraph, terms that "name the discrete seemingly disparate elements that . . . structure vernacular literary tradition [African American]. . . ."

For example, there are terms derived from techniques, themes, and forms and structures of the following: African American poetry, fiction, drama, autobiographies, essays, speeches, and folk literature such as the spirituals, sermons, blues, folktales, field cries, and rap. Also included are well-known phrases (e.g., "speaking in tongues," "the racial mountain," or "laying on the hands"); modes of discourse (e.g., the dozens "signifying" or toasts); and musical and linguistic terminology (e.g., "worrying the line," riff, or "the cut") that reflect cultural practices within the African American community. Finally, there are literary movements, spawned from unique African American experiences in the United States (the Harlem Renaissance, Chicago Renaissance, Black Arts Movement, and New Black Aesthetic).

This handbook extends familiar boundaries to include "new directions" in the reading and study of African American literature. Based on my findings in introductions, prefaces, interviews, and articles, written by major critical and creative writers of African American literature, the following are included:

1. Ages (the Age of Johnson, Age of Baraka, Age of Wright, Age of Feminist Assertion, and Age of Womanist Assertion)
2. Periods (Colonial; Antislavery; Reconstruction, reaction, and realism; Renaissances and radicalism; Cultural assertion; and Reconstruction and postmodernism)
3. Longer terms for critical and contextual studies in African American letters (ambiguity, influence, literary history, memory, repetition, representation, signifying/signification, and collective unconscious)
4. A more defined effort to link the literatures in the diaspora, particularly to the African roots and the Caribbean backgrounds that show up in the African American experience (see, e.g., African time, "spirit writing," the secret societies of "initiation," Obeah and Calypso)
5. Outlines of literary history that are inclusive of African American literature, African literature, and Anglophone Caribbean literature
6. Terms that are, for whatever reasons, regarded as Western (reader-response, structuralism, poststructuralism, and semiotics)

The Handbook of African American Literature is not intended to reinvent literature or literary criticism. It does not attempt to define criteria for admitting writers or works into some ideologically sound and privileged category. Rather, as the epigraphs by Gates, Baraka, and Pate suggest, there are terms, concepts, modes of discussion, and other elements of the vernacular literary tradition, of oral and written African American culture, worth remembering when reading and studying African American literature.

This handbook is designed also to fill a void in African American letters left by existing glossaries and handbooks of American literature and by glossaries appearing in collections of African American literature. The voids are documented. For example, in glossaries and handbooks that are familiar to most students in the humanities, such as M. H. Abrams's *A Glossary of Literary Terms* (1993) and *The Handbook of Literature* (2003), edited by William Harmon, African American literature is recognized, but it is recognized, more or less, by fewer than ten entries—the most popular entry being the Harlem Renaissance. The names of major African American writers that appear, do so under the entry *literary history*.

Less familiar glossaries have appeared in a number of specific texts of African American literature: *African American Literature: An Anthology of Nonfiction, Fiction, Poetry, and Drama* (1993), edited by Demetrice A. Worley and Jesse Perry Jr.; *Liberating Voices: Oral Tradition in African American Literature* (1991), by Gayl Jones; and *African American Literature: Voices in a Tradition* (1992), overseen by a host of advisers and reviewers such as William L. Andrews, Carole Boyce Davies, David Dorsey, Robert E. Fox, Henry Louis Gates Jr., David Adam Leeming, Phil W. Petrie, Arnold Rampersad, John Edgar Tidwell, Christopher van Wyk, and Cheryl A. Wall. As suggested by their titles, these editors give priority to African American literature.

Still, I am indebted to the editors and authors mentioned, for in many ways they have cleared literary paths and mapped the routes for me to follow. For instance, as a graduate student at Howard University, I relied heavily on Abrams's *Glossary* and *The Handbook to Literature*, then edited by William Flint Thrall and William Harmon, to compile a section of my unpublished work "Black Critics at Work" (1989). A class project, overseen by Sandra Shannon and Stephen E. Henderson, "Black Critics at Work," complete with introduction and select readings, was a chronicle of African American literary history and criticism when such a narrative did not exist. Listed also were significant terms and, at the time, perspectives by major critics of African American literary theory. The former, greatly revised by me, has become *African American Literary Criticism, 1773 to 2000* (1999), and the latter (the terms) has become what is now this handbook.

While doing research for this handbook, discoveries were made. In particular, reoccurring in writings by creative and critical writers were discussions of longer terms for critical study (ambiguity, influence, literary history, memory, repetition, representation, signifying/signification, and collective unconscious, to name a few). These discussions justify discourse untapped and the call for single texts examining such longer, critical terms. Important books have begun to appear on the term "memory" (see, e.g., *History and Memory in African-American Culture* [1994], ed. Genevieve Fabre and Robert O'Meally, and *Black Imagination and the Middle Passage* [1999], ed. Maria Diedrich, Henry Louis Gates Jr., and Carla Pedersen). For the term "influence," currently, there is *Inspiriting Influences: Tradition, Revision and Afro-American Women's Novels* (1989) by Michael Awkward. And, of course, for the term "signifying," there is Henry Louis Gates's *The Signifying Monkey: A Theory of Afro-American Literary Criticism* (1988). Also, lesser-known examinations of the term exist in Geneva Smitherman's *Talkin and Testifyin: The Language of Black America* (1977) and Claudia Mitchell-Kernan's "Signifying as a Form of Verbal Art." Mitchell-Kernan appears in *Mother Wit from the Laughing Barrel: Readings in the Interpretation of Afro-American Folklore* (1973), edited by Alan Dundes. Needed also are additional bibliographical volumes of the diasporic literatures (oral and written), especially, if, as attempted here, one wants to know what literary works were written in Africa, in the Caribbean, and in America in the same year.

How to Use the Handbook

Most of the terms in *The Handbook of African American Literature* provide history, definition, and application of the term, mostly by African American writers. Other terms, for this edition, are very brief. The terms from *A* to *Z* are listed alphabetically, and they are cross-referenced in boldface type. Most often, there are recommendations for further reading. The recommended readings follow the terms and appear also in the bibliography. In some entries, authors and works are alluded to and they appear in the bibliography, as well. The longer terms for critical study in African American letters appear in the table of contents under Criticism and Theory and in the text in essay form. These essays are intended merely to document the presence of discourse in African American texts and to broaden scholarship. Appendix 1, "Outlines of Literary History," identifies what has been written in the same year in America, in Africa, and in English-speaking Caribbean countries. Listed chronologically under African American in the outlines are major and minor African American writers and works; the year of birth and death of major African American writers; and the year of birth and death of major critics of African American literature, regardless of race. The lists are rather revealing, especially when births and deaths are in juxtaposition with literary history.

Last, there are appendices that list winners of the Pulitzer Prize and the Nobel Prize in Literature; literary societies, circles, and associations; and major archives and research centers.

Acknowledgments

As stated earlier, resources for this handbook have been the following: African American poetry, fiction, drama, autobiographies, speeches, essays, journals, letters, and oral cultural sources such as sermons, spirituals, blues, field cries, and rap. Other resources must be mentioned by title because they served the purposes of promoting accuracy and consistency in dates, titles, and modes of discussion: *The Oxford Companion to African American Literature* (1997), edited by Andrews, Foster, and Harris; more familiar anthologies of African American literature such as *The Book of American Negro Poetry, Negro Caravan, Black Writers of America, Cornerstones, The Norton Anthology of African American Literature,* and *Call and Response: The Riverside Anthology of an African American Literary Tradition*; studies of genres, authors, and/or African, African American, and Caribbean literary cultures in, but not limited to, Sterling A. Brown's *The American Negro: His History and Literature* (1969); Lawrence W. Levine's *Black Culture and Black Consciousness: Afro-American Folk Thought from Slavery to Freedom* (1977); William Barlow's *Looking Up at Down: The Emergence of Blues Culture* (1989); Houston Baker's *Blues, Ideology, and Afro-American Literature: A Vernacular Theory* (1987); Bernard Bell's *The Afro-American Novel and Its Tradition* (1988); Joseph E. Holloway's *Africanisms in American Culture* (1991); John S. Mbiti's *Introduction to African Religion* (1991); Oyekan Owomoyela's *African Literature: An Introduction* (1979) and *A History of Twentieth-Century African Literature* (2002); Janheinz Jahn's *Neo-African Literature: A History of Black Writing* (1968); Jonathan A. Peters's *English Language Fiction from West Africa* (1968); Lambros Comitas's *The Complete Caribbeana 1900–1975: A Bibliographic Guide to the Scholarly Literature* (1977); Marjorie Engber's *Caribbean Fiction and Poetry* (1970); and M. J. Fenwick's *Writers of the Caribbean and Central America: A Bibliography* (1992). Last, useful to me, were invaluable theoretical studies (in letters, articles, prefaces, introductions, interviews, and books) by major critics and creative writers (*too* numerous to name here) from the 1700s to the present.

The editor wishes to thank James R. Richardson, doctoral student at Emory University and instructor of English at Morehouse College, for his contributions to this handbook, particularly for the terms "African ontology," "biography," "the Black aesthetics," "Black Arts Movement," "Black nationalism," "Calypso," and "race." I am also grateful to SallyAnn Ferguson at the University of North Carolina at Greensboro; Dolan Hubbard at Morgan State University; Emily Williams at Morehouse College; Carol Marsh-Lockett and Elizabeth West at Georgia State University; and Carl Wade and Richard Clarke at the University of West Indies, the Cave Hill Campus, in Barbados, for their early reviews of my list of terms and for their comments and recommendations. Thank you to Jerry W. Ward Jr. at Dillard University and Richard Yarborough at UCLA for agreeing to reread selected entries. Thank you, Clenora Hudson-Weems, Consuella Bennett, and Annie Perkins.

I am indebted to Amy Gorelick, my editor at the University Press of Florida, for recognizing the need for such a handbook and especially for her patience, devotion, and support to the very end. I wish to thank also the Research and Development Committee at Morehouse College (cochaired by Cindy Lutenbacher and Jane Adams) for a research grant in 2001 to complete this book, and the Council for International Exchange of Scholars for the J. William Fulbright Award in 2001, which yielded, from numerous research projects, a useful bibliography of Barbadian writers and works. Last, my sincere thanks to the librarians at the Robert W. Woodruff Library in the Atlanta University Center, particularly to Millicent Norman, Akilah S. Nosa Khere, Sara Wilson, and Monica Riley; to my niece Cassie Murphy for her services as my research assistant on numerous occasions; to Intaba Shauri for his meticulous explanations as a researcher; and to Mattylin Hubbard for her invaluable technical support.

Terms

absurd, the A term that is used to provide explanations of purposeless existence, spiritual anguish, or irrational experience. Applications of the term are traceable to the drama of the 1950s and 1960s such as Samuel Beckett's *Waiting for Godot* (1953), Jean Genet's *Les Paravents* (1961), and Eugene Ionesco's *Le Roe se meurt* (1961); to movements such as expressionism, dadaism, and surrealism; and to the **existential** philosophy of Albert Camus in *The Myth of Sisyphus* (1942) and of Jean-Paul Sartre in *L'Existentialisme est un humanisme* (1946). Men of Western letters who are associated with the absurd are James Joyce in *Ulysses* (1922), Samuel Beckett in *Malone Dies* (1958) and *The Unnamable* (1960), and Franz Kafka in *The Trial* (1925).

In African American letters, there are works that are associated with the absurd: Bill Gunn's *All the Rest Have Died* (1944); Charles Wright's *The Wig* (1966); Kingsley Bass Jr.'s *We Righteous Bombers* (1969); Amiri Baraka's *Experimental Death Unit #1* (1969); Ishmael Reed's *Mumbo Jumbo* (1972); John Edgar Wideman's *The Lynchers* (1973); and Clarence Major's *Reflex and Bone Structure* (1975), *Emergency Exit* (1979), and *My Amputations* (1986).

Other African American works that exploit the term in efforts to dramatize the "absurdities of life" include Toni Morrison's *Beloved* (1987) and *Paradise* (1998) and Gloria Naylor's *Mama Day* (1988). Gayl Jones and Ntozake Shange admit to interviewer Claudia Tate in *Black Women Writers at Work* (1988) that writers also exploit the term in order to show that people can hold two different emotions simultaneously (i.e., to invoke simultaneously tears and laughter). Examples include Gayl Jones's *Corregidora* (1975) and Ntozake Shange's *for colored girls who have considered suicide/when the rainbow is enuf* (1974) and *Spell #7* (1979). Other examples include Ishmael Reed's *Flight to Canada* (1976) and Amari Baraka's *The Baptism* (1967).

(See also **existentialism** and **humor.**)

References for further reading: Ed Bullins, ed., *New Plays from the Black Theater* (1969); John Lowe, "Humor" (1997); Claudia Tate, *Black Women Writers at Work* (1988).

African American English (AAE) An Africanized style of standard English that gives special meaning to patterns of grammar and pronunciations; to **verbal rituals** and expressions (i.e., the **vernacular**); and to a lexicon or vocabulary. In *Talkin and Testifyin: The Language of Black America* (1977) and in *Black Talk* (1994), Geneva Smitherman traces linguistic patterns and systems of African American English (AAE) to West African speakers (e.g., Wolof, Mandingo, Ibo, **Yoruba**). Of particular interest is that West African and African American speakers do not use the English "th" sound. The "th" sound is rendered with the next closest sounds such as "d," "t," or "f." In other words, "death" becomes "def" and "with" becomes "wit." According to Smitherman, other patterns exist in certain consonants and tenses. For example:

1. The "r" sound at the end of a word and after a vowel *is not* heard in AAE. Example: "torn up" becomes "toe up." Or, "your" becomes "yo"
2. Final and medial consonants are reduced to a vowel or a single consonant sound. Example: "cold" becomes "coal"
3. Stress is placed on the first syllable. Example: "PO-leece" instead of "Police"
4. The vowel sound in words that rhyme with "think" and "ring" is pronounced as "thank" and "rang." Example: "sing" becomes "sang" and "drink" becomes "drank"
5. Tense (time) is indicated by **context,** not with "s" or "ed." Example: "Mary do anything she want to"
6. Continuous action or activity recurring infrequently is indicated with "be" and "bees." Example: "Every/time we see him, he be dressed like that"; or, "It bees dat way"
7. Verbs such as "Is" and "Are" and their contractions are not necessary to make a complete statement. Example: "What up?"

Reference for further reading: J. L. Dillard, *Black English* (1972).

African American literary criticism The explanations of the role of the writer, the functions of the work, and the artistic responsibility of the audience. The study of style and structure of the literature and the devise of general principles that govern evaluations of the literary art. In African American letters, the criticism may be called prescriptive (e.g., **Harlem Renaissance** and the **Black Arts Movement**); practical (e.g., **New Criticism**); and theoretical (e.g., **signifying; blues aesthetics; semiotics; structuralism; poststructuralism**; linguistic; **intertextuality**/historiography; mythology/**archetype**; **psychoanalysis;** gender-based; culture-based; rhetoric and **reader-response;** and **postcolonialism**).

The list of representative works on African American literary criticism and theory is exhaustive, but one would want to begin with James Weldon Johnson's preface to *The Book of American Negro Poetry* (1922); James Baldwin's *Notes of a Native Son* (1955); Addison Gayle Jr.'s *Black Expression* (1969) and *The Black Aesthetic* (1971); Ralph Ellison's *Shadow and Act* (1964); Stephen E. Henderson's introduction to *Understanding the New Black Poetry: Black Speech and Black Music as Poetic References* (1973); Larry Neal's "The Black Contribution to American Letters: Part II, The Writer as Activist—1960 and After" (1976); Stephen E. Henderson's "The Question of Form and Judgement in Contemporary Black American Poetry" (along with an essay by George Kent) in *A Dark and Sudden Beauty* (1977); Carolyn Fowler's (Carolyn F. Gerald's) preface to *Black Arts and Black Aesthetics: A Bibliography* (1976); Henry Louis Gates Jr.'s *"Race," Writing and Difference* (1985), *Figures in Black: Words, Signs, and the Racial Self* (1987) and *The Signifying Monkey: A Theory of Afro-American Literary Criticism* (1988); Houston A. Baker Jr.'s *The Journey Back: Issues in Black Literature and Criticism* (1980), *Blues, Ideology, and Afro-American Literature* (1984), and (with Patricia Redmond) *Afro-American Literary Study in the 1990s* (1989); Bernard Bell's *The Afro-American Novel and Its Tradition* (1987); John Edgar Wideman's preface as well as Terry McMillan's introduction to *Breaking Ice: An Anthology of Contemporary African-American Fiction* (1990). Edited collections include Angelyn Mitchell's *Within the Circle: An Anthology of African American Literary Criticism from the Harlem Renaissance to the Present* (1994); Hazel Arnett Ervin's *African American Literary Criticism, 1773 to 2000* (1999); and Winston Napier's *African American Literary Theory: A Reader* (2000).

References for further reading: Fred Lee Hord, *Reconstructing Memory: Black Literary Criticism* (1991); Joyce Ann Joyce, *Warriors, Conjurers and Priests: Defining African-Centered Literary Criticism* (1994); Vincent B. Leitch, *American Literary Criticism from the Thirties to the Eighties* (1988); Joe Weixlmann and Chester J. Fontenot, eds., *Black American Prose Theory: Studies in Black American Literature* (1984), and *Belief Versus Theory in Black American Literary Criticism: Studies in Black American Literature* (1986); Roger Whitlow, *Black American Literature: A Critical History* (1973); and Cary D. Wintz, *Politics and Aesthetics of "New Negro" Literature* (1996).

African American literature, periods of The divisions of African American literary history vary. Evidence of some consensus of divisions appears under "literary history" in *The Oxford Companion to African American*

Literature (1997), edited by William Andrews, Frances Smith Foster, and Trudier Harris; in the introductions to *African American Literary Criticism, 1773 to 2000* (1999), edited by Hazel Arnett Ervin, and *African American Literary Theory: A Reader* (2000), edited by Winston Napier; in *The Afro-American Novel and Its Tradition* (1987), by Bernard W. Bell; in the headnotes of *Black Writers of America: A Comprehensive Anthology* (1972), edited by Richard Barksdale and Keneth Kinnamon; and in *The American Negro, His History and Literature* (1969), by Sterling A. Brown. A consensus of periods is as follows:

1745–1831	Colonial period
1832–1864	Antislavery period
1865–1916	Reconstruction, reaction, and realism period
1917–1953	Renaissances and radicalism period
1954–1975	Cultural assertion period
1976–Present	Reconstruction and postmodernism period

Entries of these periods appear elsewhere in this book. When read in sequence, the entries on the periods give a brief history of African American literary writing.

African ethos The influences of an **African ontology** traceable to beliefs, standards, and practices of the African American community. Immediate examples include beliefs in the spirit of **ancestors** who link the living with the unseen world; in few distinctions between the sacred and the secular; and in the power of words—spoken and/or chanted. Recurring practices in African American music (**spirituals, work songs, blues**) include complex rhythmic structures—**call and response, syncopation,** and **improvisation.** Particularly in early spirituals, work songs, and blues, the music fosters an African practice of group cohesion. In **folktales** and fables that are woven out of everyday occurrences, there are powerless characters (usually animals) that use wit and guile to triumph over the powerful. Songs, tales, **proverbs, dances,** and **verbal rituals** serve dual purposes. Not only do the genres and rituals preserve communal values and standards but also they provide occasion for individuals to transcend spiritually and symbolically his or her environment, circumstances, or situations.

References for further reading: Joseph E. Holloway, *Africanisms in American Culture* (1990); Lawrence W. Levine, *Black Culture and Black Consciousness: Afro American Folk Thought From Slavery to Freedom* (1977); Albert G. Mosley, ed., *African Philosophy: Selected*

Readings (1995); George Yancy, ed., *African-American Philosophers: 17 Conversations* (1998).

African ontology The study of *being,* including how humans come to exist in the universe. More specifically, African ontology outlines how African concepts of the universe, the supernatural, nature, time, the life force, community, and family all coalesce to define and realize "being" and existence. According to scholars of African philosophy, African ontology is human-centered. To explain this worldview, some scholars have configured a triangle with humans at the center, and the Creator at the top. The **ancestors,** who exist in a fluid "living-dead" state, are on one side of the triangle. The divine spirits are on the other side. And the lower supernatural that exists as forces and spirits are at the triangle's base. According to this worldview, humans develop and become aware of their positions in the universe and of their roles in maintaining equilibrium among all the entities that compose the universe. Although equilibrium is occasionally upset, the system's overall unifying interconnected qualities are constant and indestructible.

Essential in a universe defined from an African worldview is what scholar Marimba Ani (Dona Richards) terms "Utamaroho" or "vital force." The vital force gives a culture its energy and "personality." Present in both animate and inanimate objects, the vital force can be used for good or evil by a "nyanga" (witch) or by a medicine man. Hence, all phenomena—from crop failure to weather changes to disease—are caused by a manipulation of the vital force. Unlike Western notions of time, **African time** is nonlinear and is more closely wed to solar, lunar, and seasonal cycles. The cycle of life is essential in African ontology, and a truly human self is one that is birthed in an African worldview (i.e., who participates in **naming** rites, undergoes various rites of passage, and gives birth to a child [preferably a son], and who plays his/her role in perpetuating the larger community). Thus, "being" in the ideal African ontological sense reflects the essential importance of **circularity,** community **spirituality,** and a harmonious balance of both the natural and the supernatural and the animate and inanimate. Literary works that illustrate or in some way address one or several of these aspects of African ontology include Margaret Walker's *Jubilee* (1966); Ishmael Reed's *Flight to Canada* (1976); Ernest Gaines's *The Autobiography of Miss Jane Pittman* (1971); and Toni Morrison's *Beloved* (1987).

References for further reading: Marimba Ani, *Yurugu: An African-Centered Critique of European Cultural Thought and Behavior* (1994); Edward Bruce Bynum and Linda James

Meyers, eds., *The African Unconscious: Roots of Ancient Mysticism and Modern Psychology* (1999); John Mbiti, 1992; Albert G. Mosley, 1995.

African time The dissolution of boundaries between time and place or between the past, present, and future. Nonlinear. Actual time is what is present and what is past. To quote Ishmael Reed who employs an African concept of time in *Mumbo Jumbo* (1972), "[African] time is a pendulum. Not a river." African American writers that make use of an African concept of time and place include the following: Toni Morrison, John Edgar Wideman, and Leon Forrest.

Reference for further reading: John Mbiti, *African Religions and Philosophy* (1992).

Africana womanism For the Africana womanist critic, an African cosmology is crucial in creating paradigms for the study of women writers of color. The literary history of the term suggests critics are in dialogue but are not in agreement about practice. The Africana womanist critic finds the priorities of white feminists objectionable. Often cited in Africana womanist literature are the observations of Betinna Aptheker, a white feminist, writing in "Strong Is What We Make Each Other: Unlearning Racism Within Women's Studies" (1981):

> When we place women at the center of our thinking, we are going about the business of creating a historical and cultural matrix from which women may claim autonomy and independence over their own lives. For women of color such autonomy cannot be achieved in conditions of racial oppression and cultural genocide. In short, "feminist," in the modern sense, means the empowerment of women. For women of color, such an equality, such as empowerment, cannot take place when the communities in which they live cannot successfully establish their own racial and cultural integrity. (13)

Africana womanist critics find the priorities of African American feminist critics objectionable, as well. Often cited in their literature is Alice Walker, writing in *In Search of Our Mothers' Gardens* (1983). Here Walker denounces white feminist criticism as exclusionary and controversial. She offers an alternative discourse: **womanism.** Walker defines womanism in this manner:

> Womanist: A black feminist or a feminist of color. . . . Usually referring to outrageous, audacious, courageous or willful behavior. Wanting to

know more and in greater depth than is considered "good" for one.... A woman who loves women sexually and/or non-sexually. Appreciates and prefers women's culture, women's emotional flexibility . . . and women's strength. . . . Committed to survival and wholeness of entire people, male and female. Not a separatist.... Womanist is to feminist as purple is to lavender. (xi–xiii)

For some African American female critics such as bell hooks (1990, 1992), in numerous writings, and Mary Helen Washington (1987), there is promise in Walker's womanist ethos.

However, for Africana womanist critics such as Clenora Hudson-Weems (writing in "Africana Womanism: An Overview," 2000), any critical paradigm for literature by women of color must come out of an African cosmology (an **African ethos**), and any attempts to include "white [feminist] terminology [brings to the discourse] its agenda"—that is, female empowerment, liberation within a capitalist tradition, and discriminating class differences (208). For Hudson-Weems and others, Africana womanism is family-based and community-based. Other key features include "self-namer, self-definer, genuine sisterhood, strong, in concert with male in struggle, whole, authentic, flexible role player, respected, recognized, spiritual, male compatible, respectful of elders, adaptable, ambiti[ous], mothering and nurturing" (207).

As suggested by Tuzyline Jita Allan in *Womanist and Feminist Aesthetics, A Comparative Review* (1995), at the start of the new millennium, a critique by Africana, African American, and Euro American women critics of the term "womanism" as a woman-centered approach to literature by women of color is an ongoing discussion.

References for further reading: Tuzyline Jita Allan, *Womanist and Feminist Aesthetics, A Comparative Review* (1995); Nada Elia, *Trances, Dances and Vociferations* (2000); Clenora Hudson-Weems, *Africana Womanism: Reclaiming Ourselves* (1993); Clenora Hudson-Weems, guest ed. *The Western Journal of Black Studies,* 24, no. 3 (fall 2001) (special issue on Africana womanism); Janice Lee Liddell and Yakini Belinda Kemp, *Arms Akimbo: Africana Women in Contemporary Literature* (1999); Carol Marsh-Lockett (1997); Chikwenzi Okongo Ojunyemi (1885); Sherley Anne Williams (1986).

Afrocentric/Afrocentricity A centrist perspective influenced by an African cultural center. In other words, the critic examines all data or topics from the standpoint of Africa as *subject* and from the standpoint of the African as *human agent.* According to Molefi Asante, author of *Afrocentricity* (1987), the centrist perspective has implications for other fields of study such as dance, economics, architecture, social work, politics, and psychology.

References for further reading: Nilgun Anadolu-Okur, *Contemporary African-American Theater: Afrocentricity in the Works of Larry Neal, Amiri Baraka, and Charles Fuller* (1997); William Wells Brown, *The Black Man: His Antecedents, His Genius and His Achievements* (1863); James L. Conyers and Alva Barnett, *Africana History, Culture and Social Policy* (1999); Amy Jacques-Garvey, ed., *The Philosophy and Opinions of Marcus Garvey, 1923–25* (1969).

Age of [Amiri] Baraka in African American literature   Dubbed the "father" of the **Black Arts Movement** (1960–1975/76) and a key facilitator in the maturation of a post-1960s generation of African American poets (e.g., Sonia Sanchez, Haki Madhubuti, and Nikki Giovanni) and African American playwrights (e.g., Ed Bullins and Ben Caldwell), Baraka promotes a period of experimentation with **poetry, drama,** and political activism; cultural nationalism; and Marxism. Prescriptive in his signature works—for example, in the poem "Black Art" (1969); in the coedited (with Larry Neal) *Black Fire: An Anthology of Afro-American Writing* (1968); and in several essays from *Home: Social Essays* (1966)—Baraka calls for a reordering of Western cultural aesthetics (e.g., symbolism, mythology, iconology, and metaphors) and for expressive language and characters that emerge out of an **African ethos.** Also, as stated in the poem "Black Art," poetry and drama of the **Black Arts Movement** have one concrete function—"action." In short, the poetry and the drama of the period are to function as physical entities (i.e., as "fists," "daggers," and "guns") and as personal forces.

Literature of the post-1960s generation that prescribes to the ideology of the Black Arts Movement include Sonia Sanchez's *Homecoming* (1967) and *We a BaddDDD People* (1970); Haki Madhubuti's *Black Pride* (1968) and *Don't Cry, Scream* (1969); Nikki Giovanni's *Black Feeling, Black Talk* (1968) and *Black Judgment* (1969); and Ed Bullins's *Goin' a Buffalo* (1968) and *In the Wine Time* (1968).

References for further reading: Robert Elliot Fox, *Conscientious Sorcerers: The Black Postmodernist Fiction of LeRoi Jones/Amiri Baraka, Ishmael Reed, and Samuel R. Delany* (1987); Donald B. Gibson, *Five Black Writers: Essays on Wright, Ellison, Baldwin, Hughes, and LeRoi Jones* (1970); Theodore Hudson, *From LeRoi Jones to Baraka* (1973); Larry Neal, "The Black Arts Movement," in *African American Literary Criticism, 1773 to 2000* ed. Ervin (1999); and Robert E. Washington, *The Ideologies of African American Literature: From the Harlem Renaissance to the Black Nationalist Revolt* (2001).

Age of Feminist Assertion On July 29, 1895, one hundred African American women from ten states met in Boston to organize as activists with the overall mission of uplifting the African American community. At the end of the three-day conference, familiar female leaders such as Mary Church Terrell and Ida B. Wells and others had formed the National Federation of Afro-American Women. Eventually in 1896, federations, leagues, and clubs of African American women across the United States would form the National Association of Colored Women.

Educated and well trained, African American women of the NACW redefined the "woman's sphere" or as Claudia Tate and Hazel Carby have written, the women redefined "an age [of the black woman]" and "reconstructe[ed] womanhood." While women leaders such as Hallie Q. Brown, Anna Julie Cooper, Fanny Jackson Coppin, Sarah J. Early, Fannie Barrier William, Frances Ellen Watkins Harper, Ida B. Wells, Mary Church Terrell, Margaret Murry Washington, Mary McLeod Bethune, and Charlotte Hawkins Brown promoted the nuclear family and bourgeois standards and advocated improving future generations by starting with kindergarten to educate the children, they also challenged the patriarchy for political power and suffrage for women. In addition, at the national level they opposed lynching and fought for civil rights and employment opportunities for African Americans.

While some women were assertive as educators (Mary McLeod Bethune and Charlotte Hawkins Brown), as activists (Ida B. Wells), as leaders (Mary Church Terrell), as orators (Victoria Earle Matthews), others were assertive in African American letters (Pauline Hopkins, Anna J. Cooper, Frances Harper, Alice Dunbar-Nelson, Emma Dunham Kelly, and Katherine Davis Chapman). In their literature, characters maintained similar ideals: While some women were accommodationist (i.e., they embraced Booker T. Washington's industrial training), others sided with W.E.B. DuBois and promoted academic training.

Major critics and scholars have documented the late 1880s: Paula Giddings's *When and Where I Enter* (1984); Hazel Carby's *Reconstructing Womanhood: The Emergence of the Afro-American Woman Novelist* (1987); Claudia Tate's *Domestic Allegories of Political Desire: The Black Heroine's Text at the Turn of the Century* (1992); and the many contributors to the *Schomburg Library of Nineteenth-Century Black Women Writers*, edited by Henry Louis Gates Jr. (1988).

Age of [James Weldon] Johnson in African American literature Coining the phrase in 1955 is **Harlem Renaissance** architect Charles S. Johnson in his essay "The Significance of the Negro Renaissance" (1995). A lyricist, poet, novelist, journalist, critic, and autobiographer, James Weldon Johnson is an inspiration to the creative writers of the **Harlem Renaissance** in the 1920s, and in the first issue of *New Challenge,* he can be found inspiring writers of the **Chicago Renaissance** in the early 1930s. In 1921, Johnson edited *The Book of American Negro Poetry.* In the preface, Johnson instructs writers to seek "forms" that would express an African American "racial spirit" via "symbols from within," and in their writings to express "the imagery," "the idioms," "the peculiar turns of thought," and the "distinct humor and pathos" of African Americans.

Many of the younger writers of the Harlem Renaissance are bold and persistent in their experimentations with forms, **symbols**, **imagery**, and **idioms.** In particular, critical and artistic stances are taken by Langston Hughes in the essay "Negro Artist and the Racial Mountain" (1926) and in a work such as *The Weary Blues* (1926); by Zora Neale Hurston in the essay "Characteristics of Negro Expression" (1934) and in the novel *Their Eyes Were Watching God* (1937); by Richard Wright in "Blueprint for Negro Writing" (1937) and in "The Man Who Lived Underground" (1942). Outside of the Harlem Renaissance and Chicago Renaissance, Johnson's aesthetics might be found in Ralph Ellison's "The Art of Fiction: An Interview" (1953) and in *Invisible Man* (1952); and in James Baldwin's essays "Everybody's Protest Novel" (1949), and "Many Thousand Gone" (1951), and in the novel *Go Tell It On the Mountain* (1953).

References for further reading: Charles S. Johnson, "The Significance of the Negro Renaissance"; Richard Kostelanctz. *Politics in the African-American Novel: James Weldon Johnson, W.E.B. DuBois, Richard Wright, and Ralph Ellison* (1991).

Age of Womanist Assertion In the last chapter of Hazel Carby's *Reconstructing Womanhood* (1987), the critic and scholar alludes to what might be called the Age of Womanist Assertion (1920s to the 1980s/1990s). Carby's repeated focus on "shifts," "contrasts," and "alternative discourse" before and during the **Harlem Renaissance** hint to a historical/cultural perspective in African American letters that might be called **womanist** and assertive.

According to Carby, following World War I and the Great Migration (see **migration narrative**), African American women writers in Harlem, the mecca of black writing in the 1920s, "sought artistic autonomy for their cultural practices and products and separated themselves from the task of writing for the uplifting of the race as a whole." (See **Age of Feminist Assertion** for explanations of racial uplift for the "whole.") The women writers and works of the Harlem Renaissance discussed by Carby include Jessie Fauset's *Plum Bun* (1929), Nella Larsen's *Quicksand* (1928), and Zora Neale Hurston's *Their Eyes Were Watching God* (1937). Included in these works are many or most of the following themes that mark a shift in the role of the creative and critical woman writer, starting in the 1920s: (1) challenge to romantic conventions of womanhood, (2) hypocrisy of the new black middle class, (3) black female sexuality, (4) the modern alienated individual, (5) the search for alternative possibilities of a social self, and (6) increasing fragmented discourse of "the people" (i.e., the working class), and the intellectual leadership (i.e., the new middle class). In other words, in contrast to the writers, educators, activists, and civic women of the 1880s, the creative and critical women writers of the 1920s launch a severe critique against the earlier but still influential ideology of racial uplift (Carby 166). Perhaps the most profound contrast is that the women of the 1920s reconstruct the sexual ideology of the nineteenth century and introduce race, class, *and* sex as alternative discourse of black womanhood (Carby 166).

While the novelists that follow Fauset, Larsen, and Hurston—Ann Petry in *The Street* (1946); Gwendolyn Brooks in *Maud Martha* (1951); Dorothy West in *The Living Is Easy* (1948); and the work of Toni Morrison—include many if not most of the themes of an alternative discourse of womanhood, many critics point to the tradition of African American women writers as being established from Alice Walker back through Zora Neale Hurston (see, e.g., the writings of Michael Awkward and Cheryl Wall). But, the criticism of critics such as Hazel Carby, Mary Helen Washington, and Deborah McDowell suggest perspectives of and actual shifts in reconstructions of ideology and practices start in the 1920s and extend past the 1940s and 1950s and into the 1980s.

From the 1980s, one might consider Alice Walker's *In Search of Our Mothers' Gardens: Womanist Prose* (1983). Included is her definition of womanist, which suggests shifts in perspectives of the post–World War I women writers. According to Walker, a womanist writer is as follows:

> A black feminist or feminist of color..., usually referring to audacious, courageous or *willful* behavior. Wanting to know more and in greater depth than is considered "good" for one.

Appreciate and prefers women's culture, women's emotional flexibility..., and women's strength.... Committed to survival and wholeness of entire people, male and female.... Loves the spirit.... Loves struggle. Loves the Folk. Loves herself. *Regardless.* (xi)

Age of [Richard] Wright in African American literature In his manifesto "Blueprint for Negro Writing" (1937), Richard Wright critiques the veteran **Harlem Renaissance** writers, saying many of them confined themselves to "humble novels, poems, and plays" that focused on the intellectual African American middle class. Wright insists the role of the African American writer should be more than to prove to Euro American audiences that "the African American is not inferior ... and that he has a life comparable to that of [white] people." Between 1940 and 1953, Wright charges African American writers to focus in their writings on the plight of the urban working class, using familiar African American modes of discourse or the "original contributions" of everyday folk (i.e., the **verbal** strategies, rhetorical devices, and expressive folk **rituals**).

Dubbed the "father" of modern African American literature, Wright is not always consistent in his own call to return to the "original contributions" of African Americans. See, for instance, the inconsistencies in the use of the folk or what Wright calls **"forms of things unknown"** in his autobiographies, *Black Boy* (1945) and *American Hunger* (1977, published posthumously); in his short fiction, *Uncle Tom's Children* (1938); in essays such as "The Ethics of Living Jim Crow" (1937); and in longer fiction such as *Native Son* (1940), *The Outsider* (1953), *The Long Dream* (1958), and *Lawd Today* (1963). As modernist precursor, however, Wright is persistent in his protest of urban disenfranchisement, fragmentation, and alienation of African Americans in urban America. Specific writers and works from the 1930s and 1940s that prescribe to Wright's **modernism** and literary **protest** against urban backgrounds, particularly on behalf of working-class African Americans, include Theodore Ward's play *Big White Fog* (1938); William Attaway's *Blood on the Forge* (1941); Chester Himes's *If He Hollers, Let Him Go* (1945); and Ann Petry's *The Street* (1946). See also Margaret Walker's poetry collection *For My People* (1942). According to Blyden Jackson, in *The Waiting Years* (1976), there was without question, an "age of Wright."

References for further reading: Charles T. Davis and Henry Louis Gates, *Black Is the Color of the Cosmos: Essays on Afro-American Literature and Culture 1942–1981* (1989); Jeffrey J. Folks, *From Richard Wright to Toni Morrison: Others in Modern and Postmodern American*

Narrative (2001); Robert E. Washington, *The Ideologies of African American Literature: From the Harlem Renaissance to the Black Nationalist Revolt* (2001).

allegory A term that suggests double meaning or various levels of interpretation—that is, on the surface and below-the-surface meanings. There are types of allegory: historical and political (represented by a person or event) and ideas (represented by an abstract concept, doctrine, or thesis). Unlike familiar classical myth, morality plays, and even allegorical literary art of Western literary culture such as John Bunyan's *Pilgrim's Progress* (1678), allegorical works are not readily categorized or named as such. One exception might be the mythological Shine (the only survivor of the *Titanic* due to his wit). Referenced, however, for their inclusions of allegory are Harriet Adams Wilson's *Our Nig* (1859); W.E.B. DuBois's *The Quest of the Silver Fleece* (1911); Jean Toomer's "Kabnis" in *Cane* (1923); Leon Forrest's *There Is a Tree More Ancient Than Eden* (1973) and *The Bloodworth Orphans* (1977); and Gloria Naylor's *Linden Hills* (1985).

Claudia Tate, writing in *Domestic Allegories of Political Desire: The Black Heroine's Text at the Turn of the Century* (1992), borrows from Frederic Jameson the phrase "allegorical master narrative" to identify dominant African American male texts that instruct "master allegories" such as "black liberational discourse" and "male struggle for patriarchal power" (i.e., the Oedipal complex) (8). These male texts include Frederick Douglass's *Narrative of the Life of Frederick Douglass, an American Slave, Written by Himself* (1845) and Charles W. Chesnutt's *The Marrow of Tradition* (1901). According to Tate, in a number of nineteenth-century novels by African American women writers, there are "allegorical narratives" that allow female writers on various levels "to construct, destruct, and reconstruct" Victorian ideals in order to center African American female subjectivity (8). See, for instance, Amelia Johnson in *Clarence and Corinne* (1890); Emma Dunham Kelly in *Medga* (1891); Frances Harper in *Iola LeRoy* (1892); and Pauline Hopkins in *Contending Forces* (1900).

Reference for further reading: Bernard W. Bell, *The Afro-American Novel and Its Tradition*, 1987.

alliteration A scheme using repetition of the initial stressed syllable or consonant in two or more words for emphasis or special effects. See, for instance, Gwendolyn Brooks's dramatic opening to "Boys, Black" (1972). In the poem, Brooks urges her young readers to develop proper health and sanity while in their **heroic** struggles for existence:

Be brave to *battle* for your *breath* and *bread*
Your *heads hold* clocks that strike the new time of day
(Melhem 1987:229.)

No less effective is Robert Hayden in "Runagate Runagate," as he relates an experience of runaway slaves:

Some in coffins and *some* in carriages
Some in *silks* and *some* in *shackles*
(Gates and McKay 1997:1507.)

See, also, the following:
James Weldon Johnson in the poetic verse "The Creation" (1920):

And God Stepped over to the edge of the world
And He *spat* out the *seven seas*
(Gates and McKay 1997:775.)

Margaret Walker in the ballad "Molly Means," for Molly's
heavy hair hung thick in ropes
(Hill et al. 1997:1101.)

Jean Toomer in "November Cotton Flower":

And cotton, *scarce* as any *southern snow*
(*Cane* 1923:7)

and in his "Song of the Son" (1923):

Pour O *Pour* that *parting soul* in *song*
(*Cane* 1923:21)

allusions An indirect reference made clear by an association to sources (e.g., to biblical characters and passages from the Old Testament; famous African Americans; African American literary works; African American music via **lyrics** or song titles; African American authors or public figures; and **myths**). The term is used also to give depth to an oral or written work, or to extend an experience in the African American literary tradition. See, for instance, the **spiritual** "Didn't My Lord Deliver Daniel?" In the verses, the writers (see **"O black and unknown bards"**) allude to Daniel 6:22 in the Old Testament and in the process offer a shared experience of captivity among the slaves:

Didn't my Lord deliver Daniel

Deliver Daniel, deliver Daniel?
Didn't my Lord deliver Daniel?
An' why not everyma'?

Returning to the Old Testament is W. C. Handy in the **blues** tune "Beale Street Blues." Here Handy references Heaven as the New Jerusalem:

You'll see Golden Balls enough to pave the New Jerusalem
(Gates and McKay 1997:25)

In "(What Did I Do to Be So) Black and Blue?" jazz musicians Thomas "Fats" Waller and Andy Razaf reference Ham, Noah's second cursed son. They allude to Ham's African genealogy, as viewed in Western culture:

How sad I am, each day I feel worse
My mark of Ham seem to be a curse
(Hill et al. 1997:808)

In addition to songwriters, African American authors make persistent allusions to the Old Testament. See, for instance, Arna Bontemps poem "Miracles" (1963) (Davis and Redding, eds. 1971:333, lines 5–6). He makes allusions to Jesus' miracle of changing water into wine as found in John 2:3–9 and 4:46 of the New Testament:

A jug of water in the sun
Will easy turn to wine

In Langston Hughes's short story "Feet Live Their Own Life," the author references eyes in Psalms 115:5 of the Old Testament:

You have eyes but you see not
(Reprinted in Chapman, ed. 1972:100.)

Last, Countee Cullen in the poem "The Shroud of Color" (1925) alludes to Joseph's coat of many colors in Genesis 37:3 of the Old Testament:

Unmoored, on what strange quest I willed to float;
Who wore a many-colored coat of dreams
(Gates and McKay 1997:1307.)

Incorporated into African American literary works are familiar songs or passages from specific songs. To borrow from Stephen E. Henderson, in the introduction to *Understanding the New Black Poetry* (1973), both song and passages function as poetic references, and they create **contexts** for less obvious interpretations. For instance, in James Weldon Johnson's poem "O

Black and Unknown Bards" (1908) there are references to **spirituals**. The references are to spirituals that signaled escape by and to the slaves:

> Heart of what slave poured out such melody
> As "Steal away to Jesus"? On its strains
> His spirit must have nightly floated free,
> Though still about his hands he felt his chains.
> Who heard great "Jordan roll"? Whose starward eye
> Saw chariot "Swing low": And who was he
> That breathed that comforting, melodic sigh,
> "Nobody Knows de Trouble I See"?
> (Hill et al. 1997:870–71.)

For other examples of a writer's allusions to specific song titles and passages, see Sterling Brown's poems "When De Saints Go Ma'ching Home" (1927), "Strong Men" (1931), "Revelations" (1931), and "Crossing" (1932) (Brown 1980:26–30, 56–58, 88–89, 194–95).

Allusions exist also in works that allude to other literary works. For instance, Ann Petry's character Lutie Johnson in *The Street* (1946) alludes to Benjamin Franklin's autobiography—a work that motivates Lutie's thrift and perseverance. In Ralph Ellison's *Invisible Man* (1952) references are made to Horatio Alger's *Ragged Dick* (1867) and Booker T. Washington's *Up From Slavery* (1901). See also the works of Melvin Tolson.

amanuensis (aman.'u.'en.ses) The act of collaboration; transcribers for unlettered authors. Admittance of amanuensis can be found in the prefaces to early **slave narratives** such as *A Narrative of the Life and Adventures of Venture, A Native of Africa* (1798) and to modern **autobiography** such as *The Autobiography of Malcolm X* (1965). Critical **satire** of the amanuensis exists in Sherley Anne Williams's *Dessa Rose* (1986).

ambiguity (See Criticism and Theory.)

American Dream A phrase that represents cultural ideals and values held by many Americans when it comes to economic opportunities in America. The traditional view is that with thrift, diligence, and perseverance, anyone can achieve prosperity in America. Two immediate icons of the American Dream that are referenced often in African American literary genres are Benjamin Franklin and Horatio Alger. According to Richard Yarborough—

in the essay "The Quest for the American Dream in Three Afro-American Novels: *If He Hollers, Let Him Go, The Street,* and *The Invisible Man*" (1981)—in African American culture, the traditional optimistic view of economic achievement is traceable not only to Benjamin Franklin and Horatio Alger but also to African Americanist Booker T. Washington. The latter echoes Franklin's formula of economy, thrift, diligence, and perseverance. Washington also echoes Alger's formula of honesty, virtue, courage, determination, hard work, and dedication. But, for African Americans who are fervent believers in the American Dream, when against a background of inequality, prompted by racism, discrimination, and sexism, there are major ironies, double standards, and inconsistencies in the American Dream. Negated is the cultural ideology of economic opportunity in America.

As Yarborough points out, the American Dream is a recurring **theme** in African American literature, particularly during Reconstruction (see, e.g., Frank J. Webb's *The Garies and Their Friends* [1857]) and in literature after the World Wars (see, e.g., Richard Wright's *Native Son* [1940]; Chester Himes's *If He Hollers, Let Him Go* [1945]; Ann Petry's *The Street* [1946]; Ralph Ellison's *Invisible Man* [1952]; and John A. Williams's *The Man Who Cried I Am* [1967]). But, as suggested by Yarborough, in African American literary art there is also "a dialectical tension in African American thought" (35). While writing about the failures and contradictions of cultural ideology in America, writers tend to encourage "individual responsibility" and the attempt to grasp the true promise of America.

References for further reading: Don Belton, ed., *Speak My Name: Black Men on Masculinity and the American Dream* (1997); Phillipa Kafka, *The Great White Way: African American Women Writers and American Success Mythologies* (1993); Valerie Smith, *Self-Discovery and Authority in Afro-American Novels* (1991); Richard Yarborough, "The Quest for the American Dream" (1981).

anadiplosis (an-e-di-plo'-sis) A rhetorical figure of repetition used to achieve special effects. In particular, the last word of a sentence is repeated at the beginning of the sentence or stanza that follows. For example, in *Black Like Me* (1961), John Howard Griffen writes,

> The laughter had to be gross or it would turn to sobs, and to sob would be to realize, and to realize would be to despair. (xx)

(See also **piling.**)

analogy An illustration of an idea, event, et cetera, by way of more familiar ideas, events. See, for instance, Benjamin Banneker's "Letter to Thomas Jefferson" (1791)—Banneker, the author of the **letter,** is alluding to a state of servitude:

> Sir, suffer me to recall to your mind that time in which the arms and tyranny of the British Crown were exerted with every powerful effort in order to reduce you to a state of servitude (Hill et al. 1997:159).

Anancy The Caribbean **trickster** figure, the Spider, that is endowed with the survival skills of wit and guile; **Brer Rabbit** is the African American equivalent of the folkloric Anancy.

anaphora (e-naf'-e-re) The repetition of a word or a group of words in successive clauses or lines. Examples of anaphora exist in the following: Frederick Douglass's *Narrative of the Life of Frederick Douglass, an American Slave, Written by Himself* (1845):

> I saw nothing without seeing it, I heard nothing without hearing it, and
> Felt nothing without feeling (55–56)

James Baldwin's *Go Tell It On the Mountain* (1953):

> He had read about colored men being burned in the electric chair for things they had not done; how in riots they were beaten with clubs; how they were tortured in prisons; how they were the last to be hired and the first to be fired (36).

Ann Petry's *The Street* (1946):

> Because that kitchen sink in the advertisement or one just like it was what had wrecked her and Jim. The sink had belonged to someone else—she'd been washing someone else's dishes when she should have been home with Jim and Bub. Instead she'd cleaned another woman's house and looked after another woman's child while her own marriage went to pot; breaking up into so many little pieces it couldn't be put back together again, couldn't even be patched into a vague resemblance of its former self. (29–30)

John Edgar Wideman's *Brothers and Keepers* (1984):

> I didn't need outlaw brothers reminding me how much had been lost, how much compromised, how terribly the world still raged beyond the charmed circle of my life on the Laramie plains. (30)

See also the **sermon** "Noah Built the Ark" in James Weldon Johnson's collection *God's Trombones, Seven Negro Sermons in Verse* (1927):

> Sinners came a-running down to the ark;
> Sinners came a-swimming all round the ark;
> Sinners pleaded and sinners prayed—
> Sinners wept and sinners wailed—
> But Noah'd done barred the door (36)

There are speeches such as Martin Luther King Jr.'s delivery in Selma, Alabama, following the march from Selma to Montgomery, Alabama, in 1965:

> We are moving to the land of freedom. . . . Let us . . . march to the realization of the American dream. Let us march on segregated housing. . . . Let us march on segregated schools. . . . Let us march on poverty. . . . Let us march on ballot boxes . . . until race baiters disappear from the political arena. Let us march on until the Wallaces of our nation tremble away in silence
> (Washington 1986:229.)

See also Malcolm X's delivery of "The Ballot or the Bullet" at the infamous Audubon Ballroom in Harlem:

> Why should white people be running all the stores in our community?
> Why should white people be running the banks of our community?
> Why should the economy of our community be in the hands of the white man?
> Why?
> (Breitman 1989:38–39.)

Examples of anaphora exist also in Mari Evans's "Odyssey" and "Do We Be There Waiting" located in *Nightstar* (1981).

anastrophe (a-nas'-tro-fe) A particular effect is achieved when the writer inverts the natural order of words in a sentence. See, for instance, James Baldwin, writing in the following essays (in *Notes of a Native Son* 1955), "Many Thousand Gone" (1951):

> The Negro in America, gloomily referred to as that shadow which lies athwait our national life, is far more than that. (18)

"Stranger in the Village" (1953):

> The astonishment with which I might have greeted them, should they have stumbled into any African village a few hundred years ago, might have rejoiced their hearts. (139)

"Notes of a Native Son" (1955):

> But it was, if anything, a rather shorter funeral than most, nor, since there were no over-whelming, uncontrollable expressions of grief, could it be called—if I dare to use the word—successful. (87)

ancestor A term that denotes a reverence for departed members of the family; for the living after death; for what novelist and critic Toni Morrison calls the "ancient properties" of an authentic African American culture and heritage; or for what critic Karla Holloway calls, "a posture of remembrance" (Toni Morrison's *Washerwoman*; Thérèse Jadine in *Tar Baby* [1981]; Karla Holloway in *Moorings and Metaphors* [1992]). In traditional African religion, life is a continuum, meaning that death destroys the body but not the soul/spirit. In African American literature, the ancestor portrays a deep commitment to the African American community—to the collective as well as to the individual. As suggested by Baby Suggs in Toni Morrison's *Beloved* (1987), the ancestor is a spiritual guide, instructing the African American community, for example, "to love" itself. Or, as it is with the grandmother in Ann Petry's *The Street* (1946), the ancestor is instructive as well as protective, warning young and single mothers of Harlem to trust their instincts. At other times, as in Gloria Naylor's *Mama Day* (1988) or Ntozake Shange's *Cypress and Indigo* (1982), ancestors are timeless voices. Other ancestral figures in African American literature include the following: M'Dear and Aunt Jimmy in Morrison's *The Bluest Eye* (1970); Ondine and Sydney in Morrison's *Tar Baby* (1981); Minnie Ransom in Toni Cade Bambara's *The Salt Eaters* (1980); Nanny in Zora Neale Hurston's *Their Eyes Were Watching*

God (1937); and the grandfathers in Ralph Ellison's *Invisible Man* (1952) and John Edgar Wideman's *Fatheralong* (1994).

anecdote An account of a presumably true incident. In oral **folktales,** in **autobiographies** such as John Edgar Wideman's *Brothers and Keepers* (1984) and Booker T. Washington's *Up From Slavery* (1901); in biography such as *The Life of Langston Hughes* by Arnold Rampersad (1986–88). In many of these works, there is what is called anecdotal **digression.**

anima/animus (See **collective unconscious** under Criticism and Theory.)

anthem A song of praise, sometimes to God, man, woman, or nation. An act of reverence and rejoicing. See, for instance, James Weldon Johnson's "Lift Every Voice and Sing" (1900), which is often referred to as the "Negro National Anthem."

anthropology of art A term coined by Houston A. Baker Jr. to mean the unearthing (or reconstruction) of the full **context** out of which a genre originated or evolved before taking on cultural significance.

antimetabole (an-te-me-tab'-o-le) The reversal of the grammatical order of words in successive clauses. It is also a subtype of **chiasmus.** Examples of the figure of speech appear in the following excerpts:
Zora Neale Hurston's novel *Their Eyes Were Watching God* (1937):

> Now women forget all those things they don't want to remember and remember everything they don't want to forget. (1)

Frederick Douglass's autobiographical *Narrative of the Life of Frederick Douglass, an American Slave, Written by Himself* (1845):

> His words were in perfect keeping with his looks, and his looks were in perfect keeping with his words (39);

> You have seen how a man became a slave, you will see how a slave became a man. (77)

Jean Toomer's poem "Song of the Son" (*Cane* 1923):

> To catch thy plaintive soul, leaving, soon gone,
> Leaving, to catch thy plaintive soul soon gone (21)

antinovel The experimental narrative in which writers disrupt narrative conventions to include, for instance, **myth, ritual, satire,** and/or **allegory**. The term is usually associated with the writers Alice Walker, Ishmael Reed, Clarence Major, and John Edgar Wideman.

antiphony An element of African-derived communications between speaker and audience, also known as **call and response**. Involved is a spontaneous verbal and nonverbal interaction between speaker (call) and listeners (response)—that is, between preacher and congregation; jazz soloist and ensemble; singer and audience; or storyteller and audience. The antiphonal effect appears early in the traditional **spirituals** and **work songs**. African American writers who have experimented with antiphony include Jean Toomer in, for instance, "Song of the Son" (*Cane* 1923); Langston Hughes in, for instance, *The Weary Blues* (1926); Toni Morrison in, for instance, *Song of Solomon* (1977); and Paule Marshall in *Praisesong for the Widow* (1983).

antiphrasis (an-tif-ra-sis) A very brief form of **irony**. A single word that takes on an opposite meaning. Writers and works that employ the figurative term in order to imply the opposite include Richard Wright's *Native Son* (1940); William Garner Smith's *Last of the Conquerors* (1948); and Dorothy West's *The Living Is Easy* (1948).

antislavery period During the antislavery period (1832–1864), most African Americans were slaves. The exceptions were the indentured and free African Americans of the northern cities such as New York, Boston, and Philadelphia and of southern cities such as Baltimore, Charleston, and New Orleans. While free African Americans had access to public education and some acquired fortunes (e.g., Paul Cuffe and James Forten), they were, like the majority of African Americans, subjected to racist acts of violence and to discrimination. Too, they were at risk of losing their lives in, for instance, race riots or by being lynched. Opposition to slavery, to discrimination, to murder, and to other hate crimes are expressed throughout the 1800s by slaves in slave revolts, in escape via the **underground railroad,** in **folktales,** in music, and even in their enlistments into the Union Army. The freedmen and some slave fugitives also opposed slavery and violence via **oratory,** public **letters, poetry,** and **autobiography**. As John Hope Franklin contends in

From Slavery to Freedom (1947), some of the slaves who cooked for their owners also protested bondage by slowly killing their masters with small amounts of poison or ground glass in their food.

Orators against slavery include Marie Stewart, the first African American woman to engage in public political debate against slavery; Frederick Douglass, the most well known public spokesman against slavery; and others such as Sojourner Truth, Samuel Ringgold Ward, and Henry Highland Garnet. The most prolific antislavery poets include George Moses Horton and Frances Watkins Harper. Antislavery novelists include Harriet Adams Wilson in *Our Nig* (1859) and William Wells Brown in *Clotel* (1853).

The most prolific antislavery literature to emerge from this period is the autobiography, later to be called the **slave narrative**. Included in the canon of African American literature are the following slave narratives: *A Narrative of the Uncommon Sufferings and Surprising Deliverance of Briton Hammon, a Negro Man* (1760); *Narrative of the Life of Frederick Douglass, an American Slave, Written by Himself* (1845); *Recollections of Slavery* (1838); *Narrative of William W. Brown, a Fugitive Slave* (1847); *The Fugitive Blacksmith; or Events in the Life of James W. C. Pennington* (1849); *Narrative of the Life and Adventures of Henry Bibb, Written by Himself* (1849); *The Life of Josiah Henson, Formerly a Slave, Now an Inhabitant of Canada, as Narrated by Himself* (1849); *Narrative of Henry Box Brown* (1849); Solomon Northrup's *Twelve Years a Slave* (1853); and *Running a Thousand Miles for Freedom; or, The Escape of William and Ellen Craft from Slavery* (1860). See also the Web page of William Andrews at wandrews@email.unc.edu.

Black nationalists emerge from the antislavery period. They include David Walker in *Appeal in Four Articles; Together, with a Preamble to the Coloured Citizens of the World* (1829); Paul Cuffe in *Brief Account of the Settlement and Present Situation of the Colony of Sierra Leone* (1811); and Martin R. Delany in *The Condition, Elevation, Emigration and Destiny of the Colored People of the United States, Politically Considered* (1852).

References for further reading: John W. Blassingame, *The Slave Community: Plantation Life in the Antebellum South* (1972); John Ernest, *Resistance and Reformation in Nineteenth-Century African-American Literature* (1995); George B. Handley, *Post Slavery Literature in the Americas: Family Portraits in Black and White* (2000).

antithesis (an-tith'-esis) The parallel structure of contrasting ideas. See, for example, Harriet Jacobs's *Incidents in the Life of a Slave Girl* (1861):

Whatsoever ye would that men should do unto you, do ye even so unto them, but I was her slave and I suppose she did not recognize me as her neighbor. (11)

(See also **binary opposition.**)

anxieties of influence (See **influence** under Criticism and Theory.)

aphaeresis A scheme of orthography that involves subtracting a syllable from the beginning of a word (e.g., 'neath for beneath; 'bout for about; 'cause for because) in order to accommodate the poetic diction and the rhyme (or rhythm) in verse or prose.
(See also **apocope.**)

aphorism The truth revealed in a terse statement. Insightfulness is the end function. In her speech, "Ar'n't I a Woman," Sojourner Truth renders an example of a terse statement:

If my cup won't hold but a pint, and yours holds a quart, wouldn't you be mean not to let me have my little half-measure full?
(Gates and McKay 1997:200.)
(See also **proverb.**)

apocope A scheme of orthography that involves subtracting a syllable from the end of a word (e.g., even for evening; **testifyin** for testifying; goin for going) in order to accommodate the poetic diction and rhyme (or rhythm) in verse or prose.
(See also **aphaeresis.**)

apostrophe The rhetorical means of addressing a dead person (as if still alive), or addressing an abstract or an inanimate object as if objects did exist. See, for instance, Paul Laurence Dunbar's "Douglass" (1903):

Ah Douglass, we have fall'n on evil days
(Gates and McKay 1997:903, line 1.)
James Weldon Johnson's "Go Down Death," in the collection *God's Trombones, Seven Negro Sermons in Verse* (1927):

And Death heard the summons
And he leaped on his fastest horse
Pale as a sheet in the moonlight.

Up the golden street death galloped,
And the hoofs of his horse struck fire from the gold,
But they didn't make no sound.
Up Death rode to the Great White Throne,
And waited for God's command. (28)

See also the Pharaoh Akhenaton's "The Hymn to the Aton" (1350 B.C.), which is a praise song to the sun.

Thou appearest beautifully on the horizon of heaven
Thou living Aton the beginning of life!

(Translated by John A. Wilson. In *African American Literature: Voices in a Tradition* 1992:80, lines 1–2.)

archetype (See **collective unconscious** under Criticism and Theory.)

"art is life" (See **"art of the people"** and **storytelling**.)

"art of the people" A phrase used often by Alain Locke to distinguish the following African views: **"art is life,"** "art is functional," or "art of the people" (the needs of the community determine the artist's production, or, the artist is responsible to his society). At times, Locke references the Western view of "art for art's sake" in his essay "Art or Propaganda?" (1928), but by its end, Locke appears focused on having artists pull simply from a folk poetics when producing art. He seems to decide that African American art is life. For further explanations of the traditional African view of art, read Innocent C. Onyewuenyi's essay, "Traditional African Aesthetics: A Philosophical Perspective" (1995):

> [In traditional African worldview], art is functional, community-oriented and depersonalized, *unlike Western art which is arbitrary, representative of the values and emotions of the artist, without reference to the cultural environment and the historical reality of the people.* (Emphasis added.)

References for further reading: Alain Locke, "Art or Propaganda?" in *African American Literary Criticism, 1773 to 2000* ed. Ervin (1999); Innocent C. Onyewuenyi, "Traditional African Aesthetics: A Philosophical Perspective," in *African Philosophy, Selected Readings* ed. Moseley (1995).

ascent (See **ascension narrative.**)

ascension narrative A trope of **ascent** in African American literary criticism that is introduced by Robert B. Stepto in *From Behind the Veil: A Study of Afro-American Narrative* (1979). A "consciousness" in ascension narratives, or in narratives that are of symbolic journey or pilgrimage. This level of consciousness comes while the narrator is on a quest for freedom, literacy, selfhood, and/or voice. Many times, the journey or pilgrimage is to the North. Also introduced by Stepto is the trope of immersion (i.e., group consciousness). Here, the narrator (male or female) returns usually to the South in search of knowledge about his or her culture. An example of the ascension narrative is Frederick Douglass's *Narrative of the Life of Frederick Douglass, an American Slave, Written by Himself* (1845). In Ralph Ellison's *Invisible Man* (1952) and in Zora Neale Hurston's *Their Eyes Were Watching God* (1937), tropes of ascent and immersion are present.

References for further reading: Robert B. Stepto, *From Behind the Veil: A Study of Afro-American Narrative* (1979); and Robert Burns Stepto and Dexter Fisher, eds., *Afro-American Literature: The Reconstruction of Instruction* (1978).

assimilation A term used to define a social-class phenomenon among African Americans from the late 1800s to the late 1950s. To paraphrase Langston Hughes in "Negro Artist and the Racial Mountain" (1926), in the African American middle-class home, a **color line** is drawn for the assimilationist— for example, Beethoven replaces **spirituals, ragtime,** and **jazz;** African American children attend mixed schools; white theaters, movies, and newspapers become alternative means of entertainment. According to Hughes, such aspiring middle-class African Americans have "Nordic manners, Nordic faces, Nordic hair, Nordic art (if any) and an Episcopal heaven."

Biologically, the aspiring African American middle class, particularly the near-white members of the **Blue Vein Society** elect to assimilate, espouse to rise in social standings by erasing all traces of their **blackness**. To quote a phrase by Robert Bone in *The Negro Novel in America* (1958), they strive to become "lighter and lighter [by] each generation."

A **theme** in African American literature, assimilation symbolizes the denial of one's racial identity; one's escape from or flight from race problems confronting African Americans either psychologically or physically (i.e., **passing**). Literary works that have all or predominantly white characters are referred to as assimilationist works of art: Oscar Micheaux's *The Conquest*

(1913); Paul Laurence Dunbar's *The Uncalled* (1898); James Weldon Johnson's *The Autobiography of an Ex-Colored Man* (1912); Willard Motley's *Knock on Any Door* (1947); Chester Himes's *Cast the First Stone* (1952) and *We Fished All Night* (1951); Ann Petry's *Country Place* (1947); Zora Neale Hurston's *Seraph on the Suwanee* (1948); and William Gardner Smith's *Anger at Innocence* (1950). See also any of the many novels by Frank Yerby, including *The Foxes of Harrow* (1946).

assonance A repetition of similar vowel sounds used to produce a certain effect. See, for instance, Langston Hughes's "The Negro Speaks of Rivers" (1921):

> I've known rivers ancient as the *world* and *older* than the *flow* of hu-
> man
> *Blood* in human veins
> (Gates and McKay 1997:1254, lines 1–3.)

Jean Toomer's "Beehive" (*Cane* 1923):

> *Within this* black *hive tonight*
> (Gates and McKay 1997:1117, line 1.)

Al Young's "For Poets":

> Stay beautiful
> but don't stay *down* under*ground* too long
> (Adoff 1973:361–62.)

asyndeton (a-sin'-de-ton) The deliberate omission of conjunctions, pronouns, and even articles in order to promote a hurried rhythm. See, for instance, Henry Dumas's "Strike and Fade" located in *Ark of Bones and Other Stories* (1974):

> He walkin' light, easy, pawin' (118)

or

> We hang around. Listen to talk. (119)
> (Redmond 1974: 119.)

See also John Edgar Wideman's short fiction "Newborn thrown in the trash and dies" (1992):

> Since the time between my wake-up call and curfew is so cruelly brief,

the speeded-up preview of what will come to pass, my life, my portion,
my destiny, my career, slowed down just enough to let me peak.
(Hill et al. 1997:1881.)

From longer fiction, see Ann Petry's *The Street* (1946):

Young women coming home from work—dirty, tired, depressed—
looked forward to the moment when they would change their clothes
and head toward the gracious spaciousness of the Junto. (144)

and, also,

She could feel his eyes traveling over her—estimating her, summing
her up, wondering about her. (13)

See, as well, Toni Morrison's *Sula* (1973):

The Presence of evil was something to be first recognized, then dealt
with, survived, outwitted, triumphed over. (118)

authenticating narrative A term coined by Robert B. Stepto that distinguishes phases of development in **slave narratives**. Taking into account the
fact that slave narratives were always authenticated via prefaces, **letters,** and
other documents by slaveholders, abolitionists, or others, Stepto suggests
critics can trace the moves of slaves to document their stories. For instance,
does the slave use documents that create a collective dialogue or an *eclectic
narrative?* Does the slave use documents as speech and even as actions while
he or she (the slave) has the burden of introducing and authenticating his
or her story in an *integrated narrative?* Does the slave use documents that
are integrated effortlessly into his or her story—into his or her *generic narrative?* The most integrated form of narrations by slaves that are inclusive of
the slave's story and of authenticating documents is the authenticating narrative. An example of an eclectic narrative is Henry Bibb's *Narrative of the
Life and Adventure of Henry Bibb* (1849); an example of a generic narrative is
Frederick Douglass's *Narrative of the Life of Frederick Douglass, an American
Slave, Written by Himself* (1845); an authenticating narrative resembles William Wells Brown's *Narrative of the Life and Escape of William Wells Brown*
(1852). An example of an integrated narrative is Solomon Northrup's *Twelve
Years a Slave* (1854).

References for further reading: Valerie Smith, "Form and Ideology in Three Slave Narratives," 1987. Robert B. Stepto, "Narration, Authentication, and Authorial Control in

Frederick Douglass's Narrative of 1845," in *Afro-American Literature: The Reconstruction of Instruction*, pp. 179–91, edited by Dexter Fisher and Robert B. Stepto.

autobiography An account of a person's own life that is usually chronological and unified in narrative structure. The genre has two distinct types. First, there is the *secular autobiography*—that is, recollections that have been written by freed and fugitive slaves, some more famous than others. Next, there is the *spiritual autobiography*. Not always distinguishable from secular, but in a narrow sense, the spiritual autobiography is identifiable by its multipurposes: (1) the spiritual and soulful journey of the individual, (2) the collective struggle for equality and justice, (3) travel writing, (4) communal claims to humanity and freedom, and sometimes (5) exposure to sexism within the church's hierarchy.

According to William Andrews (1986), the secular autobiography by fugitive slaves is synonymous with the **slave narrative**—a genre that has become a separate form of study in African American letters. Joanne Braxton, who has written extensively about the female secular autobiography, reveals a duel focus in autobiography by women writers: (1) an autobiographical account of the writer as African American, and (2) an autobiographical account of the writer as female and as African American female. The list of secular autobiography is exhaustive. In the canon of African American literature, however, there are the following familiar slave narratives/autobiographies: Olaudah Equiano's *The Interesting Narrative of the Life of Olaudah Equiano, or Gustavus Vassa, the African* (1789); Frederick Douglass's *Narrative of the Life of Frederick Douglass, an American Slave, Written by Himself* (1845); and Harriet Jacobs's *Incidents in the Life of a Slave Girl* (1861). Other twentieth-century secular autobiography that exists in the canon are Booker T. Washington's *Up From Slavery* (1901); Zora Neale Hurston's *Dust Track on a Road* (1942); Richard Wright's *Black Boy* (1945); Claude Brown's *Manchild in the Promised Land* (1965); and Maya Angelou's *I Know Why the Caged Bird Sings* (1970).

In the canon, the spiritual autobiography includes Briton Hammon's *Narrative of the Uncommon Sufferings and Surprising Deliverance of Briton Hammon, a Negro Man* (1760); James Albert Ukawsaw Gronniosaw's *A Narrative of the Most Remarkable Particulars in the Life of James Albert Ukawsaw Gronniosaw, an African Prince* (1770); John Marrant's *A Narrative of the Lord's Wonderful Dealings with John Marrant* (1790); Jarena Lee's *Life and Religious Experience of Jarena Lee, a Coloured Lady, Giving an Account of Her*

Call to Preach the Gospel . . . Written by Herself (1836); and Sojourner Truth's *Narrative of Sojourner Truth* (1850).

References for further reading: William L. Andrews, *To Tell a Free Story: The First Century of Afro-American Autobiography 1760–1865* (1986), wandrews@email.unc.edu; Joanne M. Braxton, *Black Women Writing Autobiography: A Tradition Within a Tradition* (1989); Frances Smith Foster, *Witnessing Slavery* (1994).

badman/"bad man"/"bad-ass(ed) nigger" A character type that can be traced to folkloric **heroes** and has been, more or less, a real man. While the badman and the "bad-ass(ed) nigger" are solitary individuals, rebellious, amoral, and antagonistic toward social order in the dominant society and in the African American community, the two character types are distinct. Thought to be a reflection of the anger and despair that grips the African American community, the badman represents the most oppressed and depressed. He avenges wrongs by subverting authority of those who exert power ruthlessly. Like the **trickster,** the badman uses wit and guile to overcome political, social, and economic oppressions. He champions for the underrepresented and oppressed in his community. In contrast, the "bad-ass(ed) nigger" has little or no concerns for communal values. He has no regrets and, if any, little remorse for his lawlessness, violence, and destruction. According to Clarence Major in *Juba to Jive: A Dictionary of African-American Slang* (1970), this person can be "a positive, courageous person; troublemaker; [and] mean person."

The badman is represented by folk characters Railroad Bill, Stagolee (Stackolee, Stackalee, Staggerlee) and John Henry; and by the mythological character Shine. The "bad-ass(ed) nigger" may be represented by fictional character Bigger Thomas in *Native Son* (1940) by Richard Wright.

Written in some places is the term "bad man," which connotes a sense of communal admiration for the male's humanizing ability and courage to defy societal order and authority. See Sonia Sanchez's *We a BaddDDD People* (1970) and Walter Mosely's *Devil in a Blue Dress* (1990).

References for further reading: Christopher C. DeSaints, "Badman," in *The Oxford Companion to African American Literature* ed. Andrews et al. (1997); Lawrence W. Levine, *Black Culture and Black Consciousness: Afro-American Folk Thought from Slavery to Freedom* (1977); and John W. Roberts, *From Trickster to Badman: The Black Folk Hero to Slavery and Freedom* (1990).

badwoman/"bad woman" A female character type that is unguided by conventional norms set by the family, church, or community. Almost always, the bad woman is characterized by her robust sexuality, moral indifference, braggadocio persona, and/or fierce independence. Familiar bad-women in lore include Bessie Smith, the Empress of the **blues**. In the 1920s, Smith is a fierce independent woman known in the real world and in the fictionalized world for her sexually aggressive lyrics. (See also Frankie [of "Frankie and Johnnie"] who resorts to violence.) According to Trudier Harris in *The Oxford Companion to African American Literature* ed. Andrews et al. (1997), the character type can be found in the following writers' fiction:

Esther in James Baldwin's *Go Tell It On the Mountain* (1953)
Faith Cross in Charles Johnson's *Faith and the Good Thing* (1974)
Sula in Toni Morrison's *Sula* (1973)
Jadine Childs in Toni Morrison's *Tar Baby* (1981)
Shug Avery in Alice Walker's *The Color Purple* (1982)
Etta Mae Johnson in Gloria Naylor's *The Women of Brewster Place* (1982)
Sarah Phillips in Andrea Lee's *Sarah Phillips* (1984)
Dessa Rose in Sherley Anne Williams's *Dessa Rose* (1986)
Sethe Suggs in Toni Morrison's *Beloved* (1987)
Mama in Terry McMillan's *Mama* (1987)

The term "bad woman" connotes a sense of communal admiration for the female's independence and humanizing courage to defy and/or to resist the patriarchy and cultural notions of womanhood.
(See also **badman.**)

References for further reading: Trudier Harris, "bad woman," in *The Oxford Companion to African American Literature* ed. Andrews et al. (1997); Lawrence W. Levine, *Black Culture and Black Consciousness: Afro-American Folk Thought from Slavery to Freedom* (1977); and John W. Roberts, *From Trickster to Badman: The Black Folk Hero to Slavery and Freedom* (1990).

Bakongo cosmology The perpetuity of life through time, space, and circumstances common to African religion. Aesthetic perceptions include:

Rising	birth, beginning, or regrowth
Ascendency	maturity and responsibility
Setting	implied death and transformation
Midnight	indicating existence in the other world and eventual rebirth

Reference for further reading: Margaret Creel, *A Peculiar People: Slave Religion and Community Culture Among the Gullahs* (1988).

ballad A story told with economy in verse and also easily set to music. Origins of the ballad are not easily identifiable, but familiar characteristics include the use of everyday language; and subjects and **themes** that are from community life, legends, folk **heroes,** historical figures, **tricksters,** and outlaws. Examples of the ballad modeled after community life include Gwendolyn Brooks's "Of De Witt Williams on his Way to Lincoln Cemetery" (Brooks 1963:10) and Margaret Walker's "The Ballad of the Free" (Hill et al. 1989:1160–61). Examples of the ballad shaped by **folklore** include "John Henry," "The Ballad of Jesse Jones," "Casey Jones," and Margaret Walker's "Molly Means." For an example of a ballad shaped by historical figures, see "The Escape of Gabriel Prosser." For an example of a ballad shaped by outlaws, see "Railroad Bill" or "Stackalee."

bard The term is used in almost any society to distinguish par excellence among its creative poets. In the poem "O Black and Unknown Bards" (1908), James Weldon Johnson assigns such a distinction to the American slave, the creators of the Negro **spirituals.**
(See also **"O black and unknown bards."**)

beat generation A 1950s generation of middle-class Euro American writers who experimented with the composition and form of **blues/jazz** in their poetry. See, for example, Allen Ginsberg's *Howl* (1956) and *Sandwiches* (1963); Jack Kerouac's *On the Road* (1957); Gregory Corso's *Gasoline* (1958); Gary Snyder's *RipRap* (1959); Lawrence Ferlinghetti's *Picture of the Gone World* (1955); and William S. Burrough's *The Naked Lunch* (1959). African American cohorts of the hip group included Ted Joans, Bob Kaufman and Amiri Baraka. Of the group, Kaufman is said to have coined the term "beat."

bildungsroman Traditionally, a narrative account of the spiritual, psychological, social, and political development of a young **hero** or **heroine** as he or she matures and integrates into dominate society or culture. Development for the African American hero or heroine (see **hero/heroine/heroism**) within the dominant culture yields narratives of various **contexts.** For instance, in W.E.B. DuBois's *The Quest of the Silver Fleece* (1911), during the hero's development, he critiques and resists the larger society that denies his validity and **blackness.** In Alice Walker's *The Third Life of Grange Copeland* (1970), the heroine's activism aids in her moral development. In James Weldon Johnson's *Autobiography of an Ex-Colored Man* (1912) and in Ralph

Ellison's *Invisible Man* (1952), the male heroes move inside and outside of dominant culture in order to emphasize **ambiguities** in identity formation and validation of blackness. Experimental bildungsromans in voice and contexts include Zora Neale Hurston's *Their Eyes Were Watching God* (1937) and Amiri Baraka's *The System of Dante's Hell* (1965).

binary opposition A rhetorical process that involves exploring similarities and differences by contrast, and then by making connections—some interpretations or points of disjuncture. According to Henry Louis Gates, Jr. in *Figures in Black* (1987), oppositions (contrasts) in their simplest forms include: presence/absence, positive/negative, on/off, up/down, left/right. In his study of the binary oppositions in Frederick Douglass's *Narrative of the Life of Frederick Douglass, an American Slave, Written by Himself* (1845), Gates finds the following for interpretation: spiritual/material; aristocratic/base; civilized/barbaric; sterile/fertile; enterprise/sloth; force/principle; fact/imagination; linear/**cyclical.**

Reference for further reading: Henry Louis Gates Jr., *Figures in Black: Words, Signs, and the Racial Self* (1987).

biography Derived from the Greek words *bio* (for life) and *graphia* (for writing), biography is both a type of literary work and a literary genre in which there is a written account of a person's life. Biographer Arnold Rampersad asserts that biographers who write biographies generically and stylistically share three important attributes: (1) academic training in historical methods; (2) research that is meticulous and sustained; and (3) freedom to contemplate and compose the subject's life story, particularly the subject's psychology. The earliest African American biographies reflected the collective biography—chapter-length accounts of each subject's life that typically focused on presenting a person's life story through the rhetoric of uncritical praise rather than through researched analysis. Examples of the collective biography include William Wells Brown's *The Black Man: His Antecedents, His Genius, and His Achievements* (1863) and William J. Simmons's *Noted Negro Women, Their Triumphs and Activities* (1893). Although the earliest known book-length biography of a single African American is *The Life and Works of Paul Laurence Dunbar* (1907) by white author Lida Keck Wiggins, African Americans have penned several biographies of African Americans, and many of these works are critically acclaimed: Wayne Cooper's *Claude McKay: Rebel Sojourner in the Harlem Re-*

naissance (1987); Arnold Rampersad's two-volume *The Life of Langston Hughes* (1986–88); David Levering Lewis's Pulitzer Prize-winning *W.E.B. DuBois: The Biography of a Race, 1868–1919* (1993); and Thadious Davis's *Nella Larsen: Novelist of the Harlem Renaissance* (1994).

Reference for further reading: Valerie Boyd, *Wrapped in Rainbow* (2002); Arnold Rampersad, "Biography, Autobiography, and Afro-American Culture" (1983).

black aesthetics, the An aesthetic that combines elements of philosophy and ideology manifesto to explain ideally what constitutes beauty and how art that seeks to create beauty should be produced and evaluated. Although placing the definite article "the" before the term may inaccurately imply a unilateral monolith, black aesthetics seeks to advance the collective human value of persons who are black-identified. Because black-identified people in America have suffered deracination and dehumanization, any black aesthetic will have at its core a political urgency. Black aestheticians of the 1960s are better known (e.g., Larry Neal, Amiri Baraka, Maulana Ron Karenga, Hoyt Fuller, Dudley Randall), but in the 1820s there were proponents of a black aesthetics (e.g., David Walker's *Appeal. In Four Articles; Together with a Preamble to the Coloured Citizens of the World, but in Preamble to the Coloured Citizens of the World, but in Particular, and Very Expressly, to Those of the United States of America* (1829); Sutton E. Griggs in *Life's Demands, or According to Law* (1916). Likewise, in the 1920s and 1930s, there were proponents of a black aesthetics (e.g., Langston Hughes in "The Negro Artist and the Racial Mountain" (1926) and Richard Wright in "Blueprint for Negro Writing" (1937). Seminal works that discuss a black aesthetics include Stephen E. Henderson in *Understanding the New Black Poetry: Black Music and Black Speech as Poetic References* (1973); Addison Gayle's *The Black Aesthetic* (1971); and the edited works of Larry Neal, Amiri Baraka, Hoyt Fuller, and Maulana Ron Karenga.

(See also **existentialism, modernism, postmodernism.**)

References for further reading: Nikki Giovanni, *Black Feeling, Black Talk, Black Judgement* (1970); William J. Harris, "Black Aesthetic," in *The Oxford Companion to African American Literature* ed. Andrews et al. (1997); Haki R. Madhubuti, 1984.

"Black Arts" A poem written in 1969 by Amiri Baraka that encompasses the ideology of the **Black Arts Movement.** Symbolizing the literature of the 1960s and the 1970s, the poem calls for writers to reorder Western cultural aesthetics. "Black Arts" (1969) encourages separate **symbolism,** mythology, and iconology that are within the African American community. Like the literature of the 1960s and 1970s, "Black Arts" exists for its action and its resistance to Western America; it functions like "fists" and "daggers."

Black Arts Movement A literary movement of mostly young, politically conscious African American artists who come of age in the 1960s and, as Kalamu ya Salaam says in "Black Arts Movement" (1997), "advance 'social engagement' as a *sine qua non* of [black] aesthetic." In other words, the Black Arts Movement proposed as one of its principal aims the grassroots mobilization and politicization of all black-identified people, using literature (particularly **poetry** and **drama**), music, **dance,** film, and other art forms to achieve both artistic and political autonomy at any price. Hence, to further advance the cause of black political and cultural empowerment, the Black Arts Movement advocated accessible art that was produced *by* blacks, *about* blacks, and *for* blacks. African American artistic productions flourished between 1960 and 1976, the generally accepted time frame of the movement. The Black Arts Movement left an impressive legacy of artistic innovations, including a valorization of the black **vernacular, subversive** orthography, and a reemphasis on **orality** and **call and response** (most successfully realized in **rap** and **"spoken word"** poetry). Profanity enters African American poetry during these years. Stephen Henderson cites profanity in the African American vernacular and in poetry as an "appropriation of the **dozens** technique." Seminal works of the period include Larry Neal's "The Black Arts Movement" (1968); Leroi Jones (Amiri Baraka) and Larry Neal's edited collection *Black Fire: An Anthology of Afro-American Writing* (1968); Harold Cruse's *The Crisis of the Negro Intellectual* (1967) and Stephen E. Henderson's *Understanding the New Black Poetry: Black Music and Black Speech as Poetic References* (1973).

References for further reading: Stephen E. Henderson, *Understanding The New Black Poetry* (1973); Larry Neal, "The Black Arts Movement," in *African American Literary Criticism, 1773 to 2000* ed. Ervin (1999); Kalamu ya Salaam, "Black Arts Movement," in *The Oxford Companion to African American Literature* ed. Andrews et al. (1997).

"black Atlantic, the" A perspective when referring to the **middle passage** that encourages interdisciplinary, comparative, and diasporic studies. As a concept, the "space in between" or the spatial and temporal continuum of a middle passage sensibility links and shapes geographical and cultural regions of Africa into a black and/or diasporic aesthetic. Exemplary works of "the black Atlantic" include Toni Morrison's *Tar Baby* (1981) and Paule Marshall's *The Chosen People, The Timeless People* (1969).

References for further reading: Geneviève Fabre, "The Slave Ship Dance," in *Black Imagination and the Middle Passage* (1999); Paul Gilroy, *The Black Atlantic: Modernity and Double Consciousness* (1995).

black gay aesthetic Questioning how major literary texts have rendered gay men invisible and invalid, Charles Nero in "Toward a Black Gay Aesthetic" (1991) turns to **signifying,** a persistent rhetorical strategy of creativity, as a critical paradigm for critiquing African American literature and African American gay literature. Via **indirection** and **irony,** African American gay male writers place their works within the African American literary tradition, a tradition that allows writers—via indirection—to deconstruct, subvert, and revise the black experience. Interpreters of gay literature are encouraged to acknowledge such **contexts.** An exemplary work remains Melvin Dixon's "The Boy with a Beer," 1978). See also Essex Hemphill's collection *Brother to Brother: New Writings by Black Gay Men* (1991).

References for further reading: Winston Napier, ed. *African American Literary Theory* (2000); Charles Nero, "Toward A Black Gay Aesthetic: Signifying in Contemporary Black Gay Literature" (1999).

black nationalism Although nationalism most often represents a strong loyalty to and identification with geographical boundaries, ethnicity, cultural customs, and language, the representative rubric that defines black nationalism is the construct of race. Hence, geography (and to varyingly lesser degrees), ethnicity, culture, and language are secondary factors in defining nation. Black nationalism transcends the normal markers of traditional nationalism, replacing those markers with race, which represents those physical, political, and cultural attributes through which people of African descent both are identified and self-identify. Black nationalism, then, is a dedication to the cultural (especially political) concerns of the black race. It is also the belief that black-identified people should collectively define themselves on the basis of race and adopt a politics that emphasizes panracial rather than global goals. Finally, black nationalism is a policy that advocates separatism from nonblack (particularly white) people and the creation of autonomous black communities worldwide. Political, social, aesthetic, and other cultural aspects of black nationalism all share an aspiration for racial independence in any region under nonblack control. Important black nationalist works include Sutton E. Griggs, *Imperium in Imperio* (1899) and *The Hindered Hand* (1905); Marcus Garvey's *Aims and Objects of Movement for Solutions of the Negro Problem Outlined* (1966–1968).

References for further reading: Rodney Carlisle, *The Roots of Black Nationalism* (1975); Moses, *The Golden Age of Black Nationalism* (1988); Madhu Dubey, *Black Woman Novelists and the Nationalist Aesthetic* (1994); Elizabeth J. West, "Black Nationalism" (1997).

blackness The state, quality, or condition of possessing those physical and cultural aspects associated with people who have been identified and self-identified as black; also the degree to which one is identified or self-identified as having the physical and cultural particulars. In the United States, notions about physical blackness have been influenced by the concept of hypodescent or "the one-drop rule," which asserts that one drop of black blood makes one racially black. As a result of hypodescent, those who are identified and who self-identify as black, range from Europeans—having skin complexions, eye colors, hair textures, and bone structures typically associated with Europeans—to sub-Saharan Africans—to skin, eye, hair, and skeletal features associated with sub-Saharan Africans, including all the physical features that exist between these two extremes. Equally challenging to define are those cultural particulars that also attempt to define blackness, and in the realm of philosophy, the markers of blackness represent African cultural vestiges present in the black diaspora—what Toni Morrison calls "Africanisms"—that deviate from Western cultural norms and that may include but are not limited to the following: a predilection for orality and the rhythm and music of speech even in writing; an emphasis on a collective identity, on the importance of community over the individual; a seamless fusion of the rational and the irrational, of the natural and the preternatural, and a prevailing view of development not as linear but as **circular** and **cyclical**. Important African American works that address blackness as a semantic, a cultural, or an artistic concern include W.E.B. DuBois's *The Souls of Black Folk* (1903); Harold Cruse's *The Crisis of the Negro Intellectual* (1967); and Henry Louis Gates Jr.'s *Figures in Black: Words, Signs, and the Racial Self* (1987).

References for further reading: Toni Morrison, "Rootedness: The Ancestor as Foundation" (1999); James A. Snead, "Repetition as a figure of black culture" (1984).

"black talk" (See **African American English.**)

"black veil" (See **double consciousness.**)

blank verse Traditionally, a form of English verse that appears close to the rhythms of everyday English speech. Blank verse consists of unrhymed and five-stress lines. Variations of the form appear in African American literature. See, for example, the variations in James Weldon Johnson's "O Black and Unknown Bards" (1908):

> O black and unknown bards of long ago
> How came your lips to touch the sacred fire?
> (Gates and McKay 1997:769, lines 1–2)

> In Jean Toomer's "Song of the Son" (1923):

> Pour O pour that parting soul in song
> O pour it in the sawdust glow of night
> (Gates and McKay 1997:1095–96.)

blaxploitation A portmanteau word created from the fusion of the words *black* and *exploitation, blaxploitation* was coined in 1972. It defines the selfish and unethical treatment of blacks and black culture by producers of black-oriented films. The term's meaning has evolved to include any cinematic, musical, visual, or written work that presents distorted, stereotypical **representations** (see under Criticism and Theory) of black people and black culture that panders to fly-by-night popular trends, and that is motivated more by the allure of financial gain than the attainment of artistic and aesthetic integrity. Typical characteristics of works deemed "blaxploitative" include the relegation of **characterization,** language, thought, and plot to spectacle; to one-dimensional, predictable characters defined by outrageous, over-the-top clothing, speech, "street-talk," and nonverbal gestures; to dialogue filled with gratuitous profanity and exaggerated black slang; to characters whose mental rationale for action is reduced to violence derived from an uncritical defense of simplistic notions of "race pride" or "black manhood"; and to a formulaic plot that features a protagonist (usually a pimp, fugitive, or other antihero) in sensationalized conflict with the forces of society. Presented also are unimaginative, predictable villains (usually corrupt white politicians or police officers); excessive depictions of graphic, interracial sex; stark, drug-infested urban or clichéd rural settings; and excessively violent melees in which evil whites and "sell-out" blacks get their comeuppance. The financial and critical success of Melvin Van Peebles's *Sweet Sweetback's Baaaaad Ass Song* (1970) initiated the first blaxploitation wave that resulted in over two hundred films being produced between 1971 and 1980, including *Shaft* (1971); *Superfly* and *Black Caesar* (1972); *Blacula* (1973); *The Mark, Trick Baby, and Coffy* (1973); *Get Christie Love* (1974); *Black Samson* (1974); *The Black Godfather* (1974); and *Dolemite* (1975). Literary works considered also to be blaxploitative include the novels of Iceberg Slim and Donald Gaines.

The second wave of blaxploitation was occasioned by the commercial and artistic success of university-trained John Singleton's *Boyz N the Hood* (1991). This film, which signaled a renewed interest in black culture, particularly Hip-hop music, spawned a series of black-male-protagonists-in-the-hood films that were seemingly driven more by Hollywood's attempt to cash in on the resurgent craze for all things black and urban than on aesthetic concerns. There are works that attempt to counter the 1990s and the millennial stereotypes with complex, fresh representations of black life. See, for example, films such as Julie Dash's *Daughters of the Dust* (1991); Carl Franklin's *One False Move* (1992); Spike Lee's *Malcolm X* (1992); Darnell Martin's *I Like It Like That* (1994); Charles Burnett's *The Glass Shield* (1995); Kasi Lemmon's *Eve's Bayou* (1997); George Tillman's *Soul Food* (1998); and Denzel Washington's *The Antwone Fisher Story* (2001).

References for further reading: Ed Guerrero, *Framing Blackness: The African American Image in Film* (1993): 83–100; bell hooks, *Reel to Real: Race, Sex, and Class at the Movies* (1996); Darius James, *That Blaxploitation: Roots of the Badasssss'Tude (Rated X by an All Whyte Jury)* (1995); Tommy L. Lott, "A No-Theory Theory of Contemporary Black Cinema" (1999); Gerald Martinez's *What It Is . . . What It Was!; The Black Film Explosion of the 70s in Words and Pictures* (1998).

Blue Vein Society An elite society of African Americans with skin that is light enough to show a blue vein. Among the members of this society, color determines class and status. In African American literature, the society functions also as an entity of intraracial prejudices and, in some instances, of false values. Portrayals of the "blue vein" appear in Charles W. Chesnutt's collection *The Wife of His Youth* (1899), particularly the stories "The Wife of

His Youth" and "A Matter of Principle." See also Wallace Thurman's *The Blacker the Berry* (1929) and Dorothy West's *The Living Is Easy* (1948).

blues A musical composition that has as its forerunners nameless songsters from the cotton fields, mills, lumberyards, levees, and railroads. As in the **spirituals, ballads, work songs, field cries,** and **hollers,** it is one of the earliest forms of music in the African American oral tradition. There are in the blues personal sentiments and collective expressions of experiences; cultural responses to oppression and suffering; and collective as well as personal struggles for survival and freedom. As cultural markers in an African American **oral tradition,** spirituals, work songs, ballads, field cries, hollers—and later the blues—evoke **race** and class solidarity. In addition, these markers, including the blues, provide sounds and rhythms that are of common struggles and pleasures; they provide **rituals** that often end in catharsis (see **cathartic release**), and allow for spiritual escape; they dramatize cultural vitality and rebelliousness; and they preserve cultural legacy as well as communal values, beliefs, standards, and practices.

With African influences such as **polyrhythms** and the **repetitions** (see under Criticism and Theory) of refrains, the blues stanza comprises a twelve-bar, three-line (*AAB*) stanza structure and a basic topic of (1) subdominant, (4) dominant, and (5) chord sequences. One of the earliest folk blues in the late 1800s is the "Joe Turner Blues." While the *AAA* stanza is replaced later by the *AAB* stanza, other elements are present in the genre (**interjection**; the repetition of refrains to strengthen the song's sense of personalization; and personal experiences expressed collectively). An example of the *AAA* stanza exists in "Joe Turner Blues" (circa 1908).

> They tell me Joe Turner been here and gone,
> Lord, they tell me Joe Turner been here and gone,
> They tell me Joe Turner been here and gone
> (Barlow 1989:33.)

An example of the *AAB* stanza exists in "Mindin My Own Business" (circa 1908), another early folk blues:

> Goin' down this road feeling bad, baby
> I'm goin' down this road feeling so miserable and sad.
> I ain't gonna be treated this way.

Critics have long studied the blues as a genre: Sterling A. Brown in "Blues as Folk Poetry" (1930); Stephen E. Henderson in *Understanding the New Black Poetry: Black Speech and Black Music as Poetic References* (1973); Amiri Baraka in *Blues People: Negro Music in White America* (1963); Albert Murray in *Stomping the Blues* (1976); Houston Baker in *Blues, Ideology, and African American Literature* (1984); Stephen C. Tracy's *Langston Hughes and the Blues* (1988); and William Barlow's *Looking Up at Down: The Emergence of Blues Culture* (1989). From such works, particularly the latter, we learn that from the blues, certain **themes** exist: railroading, leaving, death, black magic, superstition, resistance to incarceration, farming, travel, poverty, relationships between the sexes, separations, work ethics, self-reliance, self-assertion, self-worth, skin color, troubled times, political commentary, and urban experiences. Existing in the blues are also folk **heroes,** sometimes called the **badman** or rebels that symbolize cultural resistance—for example, Stagolee and Railroad Bill. In addition to characters and themes, the blues also offers proverbial wisdom, folk philosophy, and humor.

The "mother of the blues" is said to be Ma Rainy, and the "father of the blues" is said to be W. C. Handy.

(See also **blues aesthetics.**)

Reference for further reading: William Barlow, *Looking Up at Down: The Emergence of Blues Culture* (1989).

blues aesthetics The **blues** as "source" for creating and critiquing African American visual and literary art is a concept that has been promoted by art historian Richard J. Powell and literary critics such as Sterling Brown, Langston Hughes, Stephen E. Henderson, Amiri Baraka, Bernard Bell, Robert O'Meally, Houston Baker, Albert Murray, and Alvin Aubert. The blues that evolves from the earliest sacred and secular folk music in the African American community—**spirituals, work songs, field cries,** and **ballads**— has preserved beliefs, communal values, standards, and practices. Critics are particularly interested in the aspects of African American culture that are repeated in sacred and secular folk music and have been preserved in the blues: **repetition** (see under Criticism and Theory) of refrains, **improvisation, circularity, call and response,** and **interjections.** Critics are suggesting that some creative writers and visual artists function like blues musician (or like the **bards** of the spirituals, work songs, and ballads) when composing or creating their art; they pull from the culture (repetition, circularity, call and response, etc.). Interpreters are urged to begin within similar **con-**

texts. The most accomplished literary work influenced by a blues aesthetic is thought to be Ralph Ellison's *Invisible Man* (1952). Visual artists include Aaron Douglas, Archibald J. Motley, and Jacob Lawrence.
(See also **anthropology of art.**)

References for further reading: William Barlow, "Blues Origin and Influences" (1989); Richard J. Powell, "The Blues Aesthetic: Black Culture and Modernism" (1999); Lorenzo Thomas, "The Blues Aesthetic" (1997); Jerry W. Ward Jr., "Alvin Aubert: The Levee, the Blues, the Mighty Mississippi" (1999).

blues-ballad The framework of the blues-ballad, which is made up of both the traditional **ballad** and the **blues,** was introduced by Sterling A. Brown in the 1930s. Using **themes,** characters, and structures of the traditional genres—the ballad and rural blues of African American culture—Brown writes about folk **heroes** like Railroad Bill, Stackolee, and Po Lazarus; race patriots like Crispus Attucks McKoy; **trickster** figures like Slim Greer; and independent and traveling blues men like Big Boy and Lone Gone. The poet/critic Brown uses also familiar themes found in both traditional ballads and blues—for example, the ill-fated love affair, picaresque travels, and misadventures. From the African American experience, Brown adds themes of freedom, protest, and liberation.

Reference for further reading: Joanne Gabbin, *Sterling A. Brown: Building the Black Aesthetic Tradition* (1985).

body politics A term that renders **poststructuralist** approaches to critiquing black female subjectivity. Always aware of how the black female body is perceived in dominant cultures and in African American culture, critics query, for instance, that if the body is a text, then, who gets to give the official criteria and/or interpretation for reading the text? Whose **gaze** falls upon the body definitively? And how do African American women writers recover the black female body in order to reappropriate and reconstitute the body that often has been hypereroticized or exoticized and made a site of impropriety and crime?

References for further reading: Houston Baker, *Workings of the Spirit: The Poetics of Afro-American Women's Writing.* Chicago: University of Chicago Press, 1991; Michael Bennett and Vanessa D. Dickerson, eds., *Recovering the Black Female Body, Self-Representation by African American Women* (2001); Hazel Carby, "Policing the Black Woman's Body in an Urban Context" (1992): 738–55; Deborah McDowell, "Afterword: Recovery Missions: Imaging the Body Ideals" (2001).

Brer Rabbit (See **Anancy** and **trickster.**)

burlesque A kind of **parody,** but stronger. An example is when subjects of serious literary or musical works are trivialized, or when serious literary or musical works are reduced to an undignified or exaggerated style.

cakewalk A high-stepping choreographed dance that originated during slavery as a stylized caricature of the Anglo-American waltz. The cakewalk was popularized in the early 1900s (1870s–1920) in comic musicals such as *A Trip to Coontown* (1898), *Clorindy* (1989), and *Dahomey.* Also, at social gatherings, guests entertained themselves with the syncopated **dance.** The most elegant and impressive dancers received a cake as a prize. See, for instance, Ann Petry's short story "Has Anybody Seen Miss Dora Dean?" in *Miss Muriel and Other Stories* (1971).

call and response (See **antiphony** and **blues.**)

calypso An art form that is most associated with Trinidad and Tobago. The art form incorporates improvised **storytelling,** singing, and instrumental music often to **satirize,** lampoon, or comment wittily on social and political situations and events. Other calypsos emphasize "wuking out," a type of **performance** characterized by sexually suggestive lyrics and movements. Calypso's highly syncopated rhythms can be traced to the vestiges of West African songs of praise and derision. In Paule Marshall's *Praisesong for the Widow* (1983), calypso culture and music are vividly described and prominently figured in the protagonist's **spiritual** healing. Master calypsonians from Trinidad include, among others, Lord Kitchener, Chalkdust, and Mighty Sparrow.

References for further reading: Alton A. Adam, "Whence Came the Calypso?" (1955); Walter Jekyll, ed. *Jamaican Song and Story: Annancy Stories, Digging Singer, Ring Tunes, and Dancing Tunes* (1966); Massie Patterson and Lionel Belasco, *Calypso Songs of the West Indies* (1943).

capping A figure of speech that revises an original statement by adding new terms. An example is Essex Hemphill's poem "Conditions XXIV" (*Conditions* 1986).
(See also **signifying.**)

carpe diem A term of Latin origin that means to "snatch the day." Other reported meanings include "seize the day," "enjoy yourself while you can," and "make the best of the present moment."

cathartic release The release of pent-up emotions when voices, musical instruments, and/or body movements (dancing, stomping, hand clapping, and shouting) create the right atmosphere. A spiritual connection to the life force. (See also **African ontology, ecstasy,** and **sermon.**)

cento-fiction The combination of folk narrative and song.

character types (See **badman** and **badwoman**; and **representation** under Criticism and Theory.)

characterization The method of representing a character or characters in prose and **drama** include the following:

Directly   What does the author tell you about the characters?
Indirectly What do the characters reveal about themselves by their actions, appearance, private thoughts, speech?
Indirectly What do other characters reveal about the main character and about themselves?

Major writers such as W.E.B. DuBois in "Criteria of Negro Art" (1926), Ann Petry in "The Novel as Social Criticism" (1950), and Alice Walker's "Saving the Life That Is Your Own: The Importance of Models in the Artist's Life" (1976) agree that characterization is the great strength of novels. The burden of responsibility to "save a character" lies with the characters.

Reference for further reading: Hazel Arnett Ervin, ed. *African American Literary Criticism, 1773 to 2000* (1999).

chiasmus (ki-ez'-mus) The reversal or the crossover of grammatical structures in phrases or clauses, without the repetition of words. Similar to **antimetabole** in grammatical structure, but there is no repetition of words. See, for instance, what English critics did:
Samuel Johnson's "The Vanity of Human Wishes" (1749):

By day the frolic, and the dance by night.
(Abrams and Greenblatt, eds. 2000:2669, line 326.)

John Dryden's "Absalom and Achitophe: A Poem" (1681):

Exalts his enemies, his friends destroys
(Abrams and Greenblatt, eds. 2000:2092, line 711.)

Chicago Renaissance A literary movement that begins in Chicago in the 1930s. The life of the movement is from approximately 1935 to the early 1950s. Influences on the writers include the Great Migration, integration, **modernism,** the Chicago School of Sociology, theories of urbanization, and, though lost sometimes in ideology, the indigenous folk forms. Ideologically, the writers debate content over craft, or art versus propaganda. (See, e.g., Richard Wright's "How Bigger Was Born," in *Native Son* (1940); James Baldwin's "Everybody's Protest Novel" (1949) and "Many Thousand Gone" (1951); and William Gardner Smith's "The Negro Writer: Pitfalls and Compensation" (1950); and Ann Petry's "The Novel as Social Criticism" (1950). The literature of the movement, which relays the oppressions of urban America and the struggles due to racism, classism, and sexism, is referred to as **protest, proletarian,** and/or sociological. Not all of the major writers of the movement resided in Chicago. While Richard Wright, Margaret Walker, Frank Marshall Davis, Gwendolyn Brooks, William Attaway, and Willard Motley lived in Chicago, Ann Petry lived in New York. Eventually, writers Chester Himes, William Gardner Smith, and Frank Yerby lived abroad.
(See also **Age of Wright, American Dream, protest literature,** and **representation** under Criticism and Theory.)

Reference for further reading: Craig H. Werner, "Chicago Renaissance" (1997).

chorus The community, or chorus, functions as a character or as a group in African American narrations. Actively, the chorus takes part in the story's action, comments on the story's action, and provides mood and atmosphere. Refer to the community/chorus in Toni Morrison's *Sula* (1973) and the "I" narrator as community in Morrison's *The Bluest Eye* (1970).
(See also **call and response.**)

circular narration In literary art, the end is the beginning and the beginning is the end. See the works of Toni Morrison, James Baldwin, Paule Marshall, Leon Forrest, Ernest Gaines, John Edgar Wideman, Ann Petry, Zora Neale Hurston, and Ralph Ellison.
(See also **spirituals.**)

circularity (See **cyclical.**)

climax The arrangement of words, phrases, and clauses in the ascension of importance.

collective unconscious (See Criticism and Theory.)

colonial period During the colonial period (1745–1831), the greatest challenge for African American writers was to prove to white America that they were human beings with innate abilities, not only to reason but also to produce great literature. And, somewhere in between, these writers attempted to protest slavery. The major types of literature during this period are **lyrics, odes, pastorals,** and **elegies**—all of which are produced using classical devices such as the **heroic couplet, couplet, iambic pentameter, imagery,** and appeal to classical muses. The major poets that are able to use classical sensibilities are Phillis Wheatley and George Moses Horton. Jupiter Hammon, along with Wheatley, excels also in the subgenre of the **hymn.** Protest against slavery is a concise **theme** in the poetry by Horton: "The Slave's Complaint" and "On Liberty and Slavery" (Hill et al. 1997:372–73.) In more subtle and subversive ways, protest exists in poems by Wheatley (see, e.g., "On Imagination" [1773] and "To Maecenas" [1773]).

Reference for further reading: John C. Shields, "Colonial and Early National Era" (1997); *Colonial Consciousness in Black American, African, and Indian Fiction in English* (1991).

color line Coined by W.E.B. DuBois to acknowledge that concepts of racial origin and skin pigmentation tend to segregate and divide African Americans from Euro Americans within the dominant community and also divide African Americans within the African American community.

References for further reading: Gloria T. Hull, *Color, Sex and Poetry: Three Women Writers of the Harlem Renaissance* (1987); Jacquelyn Y. McLendon, *The Politics of Color in the Fiction of Jessie Fauset and Nella Larsen* (1995); Ross Posnock, *Color and Culture: Black Writers and Color and the Making of the Modern Intellectual* (2000); Henry B. Wonham, *Criticism on the Color Line: Desegregating American Literary Studies* (1996).

communal text (See **chorus.**)

conflict An element found in fiction, narrative **poetry,** and **drama.** Conflict initiates struggles between characters or between characters and external forces.

conjuring/conjurer Writing in *African Religions and Philosophy* (1970), John Mbiti explains the term: "God is the Originator and Sustainer of man: The Spirits explain the destiny of man; Man is the Centre of this ontology; the Animals, Plants and natural phenomena and objects constitute the environment in which man lives" (88).
(Mosley 1995:88)

Important to man is the unity, balance, or solidarity that exists within this universe. Existing also in this universe is a "force, power or energy" (88). While God is the source and ultimate controller of this "force," the spirits and a "few humans" have access. The latter are known as conjurers, root doctors, or root workers that "manipulate and use" this force for "the good" or for "the ill" of the community (88). For examples of the former, see Paul Laurence Dunbar's "The Conjuring Contest" (1899) and Zora Neale Hurston's *Jonah's Gourd Vine* (1934). For an example of the latter, see stories in Charles Chesnutt's *The Conjure Woman* (1899). The character Min in Ann Petry's *The Street* (1946) relies on Prophet David to return balance to her universe. Other writers to consider are Arna Bontemps, Toni Cade Bambara, Toni Morrison, Gloria Naylor, Alice Walker, Ntozake Shange, Rudolph Fisher, Tina McElroy Ansa, Joyne Cortez, and Sherley Anne Williams. Consider also Zora Neale Hurston's *Tell My Horse* (1938) and *Mules and Men* (1935)
(See **necromancy.**)

connotation An implied or suggested meaning evoked by emotions, word association, or **context.**
(See also **denotation.**)

consonance Words or phrases in which consonants are similar or identical but vowel sounds are different. Example: "hide us/heed us."

contemporary literature (See **Reconstruction and postmodernism period,** and the **novel.**)

content A term commonly used to refer to what is said in a literary work as opposed to how it is said.
(See **context.**)

context The reader may take words in a text at face value when arriving at a literal meaning, but with context, meaning depends on what Houston A. Baker, in *The Journey Back: Issues in Black Literature and Criticism* (1980), calls "the semantic fields" of language or the "underlying codes" and "neighboring signs" in the literature (Baker, 1980: 157).

Reference for further reading: Amiri Baraka, "expressive language," in *Home: Social Essays* (1966).

couplet A verse unit of two successive rhyming lines. There are various meters and line lengths for the couplet. African American poets are no exception to writers who employ the rhyming lines, but African American writers do so with various meters and line lengths. See, for instance, Paul Laurence Dunbar in "Philosophy" (1903):

> I been t'inkin' 'bout de preachah; what he said de othah night,
> 'Bout hit bein' people's dooty, fu' to keep dey faces bright;
> (Gates and McKay 1997:903–4, lines 1–2)

Countee Cullen in "Heritage" (1925):

> What is Africa to me:
> Copper sun or scarlet sea:
> (Gates and McKay 1997:1311–14, lines 1–2.)

Gwendolyn Brooks in "The Mother" (1945):

> Abortions will not let you forget.
> You remember the children you got that you did not get.
> (Gates and McKay 1997:1579, lines 1–2.)

and in Brooks's "Maxie Allen" (1949):

> Maxie Allen always taught her
> Stipendiary little daughter.
> (Gates and McKay 1997:1585–86, lines 1–2.)

Creole A term to suggest that similarities in African languages are mixed with another language (i.e., English) to form, for instance, **African American English** and **Gullah**/geeche. The term is used also to distinguish a racially mixed people who are of African and French or Spanish ancestry, especially in Louisiana's Creole communities.

crossroads In **Yoruban folklore,** a crossroads symbolizes the junctions between physical and **spiritual** worlds; a place where mortals seek out the god **Legba** in order to learn their fate. The lore is reiterated in music, such as Robert Johnson's "Crossroad Blues" and in many of the **trickster** tales.

References for further reading: Henry Louis Gates Jr., *The Signifying Monkey: A Theory of Afro-American Literary Criticism* (1988); Ropo Sekoni, *Folk Poetics: A Sociosemiotic Study of Yoruba Trickster Tales* (1994).

cultural assertion period (1955–1975) In 1926, in "The Negro Artist and the Racial Mountain," Langston Hughes anticipates a new group of artists that would, in essence, declare a cultural autonomy:

> We younger Negro artists who create now intend to express our individual dark-skinned selves without fear or shame. If white people are pleased we are glad. If they are not, it doesn't matter. We know we are beautiful. And ugly too. . . . If colored people are pleased we are glad. If they are not, their displeasure doesn't matter either. We build our temples for tomorrow, strong as we know how, and we stand on top of the mountain, free within ourselves.
> (Ervin 1999:48)

In 1968, echoing Hughes, Larry Neal, in "The Black Arts Movement," introduces this anticipated generation of artist. According to Neal, this generation of writers

> envision[s] art that speaks directly to the needs and aspirations of Black America . . . [that relates] broadly to the Afro-American's desire for self-determination and nationhood.
> (Ervin 1999:122)

Unlike Hughes and other Harlem Renaissance writers that experimented with African American cultural forms to shape their literature and thought (e.g., **repetition** (see under Criticism and Theory), **improvisation,** or **call and response** from the **spirituals, work songs,** and other oral traditions), the new generation of artists maintained an interest in the oral cultural forms but required what Larry Neal called "a separate symbolism, mythology, critique and iconology [that emerged] from the black community" ("the Black Arts Movement" (1968) (Ervin 1999:122). As instructed by LeRoi Jones (Amiri Baraka) in "The Myth of Negro Literature" (1966), the new generation was to employ methods used earlier by the songsters of, for instance, "blues, jazz, and spirituals." Or, as instructed by Larry Neal in the afterword to *Black Fire: An Anthology of Afro-American Writing* (Jones and Neal 1968)—the anthology thought to usher in this new generation—the "poets [were to] learn to sing, dance, and chant their works, tearing into the substance of their individual and collective experiences" (655).

In addition to Amiri Baraka and Larry Neal, major poets of this period include Haki Madhubuti, Carolyn Rodgers, Sonia Sanchez, Nikki Giovanni, and Bob Kaufman. In addition to Baraka as dramatist, others include Ed Bullins and Ben Caldwell.

(See also **Age of Baraka** and **Black Arts Movement.**)

cultural nationalism (See **black nationalism.**)

cultural pluralism An openness to participation in national life. Similar to "the melting pot" paradigm, but according to philosopher Alain Locke, with the latter, African Americans and other distinctive minority groups are excluded. Locke advocates cultural pluralism.

Reference for further reading: Alain Locke, "Black Watch on the Rhine" (1924); E. Ethelbert Miller, *First Light: New and Selected Poems,* 1994.

"cut, the" The repetitive nature of blues-jazz that abruptly skips back to another beginning already heard. Rupture does not cause dissolution of rhythm; it strengthens it. Musicians such as James Brown and John Coltrane are often recognized for their use of "the cut," but studies include also the **folk preacher** who may interrupt himself with rhythmic phrases such as "praise God." Recognized also are writers such as Toni Morrison, Amiri Baraka, John Edgar Wideman, and John Williams.

References for further reading: James A. Snead, "Repetition as a figure of black culture" (1999); Eleanor W. Traylor, "A Blues View of Life (Literature and The Blues Vision)" (1999).

cyclical Recurrences; cyclic repetition.

(See also **circular narration, "the cut"**; and **repetition** under Criticism and Theory.)

Reference for further reading: James A. Snead, "Repetition as a figure of black culture" (1999).

dance (See **cakewalk, ring shouts.**)

deconstruction A term that denotes the process of destabilizing and transforming the usual understanding of a work, especially when language shows gaps or is susceptible to dissemination. What is not said constitutes gaps in the work. Dissemination of a text (dismantling or taking a text apart) can reveal its gaps as well as its inherent, **subversive,** or contradictory elements. Meaning in a work that gets postponed or that is ceaselessly deferred will signal **diffe'rance/diffe'rence** (a key distinction of deconstruction).
(See also **deictic/deixis.**)

References for further reading: Houston Baker, *Blues, Ideology, and Afro-American Literature: A Vernacular Theory* (1984); Peter Barry, *Beginning Theory: An Introduction to Literary and Cultural Theory* (1995); Paul de Man, *Blindness and Insight: Essays in the Rhetoric of Contemporary Criticism* (1985); Jacques Derrida, *Writing and Difference* (1980).

def-jam poetry According to Clarence Major in *Juba to Jive: A Dictionary of African-American Slang* (1970), jam means a party of musicians who are making music and enjoying the times socially. The term "jam session" is an occasion where jazz musicians get together and play for their own pleasure. Influenced also by **Hip-hop culture,** *def* denotes "a standard of excellence, or "the bomb"; *jam* denotes "a song, a cut, or a track." Like the DJs and MCs or rappers of Hip-hop culture, **"the spoken word"** poet must be spontaneous, original, and creative. Hip-hop, which began as an urban experience in the 1970s, reached the public via theater, parks, et cetera, and has become a global industry. In America, spoken-word artists reach audiences via the media (e.g., Russell Simmons's "Def-Poetry Jam," which first appeared on Broadway and then the cable station HBO).
(See also **Age of Baraka, bard, Black Arts Movement, griot, haiku, Hip-hop culture, last poets, performance, rap,** and **"the spoken word."**)

deictic/deixis Time markers (now/then, yesterday/today), place markers (here/there, this/that), and markers of the person (I/you, us/them) identify situations, events, objects, or perspectives by pointing *outside* of the text. According to Geoffrey Leach in *Semantics* (1975), to arrive at the significance of deictic expressions, the reader must define "the speaker and hearer and ... the time and place of [the text's] production" (76). Then, the reader must read the work within this time and place. For example, in *The Street* (1946), Ann Petry's "that kitchen" points to cultural situations of the 1940s—such as the woman's place being in the kitchen or the home. See, also Toni Morrison's opening sentence in *Sula* (1973): "In *that* place, where they tore the nightshade and blackberry patches..., there was once a neighborhood." In both Petry and Morrison, meaning depends on understanding "that" place.

Reference for further reading: Geoffrey Leach, *Semantics* (1975).

deities According to Robert Farris Thompson, author of *Flash of the Spirit: African and Afro-American Art and Philosophy* (1984), the most widely worshipped deities that survived the Atlantic trade were of the **Yoruba** culture. The deities—the Orisha—include

> Eshu, spirit of individuality and change
> Ifa', god of divination
> Ogún, lord of iron
> Yemoja (Yemayá), goddess of the seas
> Oshun, goddess of river, sweet and giving
> Oshoosi, god of hunting
> Obaluaiye, earth deity of dread disease
> Nana Bukúu, mother of Obaluaīye
> Shàngó, the fiery thunder god
> Osanyin, god of herbalistic medicine
> Obatala, god of creativity

References for further reading: Robert Farris Thompson, *Flash of the Spirit, African and Afro-American Art and Philosophy* (1984) and *Black Gods and Kings: Yoruba Art at UCLA* (1976).

denotation The literal meaning of words; the dictionary meaning of words. (See also **connotation.**)

denouement The final unraveling or unknotting of a plot in fiction or **drama;** the final outcome or revelation of plot.

desire (See **psychoanalysis.**)

diachronic and synchronic The terms were coined by Ferdinand de Saussure (1857–1915) in *Cours de linguistique générale* (1915). When gram-

matical features within language are studied or are related to as evolving across time (origin, development, history, and change), the language is diachronic. When the grammatical features of language are with reference to a given time or moment—in the same space—the language is synchronic. According to Karla Holloway in *Moorings and Metaphors: Figures of Culture and Gender in Black Women's Literature* (1992), black women writers (African, African American, and Caribbean) often "dissolve the distinctions between across time (diachronic) and together time (synchronic) in their literature." Holloway writes further that "Simultaneity (synchrony) is often compatible with, rather than distinctive from, the long expanse of historic time and the changes that occur within this expanse (diachrony)." The critic insists that for black women writers, "historic events often exist in the same space as the events of the present."
(See also **African time.**)

dialect Linguistically, the term means a variation of languages, of grammatical habits, and pronunciations, although it has come to suggest a form of speech that is regional, substandard, or inferior to a national or standard language due to social, political, and/or economic reasons. As for a "real" language, modern linguists, including Geneva Smitherman in *Talkin and Testifyin: The Language of Black America* (1977), point out that the "real" language exists only in abstract. Some writers who adapt the rhythms and modalities of an African American **vernacular** include Paul Laurence Dunbar in *Oak and Ivy* (1893), *Major and Minors* (1895), and *Lyrics of Lowly Life* (1896); Frances Harper in *Sketches of Southern Life* (1870); James Edwin Campbell in *Drifting and Gleamings* (1887) and *Echoes from the Cabin and Elsewhere* (1895); Sterling Brown in *Southern Road* (1932); Zora Neale Hurston in *Their Eyes Were Watching God* (1937); and Alice Walker in *The Color Purple* (1982). Dialect of African Americans in their urban settings might be represented in the works of Langston Hughes, Cecil Brown, and Haki Madhubuti.

dialogic (See **polyphonic.**)

diary and journal In these genres, which emerge in the nineteenth-century, writers record their observations of southern and northern community life, their travels abroad and to the South, and their occasional revelations about personal and religious aspirations and experiences.

Reference for further reading: Geneva Cobb-Moore, "Diaries and Journals," eds. Andrews et al., 1997.

diasporic literature The writers are of African descent and of shared history and culture, particularly aesthetic patterns such as **call and response** and **polyrhythms** and cultural figures such as the **trickster**. Shared **themes** include, among others, physical and/or mental dispersion; alienation and displacement; a return to a place called home; escape and liberation; colonization and repatriation; migration; the return to Africa (or Africans to America); and the meaning of community.

References for further reading: Margaret Busby, *Daughters of Africa*, 1992; Carole Boyce Davies, *Black Women, Writing and Identity*, 1994, and *Moving Beyond Boundaries*, vols. 1– 2 (1995); Frances Smith Foster, "Diasporic Literature," 1997.

diction The choice of words by a writer or speaker—words that help to signal **tone, context,** and style.

didactic literature Beginning in some of the earliest narratives and poems, and particularly in literature by some of the writers of the **Harlem Renaissance,** there is literature that purposely instructs and testifies.
(See also **propaganda.**)

References for further reading: Arlene R. Keizer, "Poetry, Religious and Didactic," 1997; Sondra A. O'Neale, *Jupiter Hammon and the Biblical Beginnings of African American Literature* (1993).

diegesis A term used to designate the reporting in narration of events. In contrast, there is mimesis, which is the imitative representation of events. In modern narratology, diegesis is "showing" and **mimesis** is "telling."

diffe'rance/diffe'rence (See **deconstruction.**)

digression A technique used to depart from the main plot or **theme** in **storytelling** and **oratory**.

double consciousness A term used by W.E.B. DuBois in *The Souls of Black Folk* (1903) to characterize a psychic duality in African American identity: "One ever feels his twoness—an American, a Negro; two souls, two thoughts, two reconciled strivings, two warring ideals into one dark body, whose dogged strength alone keeps it from being torn asunder" (83).

double-voiced (See **duality** and **signifying.**)

dozens, the dirty Verbal dueling that includes "put downs" by **analogy** or **signifying.** Usually the verbal insult is used to test the emotional strength of the African American male, especially when signifying turns to a relative like the mother. The first to become angry loses the duel.
(See also **signifying.**)

drama A work that is written for and performed on the stage. Elements of drama include **conflict, characterization,** dialogue, and setting. For most major plays after the 1960s, the setting is urban America (e.g., New York City, Pittsburgh, South Philadelphia, and Chicago). Exceptions include the train, as in Amiri Baraka's *Dutchman* (1964); the museum, as in George Wolf's *The Colored Museum* (1986); and the army base, as in Charles Fuller's *A Soldier's Play* (1984).

Dialogue in African American drama is usually realistic and accurate. It is also used to complicate the plot, as in Louis Peterson's *Take a Giant Step* (1953); in Adrienne Kennedy's *Funnyhouse of a Negro* (1964); in Baraka's *Dutchman* and Charles Fuller's *A Soldier's Play.* Dialogue is used also by playwrights to unify the plot, as in August Wilson's *Fences* (1987), Charles Gordone's *No Place to Be Somebody* (1969), and Joseph Walker's *The River Niger* (1973). In nearly all of these plays, conflict is either external—that is, the struggles are between characters and external forces such as society or the environment; or, conflict is internal—that is, the characters battle with internalized tensions that begin to affect the family (e.g., *Fences*); or the self (e.g., *No Place to Be Somebody*); or, the battle within man to compromise human values (e.g., Lorraine Hansberry's *A Raisin in the Sun* [1959]). Conflict also exists between characters (e.g., *Dutchman, Take a Giant Step, A Raisin in the Sun,* and Ed Bullin's *Clara's Ole Man* [1965]).
(See also **Federal Theatre Project.**)

References for further reading: Esther Arata, *More Black American Playwrights: A Bibliography* (1978); James V. Hatch and Omani Adbullah, *Black Playwrights, 1823–1977: An Annotated Bibliography* (1977); Bernard L. Peterson Jr., "Drama" (1997).

duality/double-voiced A term that denotes structural merging of two almost **antithetical** "selves" or the dual voices of the narrator and protagonist. Also referred to as coded intertexts (two contexts and two traditions). A number of novels by African American women writers are considered double-voiced, including Zora Neale Hurston's *Their Eyes Were Watching God* (1937), Toni Morrison's *The Bluest Eye* (1970), and Alice Walker's *The Color Purple* (1982).

ebonics (See **African American English.**)

ecstasy A term used within African American culture to denote a vital force; spirit possession; or a sense of **cathartic release.**
(See also **magara.**)

elegies A form of **poetry** that has poets lamenting the passing of a specific person or a specific way of life. See, for instance, Margaret Walker's "For Malcolm X" (1970):

Gather round this coffin and mourn your dying swan
(Gates and McKay 1997:1575, line 8.)
See also, the latter poetry by Phillis Wheatley, particularly, "An Elegy on Leaving" (1784):

No more my hand shall wake the warbling lyre
(Shields, 1989:156–57.)
The elegy may serve also as an epitaph or as a commemorative verse. See, for example, Rita Dove's "David Walker (1785–1830)" (1980):

Free to travel, he still couldn't be shown how lucky / he was.
(Gates and McKay 1997:2584, lines 1–2.)

ellipsis The deliberate omission of a word or words in order to achieve a compact expression.
(See also **asyndeton.**)

encoding (See **folktales, signifying, spirituals.**)

environmental determinism A term used to identify novels written mostly in the 1940s and 1950s that have a **naturalistic** thesis. The premise in naturalistic novels is that the environment exerts a tremendous influence on an individual's life. In poverty-stricken and crime-ridden environments, the African American character is doomed to meet disaster. See, for instance, Richard Wright's *Native Son* (1940) and Ann Petry's *The Street* (1946).

References for further reading: Carl Milton Hughes, *The Negro Novelist: A Discussion of the Writings of American Negro Novelists, 1940–1950* (1953); Richard Wright, "How Bigger Was Born," in *Native Son* (1940).

epic, the A long narrative that emerges from an oral tradition and for centuries has been recited and passed on by **griots** and others. Incorporated in the narrative are historical events as well as communal values. As a model, the **hero** is one who in his journey and adventures seeks knowledge and mystical powers. Examples of the epic narrative include *The Mwindo Epic, Sunjata* (or *Sundiata* or *Sunyetta*), *Kambili,* and *The Ozidi Saga.* Also considered epic narratives are the early Negro **spirituals** such as "Go Down, Moses."

epistolary novel A genre that uses **letters** as a form of narration. See, for instance Alice Walker's *The Color Purple* (1982). Variations of personal writing have been used to reflect an epistolary tradition. See, for instance, Sherley Anne Williams's *Dessa Rose* (1986) and Trey Ellis's *Platitudes* (1988).

Reference for further reading: Keith E. Byerman, "Epistolary Novel" 1997.

epigram A situation or philosophy that might be summed in a few concise words or lines. See Countee Cullen's "For a Lady I know" (1925):

> She even thinks that up in heaven
> Her class lies late and snores. . .
> (Early, ed., 1990:111, lines 1–2.)

epistrophe (e-pis'tro-fe) The repetition of the same word or words at the end of successive sentences for, among others, emphasis. See, for instance, a line from a folk **sermon:**

> Give your life to the Lord; give your faith to the Lord;
> raise your hands to the Lord

Or, lines from a speech by Malcolm X:

> As long as the white man sent you to Korea, you bled. He sent you to Germany, you bled. He sent you to the South Pacific to fight the Japanese, you bled.
> (Breitman, "Message to the Grass Roots" (1963); Breitman, ed. 1989.)

epithet A word or phrase used to characterize a person, place, or thing. Praise names in African societies are considered epithets. In **spirituals,** "God is a God" is considered an epithet.

Eshu-Elegba/Esu-Elegbara A **Yoruban** god associated with the **crossroads** (the junction between the physical and the spiritual worlds; the point where a person has to make decisions that may affect his or her life). Written sometimes as Legba (of Fon), which is also associated with crossroads. (See also **crossroads, deities,** and **Legba.**)

Reference for further reading: Robert Farris Thompson, "Portraits of Major Orisha," in *Flash of the Spirit* (1984), 18–19.

essay A composition that could be either formal or informal in organization, and that could have a purpose that is personal, argumentative, analytical, polemical, or political. Examples of essays by noted essayists that are largely personal and analytical include James Baldwin's *Notes of a Native Son* (1955) and *The Evidence of Things Not Seen* (1985) and Alice Walker's *In Search of Our Mothers' Gardens: Womanist Prose* (1983). For examples of argumentative and analytical essays, see Ralph Ellison's *Shadow and Act* (1964) and *Going to the Territory* (1986). For examples of polemical and political essays, see LeRoi Jones's (Amiri Baraka's) *Home: Social Essays* (1966); Eldridge Cleaver's *Soul on Ice* (1968); and Richard Wright's *White Man, Listen* (1957). Collections that include a variety of presentations, include W.E.B. DuBois's *The Souls of Black Folk* (1903); James Baldwin's *The Price of the Ticket* (1985), and Barbara Smith's *The Truth That Never Hurts* (2000).

Reference for further reading: Gerald Early, *Speech and Power: The African-American Essay and Its Cultural Content from Polemics to Pulpit*, 1992.

essentialism Cultural experiences and **representation** (see under Criticism and Theory) are pervasive and intimate; writers represent experiences and identities, as if inherent.

Esu (See **trickster.**)

ethos A habitual way of life based on beliefs, aesthetic principles, standards, and practices.
(See also **African ethos.**)

euphony A smooth, richly flowing sound usually produced by long vowels and liquid consonants. See, for instance, the opening line from Ann Petry's *The Street* (1946):

There was a cold November wind blowing through 116th Street.

The opening line from Toni Morrison's *Sula* (1973):

In that place, where they tore the nightshade and blackberry patches from their roots to make room for the Medallion City Golf Course, there was once a neighborhood.

A line from Henry Dumas's title story in *Ark of Bones and Other Stories* (1970):

Headeye, he was followin me. I knowed he was followin me. But I just kept goin, like I wasn't payin him no mind.

(Dumas 1970:1616, lines 1–3.)

existentialism According to Jean-Paul Sartre, writing in *L'Existentialisme est un humanisme* (1946), man is born into a kind of void (*lenéant*). He makes himself what he is ("existence precedes essence"). Forging his own values, man gives meaning to his existence and universe; or, in a less conscious state, man leads a passive, acquiescent existence (1–10).
(See also **the absurd**.)

expatriate The African American writer has a long history of seeking psyche equilibrium in Europe. Starting early in the nineteenth century, Paris, France, became the most popular residency of expatriate communities. From these communities, African American writers have produced many novels (see Jessie Fauset's *Plum Bun* [1929]; Walter White's *Rope and Faggot* [1929]; Chester Himes's *Case of Rape* [1963]; Richard Wright's *The Outsider* [1953], *Savage Holiday* [1954], and *The Long Dream* [1958]; James Baldwin's *Another Country* [1962], *Tell Me How Long the Train's Been Gone* [1968], *If Beale Street Could Talk* [1974], and *Just Above My Head* [1979]); essays (see James Baldwin's *Notes of a Native Son* [1955]); and **autobiography** (see Langston Hughes's *I Wonder as I Wander* [1956]); and travelogue (see Alain Locke, Booker T. Washington, Jessie Fauset, and others in *A Stranger in the Village, Two Centuries of African-American Travel Writing*, ed. by Farah J. Griffin and Cheryl J. Fish, [1998]). While a number of writers flirted with the idea of obtaining permanent residence in France, only the following major writers remained expatriates: Richard Wright, James Baldwin, Chester Himes, Frank Yerby, and William Gardner Smith.

References for further reading: Jean-Claude Baker and Chris Chase, *Josephine: The Hungry Heart* (2001); Lloyd W. Brown, "The Expatriate Consciousness in Black American Literature" (1999); Michel Fabre, ed. *From Harlem to Paris: Black American Writers in France, 1840–1980* (1993); Kenneth R. Janken, "Expatriatism" (1997); Stanley Schatt, "You Must Go Home Again: Today's Afro-American Expatriate Writers" (1973).

exposition A type of writing that informs and explains—for example, **essays,** newspapers, magazines, **biographies,** and **autobiographies.** It is also the opening part of a play, **novel,** or **short story** that provides information about, for instance, plot and characters.

fantasy (See **speculative fiction.**)

Federal Theatre Project (FTP) Under Franklin Roosevelt's administration and his New Deal Program of the late 1930s, particularly the Works Progress Administration (WPA), a prolific number of writers were hired as resident playwrights in New York City, Chicago, Seattle, and Newark to write and to produce plays. Writers such as Langston Hughes, Shirley Graham (DuBois), Theodore Ward, and Hall Johnson wrote and produced local plays, many of which appeared also on Broadway.

Federal Writer's Project (FWP) Under Franklin Roosevelt's administration and his New Deal Program of the late 1930s, the Works Progress Administration (WPA) brought together unemployed writers to research and publish among other things, a treasury of **folklore,** African American history, and **slave narratives** in the *American Guide* series. Writers associated with the program included Sterling A. Brown, Zora Neale Hurston, Arna Bontemps, Claude McKay, Margaret Walker, Willard Motley, Frank Yerby, Richard Wright, and Ralph Ellison.

feminism Alice Walker once wrote, "I am preoccupied with the spiritual survival . . . of my people. . . . . But beyond that, I am committed to exploring the oppression, the insanities, the loyalties, and the triumphs of black women." (Quoted in "About the Author," *African American Literature: Voices in a Tradition,* 1998:541.) Critic Patricia Hill Collins has written, "Diversity among black women [e.g., historical era, age, social class, sexual orientation, or ethnicity] produces different concrete experiences that in turn shape various reactions to the core themes [e.g., struggle against racism and sexism, denigrated images of black womanhood with self-defined images, black women's activism as mothers, teachers, and black community leaders, and a sensitivity to sexual politics]" (22–23). Since the 1970s, black feminism has been tied to theory and aspects of the culture. For instance, Karla Holloway has written, "black women's literature reflects its community—the cultural ways of knowing as well as ways of framing that knowledge in language" (1). Holloway directs readers to "figures of language that testify . . . to inversive, recursive and sometimes even subversive structure that layer the black [female's] text and give it a dimension only accessible when its cultural context is acknowledged" (1–2). Critic Hazel Carby contends "novels of black women should be read not as passive representations of history but as active influences within history" (95). In the later twentieth century, critics have been determined to add individual and collective explorations of the black female body—historically, socially, politically, and economically—within an African American literary tradition and within an African American women's literary tradition.

References for further reading: Toni Cade Bambara, *The Black Woman* (1970); Michael Bennett and Vanessa D. Dickerson, eds., *Recovering the Black Female Body: Self-Representation by African American Women* (2001); Hazel Carby, *Reconstructing Womanhood: The Emergence of the Afro-American Woman Novelist* (1987); Patricia Hill Collins, *Black Feminist Thought: Knowledge, Consciousness, and the Politics of Empowerment* (1991); Beverly Guy-Sheftall, *Words of Fire: An Anthology of African-American Feminist Thought* (1995); Karla Holloway, *Moorings and Metaphors: Figures of Culture and Gender in Black Women's Literature* (1992); Gloria Hull, Patricia Bell Scott, and Barbara Smith, eds., *All the Women Are White, All the Blacks Are Men, But Some of Us Are Brave* (1986); Barbara Smith, "Toward a Black Feminist Criticism," in *African American Literary Criticism, 1773 to 2000,* (1999) and also her *Home Girls: A Black Feminist Anthology* (1983); Alice Walker, *In Search of Our Mothers' Gardens: Womanist Prose* (1983).

field cries (See **folk cries.**)

film (See **blaxploitation.**)

Fisk Jubilee Singers Student singers from Fisk University, Nashville, that toured the United States and Europe, starting in the late 1870s, under the leadership of George White. From their slave parents, the students learned traditional Negro **spirituals,** and on tour, mannered renditions of the songs. The concerts raised funds to erect the notable Jubilee Hall at Fisk. In the twenty-first century, choral organizations at historically black colleges and universities (HBCUs) such as Morehouse College, Spelman College, and Hampton University, have maintained the tradition of touring nationally and internationally to perform, among others, Negro spirituals.

flashback A scene or episode in prose, verse, or **drama** that takes place earlier than its given moment. Modern novelists who frequently employ the technique are Ann Petry in *The Narrows* (1953); Ralph Ellison in *Invisible Man* (1952); and John Edgar Wideman in *Hurry Home* (1970).

flying African A tale that recounts the belief in the ability of native-born Africans to call on a special African-derived power to lift them up from the burden of slavery in America and return them to Africa. As **myth,** the suggestion is that the African American is bound in body and weighed down in chains, but his spirit is not to be enslaved. The flying **motif** occurs in Ralph Ellison's story "Flying Home" (1944); Toni Morrison's *Song of Solomon* (1977); and Paule Marshall's *Praisesong for the Widow* (1983). The motif occurs also in Julius Lester's collection *Black Folktales* (1991) and Virginia Hamilton's children collection *The People Could Fly: American Black Folktales* (1985).

folk cries A form of folk music sung without instruments, initially in fields while work was in progress. According to William Barlow in *Looking Up at Down: The Emergence of Blues Culture* (1989), the folk/field cries "were short signature pieces—the vocalization of a field hand's identity and mood" (18). The vocal utterances turned into verbal phrases and then into verses. According to Willis James in "The Romance of the Negro Folk Cry in America" (1950), folk cries range from simple to elaborate: plain cries, florid cries, and coloratura cries. The plain cries are found in simple calls such as street cries and dance cries. Florid cries, the more stylistic, are religious cries, field cries, hollers, and night cries that are found in, for instance, **spirituals, work songs, blues, folk preaching,** and **jazz.** Coloratura cries, the more elaborate, are derived from water cries and are best exemplified in the works of Louis Armstrong and Mahalia Jackson.
(See also **blues.**)

References for further reading: William Barlow, "I Been 'Buked and I Been Scorned" (1989); Willis Laurence James, "The Romance of the Negro Folk Cry in America" (1950);

and Patricia Liggins Hill, introduction to *Call and Response, The Riverside Anthology of the African American Literary Tradition* (1997): 29–30.

folklore The sum of what a group traditionally says in **proverbs, folktales, ballads, spirituals, work songs,** and **toasts** and traditionally does in **rituals, dances,** customs, and practices. Preserved is a heritage as well as the spirit of a race within folk songs, stories, sayings, rites, manners, and customs. The mythological carriers of African American folk traditions have been **Brer Rabbit,** the Signifying Monkey, John de Conquer, Shine, Stackolee, and Railroad Bill. Actual carriers have been the slaves and their descendents who have recounted lessons about life and survival, communal values, and tradition, even in new situations and changing realities.

Reference for further reading: Ralph Ellison, "Change the Joke and Ship the Yoke" (1964).

folk preacher A product and producer of an aesthetic tradition in African American culture. A skilled orator. A performer. He uses black speech and black music as vehicles by which to move his audience to **ecstasy** or to regenerate the spirits of his downtrodden community. He humanizes figures in the Old Testament via vibrant folk idioms, vivid **imagery,** and apt metaphors, and using his one instrument—the voice and its various ranges—he connects the situations and experiences of the African American community to the parables of the Old Testament. In short, he revises reality, offering hope and a sense of spiritual wholeness.

References for further reading: Daryl Cumber Dance, *Shuckin' and Jivin': Folklore from Contemporary Black America* (1978); Dolan Hubbard, *The Sermon and the African American Literary Imagination* (1994); Henry H. Mitchell, *Black Preaching,* 1970.

folktale A genre that entertains, but also through **indirection** teaches lessons about life and survival (e.g., the **Gullah's** moralizing tale). The folktale nearly always shows how the powerless can overcome one's adversity (e.g., the **trickster** tale and the **conjure** tale). The carriers of the folktale have been the mythological animal characters **Brer Rabbit** and the Spider (e.g., **Anancy** stories in the Caribbean) and the actual slaves and their descendents. The latter passed on the tales—also called "lies"—orally. Analytical criticism of the folktale, particularly the trickster tale, reveals that there are recurring **themes:** escape, confronting overseers and masters, and the protection of (or attempts at protecting) loved ones. **Representations** (see under Criticism and Theory) of the folktale appear in the following collections: Charles W. Chesnutt's *The Conjure Woman* (1899); Rudolph Fisher's *The Conjurer Man* (1932); and Tina McElroy Ansa's *Baby of the Family* (1989). Other writers who pull from the folktale include Zora Neale Hurston in *Moses, Man of the Mountain* (1939) and Toni Morrison in *Tar Baby* (1981).

References for further reading: John Mason Brewer, *The Word on the Brazos: Negro Preacher Tales from the Brazos Bottoms of Texas* (1958); Harold Courlander, *A Treasury of Afro-American Folklore* (1996); Zora Neale Hurston, *Mules and Men* (1935); Charles C. Jones, *Negro Myths from the Georgia Coast* (1969).

foreshadowing When information or events are used early in a literary work to give a hint to a later outcome. See, for instance, the opening chapters in Richard Wright's *Native Son* (1940) and Ann Petry's *The Street* (1946).

"forms of things unknown" A phrase coined by Richard Wright (though expressed earlier by William Shakespeare and Marcel Proust) to suggest a dialectic between the spoken and the written—between the folk and the traditional; levels of crisscrossing that are not discrete entities.

References for further reading: Stephen E. Henderson, *Understanding the New Black Poetry: Black Music and Black Speech as Poetic References* (1973); Geneva Smitherman, *Talkin and Testifyin: The Language of Black America* (1977).

framed narrative A story or a series of stories that will be enclosed or embedded in another story—"a tale within the tale." Usually a **vernacular** story is framed within a standard story for regional and local color effects. According to John Edgar Wideman, sometimes a vernacular story is framed within a vernacular story (e.g., Ernest Gaines's *The Autobiography of Miss Jane Pittman* (1971) as a way of **signifying** on standard Western tradition. Other examples of the framed narrative include Janie Crawford's story to Phoeby within Zora Neale Hurston's *Their Eyes Were Watching God* (1937) and the readings of Nettie's letters by Shug and Celie in Alice Walker's *The Color Purple* (1982).

free indirect discourse A mode of bivocal narration, with third-person narrative voice attempting to represent first-person **point of view** without the appearance of an intruding narrator. The result is two voices that co-occur to represent the consciousness and point of view of first-person. The reader is often forced to ask who is speaking? An example of free indirect discourse is found in Zora Neale Hurston's *Their Eyes Were Watching God* (1937):

> Joe Starks was the name, yeah Joe Starks from in and through Georgy. Been workin' for white folks all his [my] life. Saved up some money—round three hundred dollars, yes indeed, right here in his [my] pocket. Kept hearnin' 'bout then buildin' a new state down heah in Floridy and sort of wanted to come. But he [I] was makin' money where he [I] was. But when he [I] heard all about 'em makin' a town all outa colored folks, he [I] knowed dat was de place he [I] wanted to be. He [I] had always wanted to be a big voice, but de white folks had all de sayso where he [I] come from and everywhere else, exceptin' dis place dat colored folks was buildin' theirselves. Dat was right too. De man dat built things oughta boss it. Let colored folks build things too if day wants to crow over somethin'. He [I] was glad he [I] had his [my] money all saved up. He [I] meant to git dere whilst de town wuz yet a baby. He [I] meant to buy in big. (47–48)

An example of free indirect discourse is found also in Ann Petry's *The Street* (1946):

> Her grasp on the subway strap tightened until the hard enameled surface cut into her hand and she relaxed her hand and then tightened it. Because that kitchen sink in the advertisement or one just like it was what had wrecked her [me] and Jim. The sink had belonged to someone else—she'd [I'd] been washing someone else's dishes when she [I] should have been home with Jim and Bub. Instead she'd [I'd] cleaned another woman's house and looked after another woman's child while her [my] own marriage went to pot. (29–30)

In Alice Walker's *The Color Purple* (1982), Celie appears to give her account of Mr. ___'s sister, but in the following passage, the narrator leaves the reader to question who is speaking? Carrie, Kate, Celie, or all three?

> Well that's no excuse, say the first one. Her name Carrie, other one name Kate. When a woman marry she spose to keep a decent house and a clean family. Why, wasn't nothing to come here in the winter time and all these children have colds, they have flue, they have direar, they have new monya, they have worms, they have the chill and fever. They hungry. They hair ain't combed. They too nasty to much. (19)

(See also **double-voiced.**)

Reference for further reading: Henry Louis Gates Jr., *The Signifying Monkey: A Theory of Afro-American Literary Criticism* (1988).

freedom (See **theme**.)

free verse Verse that lacks standard meter, line length, and measured syllables (stressed or unstressed) and is modeled after rhythms of natural speech. See, for instance, the consistent use of free verse by Langston Hughes in a poem such as "Mother to Son":

> Well, son, I'll tell you:
> Life for me ain't been no crystal stair
> (Gates et al. 1997:1254–55, lines 1–2.)

In a poem such as Margaret Walker's "For My People" (1942):

> For my people everywhere singing their slave songs repeatedly: their dirges and their ditties and their blues and jubilees, praying their prayers nightly to an unknown god, bending their knees humbly to an unseen power
> (Gates et al. 1997:1572–73, lines 1–4.)

In a poem such as James Weldon Johnson's "The Creation" (1920):

> And God stepped out on space,
> And he looked around and said:
> I'm lonely—
> I'll make me a world.
> (Gates et al. 1997:775–77, lines 1–4.)

In a poem such as Robert Hayden's "Those Winter Sundays" (1962):

> Sundays too my father got up early
> And put his clothes on in the blueblack cold
> then with cracked hands that ached
> from labor in the weekday weather make
> banked fire blaze. No one ever thanked him.
> (Glaysher 1985:41, lines 1–5.)

as well as Hayden's "The Whipping" (1962):

> The old woman across the way
>   Is whipping the boy again

and shouting to the neighborhood
    Her goodness and his wrongs
(Glaysher 1985:40, lines 1–4.)

Contemporary writers to Hughes, Walker, and Hayden continue to employ free verse. See, for instance, Michael Harper's poem "Effendi" (1977):

The piano hums
again the clear
story of our coming,
enchained, severed
(Hill, 1997:1650, lines 1–4.)

funk Slang used often among musicians and African American writers to mean groove and **soul.**

Reference for further reading: Stephen E. Henderson, "Inside the Funk Shop: A Word on Black Words" (2000).

"furious flower" A phrase coined by Gwendolyn Brooks in her poem "The Second Sermon on the Warpland" (1968). As **motif,** "furious flower" suggests two significant intertwining developments in African American **poetry**: radical and aesthetic.
(See also **appendix 2.**)

Reference for further reading: Joanne Gabbin, *Furious Flower: A Video Anthology of African American Poetry 1960–95* (1998); www.newsreel.org

Garveyism The term has come to represent the new awakening among the masses of African Americans in the early 1900s, which was spawned by Marcus Garvey and his organization, the Universal Negro Improvement Association (UNIA). The UNIA was founded on the basic beliefs of pride, self-determination, **black nationalism,** loyalty among the black masses, and on a determined back-to-Africa effort.

"gaze, the" According to bell hooks in *Black Looks: Race and Representation,* the imperial gaze is "the look that seeks to dominate, subjugate and colonize" in and out of literary art.

References for further reading: Carolyn Gerald, "The Black Writer and His Role" (1999); bell hooks, "Revolutionary Attitudes" (1992); Mary Helen Washington, introduction to *A Voice from the South* (1988).

genealogical narrative A narrative that was once indebted to oral and written testimonies of African American **ancestors,** particularly former slaves. Following the Civil Rights movement, the term came to mean narrated accounts of searches of family lineages—for example, Alex Haley's *Roots* (1976).

"girlfriend culture" Popular novels of the 1990s that maintain similar **themes** of women at odds with the residual elements of contemporary African American male culture. The novels are also rooted in the everyday lives of African American women, and these women, among others, battle to save their own souls. See, for instance, Terry McMillan's *Disappearing Act* (1989), *Waiting to Exhale* (1992), and *How Stella Got Her Groove Back* (1996); Connie Briscoe's *Sisters and Lovers* (1994); and J. California Cooper's short story collections *A Piece of Mind* (1984), *Homemade Love* (1986), *Some Soul to Keep* (1987), *The Matter Is Life* (1991), and *Some Love, Some Pain, Sometime* (1995).

Reference for further reading: Maryemma Graham, "Novel" (1997).

goopher Grave dirt used in **conjure** or magic, particularly when attempting to call up spirits of dead **ancestors.** An African tradition from the Kongo civilization derived from the KiKongo verb *kufwa* that means "to die." According to tradition, earth from a person's grave is considered to be one with the person's spirit. The use of goopher is found in the conjure stories in Charles W. Chesnutt's *The Conjure Woman* (1899) and Zora Neale Hurston's *Mules and Men* (1935).

gospel songs The term was coined by Thomas Dorsey to describe African American religious music emanating from urban culture in the late 1920s and early 1930s. Influences of gospel are the **spirituals** and **blues.** Classic gospel songs written by Dorsey include "Take My Hand, Precious Lord" and "Peace in the Valley."

grammar of the sermon A sermonic mode that conjures up the **performance** of the **folk preacher**—as product of and as producer of an aesthetic tradition. Through speech acts (sermons) the preacher provides the vehicle by which a community may participate in emotional and affective witnessing. His sermon moves from complication to **climax** to resolution and then to **cathartic release** or ecstasy. It is in the latter that the community seeks and finds a vital force or a sense of spiritual ecstasy or a sense of spiritual wholeness. According to Marcellus Blount, the "vernacular sermonic performance [is] a cite of authority, authenticity, and artistic creativity." According to Dolan Hubbard in *The Sermon and the African American Literary Imagination* (1994), writers function like preachers; they attempt to engage the community in emotional and affective witnessing and to bring about some sense of spiritual wholeness. The fiction and nonfiction by the following writers show evidence of the grammar of the sermon performance (complication, climax, resolution, and cathartic release): Frances Ellen Watkins Harper, Jean Toomer, Zora Neale Hurston, Richard Wright, Ishmael Reed, Leon Forrest, Alice Walker, Ernest Gaines, Toni Morrison, Gloria Naylor, Julius Lester, and C. Eric Lincoln. One may add unlikely writers such as Paul Laurence Dunbar in "Ode to Ethiopia" (1893) and contemporary songsters R. Kelly in "I Believe That I Can Fly" and Curtis Mayfield in "New World Order." A writer like James Baldwin in *Go Tell It On the Mountain* (1953) and a singer like Jill Scott in "A Long Walk" employ sermonic rhetoric for effect or outcome.

(See also **ecstasy, magara,** and **sermon.**)

Great Chain of Being A belief that denotes an idea of a natural hierarchy. As expressed by Alexander Pope in *Essay on Man* (1733):

Vast chain of being which from God began,
Natures ethereal, human, angel, man,
Beast, bird, fish, insect, what no eye can see
(Abrams and Greenblatt, eds. 2000:2560, lines 237–39.)

The persistent attitude since colonial times in America has been that in this hierarchal order, the slave, supposedly due to his lack of innate abilities to reason, was between man and beast.

griot (gre'o) The oral carrier of African American culture. In traditional Africa, the griot functions as poet, storyteller, genealogist, historian, teacher, musician, singer, and entertainer. The tribal figure is regarded widely as "the library," for, as stated in the West African **proverb,** when an old man dies, a library burns to the ground. The griot figure exists in *Daughters of the Dust* (1991), a film by Julie Dash, and in the character of Pilate in Toni Morrison's *Song of Solomon* (1977).

Gullah African practices, beliefs, manners, customs, and literary art that are maintained on the coastal islands of South Carolina and Georgia by descendents of African slaves. Gullah is an African language that maintains African word order and etymological meanings with English words added. The African word order can be traced to African countries such as Senegal, Gambia, Sierra Leone, Ghana, Nigeria, and Anglo. Gullah is also an African culture that has been preserved largely **orally** via **proverbs, trickster** tales, riddles, and in art forms such as basket weaving, netting, quilting, rootwork, and African languages.

References for further reading: Muriel Miller Branch, *The Water Brought Us: The Story of the Gullah-Speaking People* (1995); Margaret W. Creel, *A Peculiar People: Slave Religion and Community Culture Among the Gullah* (1988); Patricia Jones-Jackson, *When Roots Die* (1987); Charles Joyner, *Down by the Riverside: A South Carolina Slave Community* (1986); Lorenzo D. Turner and Kathera Wyly Mills, *Africanisms in the Gullah Dialect* (2000); Mary A. Twining and Keith Baird, *Sea Island Roots: African Presence in the Carolinas and Georgia* (1991).

haiku (hi'koo) A Japanese verse form with, among other, natural images, feelings, and scenes that are portrayed indirectly in seventeen syllables: arranged in three unrhymed lines of five, seven, and five syllables. While Richard Wright, Mari Evans, and Etheridge Knight are early poets who experimented with the verse form, Lenard Moore is one of the more familiar haiku poets. See, for instance, Moore's *Gathering at the Crossroads: A Chapbook of Haiku and Photographs of the Million Man March* (2003):

the cadenced footsteps
of one million black men
a warm fall day

Harlem Renaissance According to Sterling A. Brown, between 1917 and 1935, a host of writers, particularly in Harlem, shared common literary experiences: "(1) a discovery of Africa as a source for race pride, (2) a use of Negro heroes and heroic episodes from American history, (3) propaganda of protest, (4) a treatment of the Negro masses ... with more understanding and less apology, and (5) franker and deeper self-revelation" (Sterling A. Brown, 1969:61). The older members of the group of writers included W.E.B. DuBois, Alain Locke, Charles S. Johnson, and James Weldon Johnson. The younger members of the group included Langston Hughes,

Jean Toomer, Countee Cullen, Claude McKay, Zora Neale Hurston, Georgia Douglas Johnson, Nella Larsen, and Jessie Fauset. (See also **Renaissances and radicalism period.**)

healing (See **"laying on the hands."**)

hero/heroine/heroism Gayl Jones has written in *Liberating Voices: Oral Tradition in African American Literature* (1991):

> African American writers frequently draw upon archetypes from African and African American mythology, folklore and history as paradigms for the heroic qualities of their protagonists. (199)

Jones is referencing some of the earliest paradigms of resistance and of "getting over" in African American culture (e.g., see heroes in the **trickster** tales and **conjure** tales). Referenced also as heroes are actual African Americans fighting for their rights, from slavery to present. Like the trickster and conjure tales, heroic figures are remembered best orally. Eventually making their way into written texts are the better known ones: **Brer Rabbit, High John de Conqueror,** John (of the John and Massa tales), the **badman,** the **"bad-ass(ed) nigger,"** **hoodoo** or conjure women and men, John Henry, Shine, Stackolee, and the countless slaves remembered in stories passed on within African American families.

References for further reading: Robert B. Stepto, *From Behind the Veil: A Study of Afro-American Narrative* (1979); Sherley Ann Williams, "Some Implications of Womanist Theory" (2000).

heroic couplet A literary device of two successive rhyming lines in a verse unit that are mostly in **iambic pentameter.** Phillis Wheatley is the most recognized poet to use the elevated English form. See, for instance, Wheatley in "To Maecenas" (1773):

> Maecenas, you, beneath the myrtle shade,
> Read o'er what poets sung, and shepherds play'd
> (Gates and McKay 1997:169–70, lines 1–2.)

and in her "On Imagination" (1973):

> Thy various works, imperial queen, we see,
> How bright their forms! How deck'd with pomp by thee!
> (Gates and McKay 1997:173–74, lines 1–2.)

As demonstrated by Frances Watkins Harper in "Bury Me in a Free Land" (1864), there were other early African American poets who used the *AB* rhyming scheme, as well:

Make me a grave wher'er you will,
In a lonely plain or a loftly hill;
(Gates and McKay 1997:173–74, lines 417–18.)

heteroglossia A term coined by Mikhail Bakhtin in "Discourse in the Novel" (1934–35) (in Leitch et al. 2001:1190–1220) to denote the "internal stratification" of language or the "centrifrugal forces" at work in language. Not only is there evidence via the language of differences between the narrative voice and the voices of the characters (e.g., class, ethnicity, age, generation) but reflected also via language are different attitudes and opinions of the characters and narrators.
(See also **dialogic** and **"speaking in tongues."**)

Reference for further reading: Vincent B. Leitch et al., *The Norton Anthology of Theory and Criticism* (2001).

Hip-hop culture Emerging in the 1970s is a younger culture of **performance: rap** musicians that freestyle and **improvise**. Other markers include verbal dualing (i.e., playing the **dozens**), graffiti art, and break dancing. A shift in **"black talk"** takes place, as well. For instance, "jiggy" denotes "lots of money"; "end" denotes "money"; "PJs" denotes "the projects"; "dis" denotes "to insult"; and "jam" denotes "a song, a cut, or a track." Unchanged is the term **"the word,"** which denotes still "the truth" or one's "word is bond."

Out of the Hip-hop culture have come rap music and **def-jam** or **"the spoken-word"** poetry. According to Mtume ya Salaam in "The Aesthetics of Rap" (1995) (in Ervin, 1999:445–52), the first period of rap development can be traced to the 1970s to DJs perfecting their craft in parks and house parties:

Using the bass and drum while the melodic instruments and the singer(s) sat out. . . . this "break" was the most affective part of the record. . . . Then using two turntables and a stereo mixer, the DJs would extend and combine the few bars customary on the recordings into new creations that would last as long as the DJ wanted. (Ervin, ed. 1999:450.)

The rapper or MC—short for Master of Ceremonies—becomes as influential as the DJ (if not more influential), for titles such as the Sugar Hill Gang's "Rapper's Delight," and debut albums such as Run-D.M.C.'s *Run-D.M.C.* appear in the late 1970s. Since the late 1980s, overt commercialism, public opinions, and individual tastes and "morals" (or lack thereof) by artists have shaped the creative climate of the rap world.

According to Michael Dyson in "The Culture of Hip-Hop" (1993), rap is "a profound musical, cultural, and social creativity" (Donalson, ed. 1996: 843). It expresses the desire of young black people to reclaim their history, reactivate forms of black radicalism, and contest the powers of despair and economic depression that presently besiege the black community. Rappers (like other musicians) acknowledge African history and sources.
(See also **Age of Baraka, bard, Black Arts Movement, griot, haiku, last poets, performance, rap, "the spoken word."**)

References for further reading: Houston A. Baker Jr., "Hybridity, the Rap Race, and Pedagogy for the 1990s" (1991); Michael Eric Dyson, *Between God and Gangsta' Rap: Bearing Witness to Black Culture* (1995) and *Reflecting Black: African American Cultural Criticism* (1993); Marvin Gladney, "The Black Arts Movement and Hip Hop" (1995); Tricia Rose, *Black Noise: Rap Music and Black Culture in Contemporary American Music/Culture* (1994); Mtume ya Salaam, "The Aesthetics of Rap," in *African American Literary Criticism, 1773 to 2000* (1999).

historical novel A narrative set in a specific historical period with both fictional and historical characters. Writers of the historical novel before 1970 strived for **verisimilitude** (see, e.g., Arna Bontemps's *Black Thunder* (1936) and Margaret Walker's *Jubilee* (1966). Writers after the 1970s experimented with conventions of narrative voice and form (see, e.g., Ernest Gaines's *The Autobiography of Miss Jane Pittman* (1971); Alex Haley's *Roots* (1976); David Bradley's *The Chaneysville Incident* (1981); Toni Morrison's *Beloved* (1987); Barbara Chase-Riboud's *Echo of Lions* (1989); and Charles Johnson's *Middle Passage* (1990).

historical revisionist The writer revises actual historical records or so-called truth, offering history and truth from an alternative perspective. When offered as a literary form, revisionist writing offers insightful commentary. Such writings are postmodern in style due to the author's fusion of fact and fiction. Historical revisionists include John A. Williams in *The Man Who Cried I Am* (1967); Randall Kenan in *A Visitation of Spirits* (1989); Charles Johnson in *Middle Passage* (1990); Ishmael Reed in *Flight to Canada*

(1976); Toni Morrison in *Beloved* (1988); David Bradley in *The Chaneysville Incident* (1981); and Ann Petry in *Tituba of Salem Village* (1964).

hollers (See **folk cries.**)

"homespace" (See **"urban space."**)

hoodoo A variation of **voodoo/vodun**. See variations of hoodoo in Paule Marshall's *Brown Girl, Brownstones* (1959); Toni Cade Bambara's *The Salt Eaters* (1980); Toni Morrison's *Tar Baby* (1981); and John Edgar Wideman's *Damballah* (1981).
(See also **neo-hoodoo aesthetic** and **voodoo/vodun.**)

humor Subversive. Mocking. Heroic. Creative and exuberant. In African American literature humor is used to display wit and to bring about change. (See also **the absurd** and **parody.**)

References for further reading: Daryl Dance, *Honey Hush! An Anthology of African American Women's Humor* (1998); Zora Neale Hurston in *Mules and Men* (1935); John Lowe, "Humor," in *The Oxford Companion to African American Literature* (1997).

hymn A lyric poem of religious theme that is meant to be sung.

hyperbole A term that means an exaggeration for emphasis or heightened effect. See, for instance, Amiri Baraka's use of the term in *Preface to a Twenty Volume Suicide Note* (1961):

> Lately, I've become accustomed to the way
> The ground opens up and envelopes me
> Each time I go out to walk the dog
> Or the broad edged silly music the wind
> Makes when I run for the bus . . . (5)

See also J. California Cooper's use of the term in "The Life You Live (May Not Be Your Own):

> He was even stingy at the dinner table. Grow it or don't get it! Even his horses and cows was thin. Everything on his farm didn't like him.
> (Cooper, 1987: 47; reprinted in McMillan, 1990:147.)

iambic pentameter A line of a verse that contains five iambs (unaccented syllables followed by an accented syllable). Countee Cullen uses the rhythmic pattern in "From the Dark Tower" (1927):

> We shall not always plant while others reap
> The golden increment of bursting fruit
> (Gates and McKay 1997:1315, lines 1–2.)

Ibo Landing In 1858, on St. Simon Island, Georgia, shortly after the slave ship *Wanderer* landed, eighteen African men of the Ibo tribe decided to die rather than be enslaved. Linked together they waded into Dunbar Creek, proclaiming "Water brought us, and water's gonna take us away." According to Muriel Miller Branch in *The Water Brought Us: The Story of the Gullah-Speaking People* (1993), the rebellion at Dunbar Creek is now commemorated as Ibo Landing. The rebellion also is said to be the origin of the Negro **spiritual** "Oh, Freedom."

ideophones The descriptive words that convey images and meaning through their sounds. As a communicative device, listeners are able to identify a feeling, sound, color, texture, expression, movement, and even silence through their own senses. A verbal technique used first by slaves in the **spirituals** (e.g., "the blood ran twinkling down" [the spiritual "He Never Said a Mumbaling Word," in Davis et al. 1941:438]) and by oral storytellers. See, also novelist Toni Morrison in *Song of Solomon* (1977):

> She spent her days, her tendril, sapgreen days.

Or, Morrison in part two of *Sula* (1973), as the novelist describes Nel's loneliness after Jude, Nel's husband, has left. According to Morrison, this is a loneliness that does not scream its pain but hovers over Nel like a "quiet, gray dirty . . . ball of muddy strings . . . , without weight, fluffy but terrible in its malevolence" (109). Following Sula's death, Nel's call to Sula is via ideophones. As Nel "gaz[es] at the top of trees,"

> Leaves stirred; mud shifted; there was the smell of overripe green things. A soft ball of fur broke and scattered like dandelion spores in the breeze (174).

See, also Ann Petry in *The Street* (1946):

> It was the woman's eyes. They were as still and as malignant as the eyes of a snake. She could see them quite plainly—flat eyes that stared at her—wandering over her body, inspecting and appraising her from head to feet (6).

Reference for further reading: Isidore Okpewho, *African Oral Literature: Backgrounds, Character, and Continuity* (1992).

idiom Refers to a turn of phrase that cannot be translated into another language and maintain its meaning. There are regional differences in idioms due to customs. Writers use idioms to lend authenticity to the characters (see Langston Hughes's character Jesse B. Semple in *The Best of Simple* [1961]); to the narrative (see Zora Neale Hurston's "How the 'Gator Got Black"); and to regionalism (see Ernest Gaines's "Robert Louis Stevenson Banks, aka Chimley").
(See also **dialect.**)

Ifa divination (See **deities.**)

imagery The use of words to create pictures or images in a reader's mind. Consider, for instance, the poems "Southern Mansion" (1931) by Arna Bontemps and "Heritage" (1925) by Countee Cullen.

Reference for further reading: Stephen Henderson, *Understanding the New Black Poetry: Black Speech and Black Music as Poetic References* (1973).

images (See **representation** under Criticism and Theory.)

immersion narrative (See **ascension narrative.**)

imperial gaze (See **"the gaze."**)

improvisation Spontaneity expressed in the delivery of traditional folk forms such as **work songs, spirituals, blues, jazz,** and **sermon.** A practice by musicians, orators, and preachers that is dependent upon spontaneity and variety in delivery. As technique, improvisation means a break with established rhythm or melodic line in order to explore solo. The solo becomes the improvisation. The break is also called **riff** or "improv."

indeterminacy (See **ambiguity** under Criticism and Theory.)

indirection A discourse strategy used to meander around a point or to avoid confronting it head-on. It is also subtle circumlocution. (See **signifying.**)

influence (See Criticism and Theory.)

initiation (See **secret societies.**)

in medias res A technique that allows authors to begin their stories in the middle of an action or at some heightened moment.

inspiriting influences (See **influence** under Criticism and Theory.)

interjections The inclusion of emotion words that may have been handed down through the **spirituals**. See, for example, Jean Toomer's "Song of the Son" (1923):

> Pour O pour that parting soul in song
> (Gates and McKay 1997:1095–96, line 1.)

intertextual/intertextuality A term that denotes the nonthematic manner by which texts—**slave narratives,** poems, and **novels**—absorb, transform, or respond to other texts. Interconnected to **poststructuralism** via textuality or the concept that textuality is conditioned by the inescapable historical intertext—a "textual subconscious." See, for instance, how Gloria Naylor's *The Women of Brewster Place* (1982) becomes what critics call "a new articulation" of Ann Petry's *The Street* (1946) or how Ishmael Reed's *Mumbo Jumbo* (1972) becomes a "new articulation" of Richard Wright's *Native Son* (1940) and Ralph Ellison's *Invisible Man* (1952). (See also **signifying.**)

References for further reading: Vincent B. Leitch et al., *The Norton Anthology of Theory and Criticism,* 2001; Robert B. Stepto and Dexter Fisher, eds. *African American Literature: The Reconstruction of Instruction* (1979); Henry Louis Gates Jr., *Figures in Black: Words, Signs, and the Racial Self* (1987).

intonation A pattern of variations in pitch during a spoken utterance. In the preface to *God's Trombones, Seven Negro Sermons in Verse* (1927), James Weldon Johnson defines intonation as an artful practice by old-time preachers that is extremely difficult to imitate and next to impossible to describe. While intonation must be heard to be appreciated, Johnson says the artful practice might be called

> A matter of crescendo and diminuendo in the intensity—a rising and falling between plain speaking and wild chanting. Often a startling effect is gained when the preacher breaks off suddenly at the highest point of intensity and drops into a monotone of ordinary speech. (10)

Johnson identifies the following sermons from the collection that would better be toned than read: "Listen Lord," "The Crucifixion," and "The Judgment Day."
(See also **improvisation.**)

intrusive narrator (See **point of view.**)

inversion The reversal of normal word order in a sentence in order to preserve rhyme scheme or to place special emphasis on particular words. See, for example, Claude McKay's "Baptism" (1953):

> You will not note a flicker of defeat
> My heart shall tremble not its fate to meet
> (Hill, ed. 1997:883–84, lines 6–7.)

invisibility (See **theme.**)

irony A subtle practice with outcomes incongruent with expectations or proper effects. Types of irony include:

Verbal irony: When a person says one thing but means something different
Dramatic irony: When the audience realizes something that a character does not realize
Irony of situation: When there is a discrepancy between what is expected as a result of an action or situation and what is the actual result

Italian sonnet A verse form that consists of fourteen lines in **iambic pentameter**. The verse form is made up of two parts: an octave (the first eight lines, rhyming *abba, abba*) and a sestet (remaining six lines, varying in rhyme scheme, although usually *cdcdcd* or *cdecde*). In the first eight lines, a **theme** is established. In the remaining six lines, the theme is developed or the problem is resolved. With African American poets, familiar themes of the Italian sonnet such as love, passion, or regret, are often eclipsed by some aspect of the African American experience or some problem experienced by the African American. For example, in "From the Dark Tower" (1927), Countee Cullen establishes a problem from the African American experience in the octave:

We were not made eternally to weep

In the sestet, Cullen offers the resolution:

So in the dark we hide the heart that bleeds
And wait, and tend our agonizing seeds
(Gates and McKay 1997:1315.)

Other poets who wrote in this verse form include Henrietta Cordelia Ray, Thomas Fortune, and Melvin B. Tolson.
(See also **Petrarchan sonnet** and **Shakespearean sonnet.**)

jazz Musician Max Roach has defined "jazz" as "a kind of music, generally improvised but somehow arranged, achieving its effects by syncopation, heavily accented rhythms, dissonance, melodic variation, and particular tonal qualities of the saxophone, trumpet, clarinet, and other instruments" (Ervin, ed. 1999:113). The art form was originated by African American musicians in New Orleans, although the music is generally said to have been derived from **blues, work songs,** and **spirituals.**

John the Conqueror/High John the Conqueror A folk term associated with **conjuring** (or magical) powers. Also referred to as a root ("High John") that comes in a variety of forms: nonprocessed root, powder, liquid, or diced. The root is used to protect against evil spirits or to improve one's fortune. In Ann Petry's *The Street* (1946), to improve Min's fortune and to protect her against her live-in husband who wants to expel her from their apartment, the root doctor gives Min "a red liquid," one drop of which every morning she is to put into Jones's coffee, and a "powder" that she is to carry with her at all times. According to Clarence Major in *Juba to Jive: A Dictionary of African-American Slang* (1970) in myth, "[Big] John [the] Conqueror" is the one who "tore off the Devil's arm and whipped him with it" (261).

journey (See **theme.**)

jump(ing) the broom A **ritual** initiated in the African American community by slaves to symbolize commitment between married couples.

Juneteenth Following the signing of the Thirteenth Amendment that abol-
ished slavery in the United States in 1864, Union officers made their way
through the Southeast in order to read the Emancipation Proclamation. On
June 19, 1865, an emancipation celebration took place in Texas, Louisiana,
Arkansas, and Oklahoma. The nineteenth of June has become the southwestern freedom day, and it is called Juneteenth. To commemorate the celebration, writers include in their works either festival picnics (see Maya
Angelou's *I Know Why the Caged Bird Sings* [1970]) or celebration **rituals**
(see Ralph Ellison's "Juneteenth" [1965] and the posthumously published
Juneteenth [1999]).

Kwanzaa A cultural holiday, first observed by African Americans on December 26, 1976, and now celebrated from December 26 to January 1. Taken
from the Swahili phrase "matunda ya Kwanza" ("first fruits") and rooted in
the first harvest celebration by West African cultures, Kwanzaa reinforces a
connectedness to African cultural identity, to community, and to certain
values spelled out in seven social and spiritual principles (one for each day):

> Umoja (oo-moe-jah): unity
> Kujichagulia (koo-jee-cha-goo-LEE-ah): self-determination
> Ujima (oo-JEE-mah): collective work and responsibility
> Ujamaa (oo-JAH-mah): cooperative economics
> Nia (nee-AH): purpose
> Kuumba (koo-OOM-bah): creativity
> Imani (ee-MAH-nee): faith

Kwanzaa was conceived and developed in America by **black aesthetician**
Maulana Ron Karenga.

last poets The **"spoken word"** artists and rappers of the Civil Rights era. As
revolutionists, these spoken-word poets have become the precursors of
modern day rappers: David Nelson, Gylan Kain, Abiodun Oyewole, Felipe
Luciano, Umar Bin Hassan, Jalal Nurridin, and Suliman El Hadi.

"laying on the hands" A folk phrase that refers to the **ritual** of healing the body physically and the mind psychologically. Performed mostly by a **conjurer** or a spiritual guide, the act of "laying on the hands" is to remove a spell or to cast off psychological injury. The conjurer or spiritual guide is set on the use of ritual to restore a sense of spiritual wholeness in individuals or to restore communal harmony. The conjurer and spiritual guide appear in Charles W. Chesnutt's *The Conjure Woman* (1899); Gloria Naylor's *Mama Day* (1988) and *The Women of Brewster Place* (1982); Margaret Walker's *Jubilee* (1966); and Toni Cade Bambara's *The Salt Eaters* (1980). See also Ntozake Shange's play *for colored girls* (1974).

Legba (See **Eshu-Elegba.**)

legend A story that is handed down in oral traditions such as **work songs** and **ballads** and that is usually based on **myth** or historical accounts of particular figures or persons. Postbellum folk **hero** John Henry, who in real life died while driving steel for the railroad in West Virginia in the early 1870s, is probably the most immortalized of historical figures in work songs and ballads. Interpretations of John Henry exist in John O. Killens's *A Man Ain't Nothin' But a Man* (1975), and Ernest Gaines's character Joe Pittman in *The Autobiography of Miss Jane Pittman* (1971) and Raoul Carmier in *Catherine Carmier* (1964). See also James Alan McPherson's Doc Craft in "A Solo Song: For Doc" (McPherson, *Hue and Cry: Short Stories* by James Alan McPherson. Boston: Little, Brown, 1969). For additional examples, see the poetry of Margaret Walker, Sterling Brown, and Melvin B. Tolson. Ann Petry's essay "New England's John Henry" (1945) immortalizes yet another man of African descent who ignites the collective folk imagination about African Americans' triumph over doom. Petry's New England John Henry is named Venture Smith, a slave from Rhode Island and later of Connecticut, who in real life labored with his nine-pound axe to buy his freedom. As a freedman, he started a successful New England shipping business.

References for further reading: Guy B. Johnson, *John Henry: Tracking Down a Negro Legend* (1929); Ann Petry, "New England's John Henry" (1945); Dorothy Porter, *Early Negro Writing: 1760–1837* (1971).

leitmotif A recurrent **theme** in an author's work or in an artist's work. For example, in John Edgar Wideman's Homewood trilogy—*Damballah* (1981), *Hiding Place* (1981), and *Sent for You Yesterday* (1983)—there is the leitmotif of journeying back to the historical self. In Lynn E. Harris's trilogy *Invisible Life* (1991), *Just as I Am* (1994), and *And This Too Shall Pass* (1996), there is the recurring theme of invisibility for the black gay male in African American and in American communities. In Gayl Jones's novels *Corregidora* (1975) and *Eva's Man* (1976) and in her short story collection *White Rat* (1977), the recurring theme is often the way that racism and sexism build and victimize African American men and women.

letter A genre that can be distinguished as private or as public—informal or formal. Addressed mostly to family, friends, and other close acquaintances, the private letter has been limited to observations, requests, and testimonies of life. See, for instance, the private letters of slaves and of former slaves in John Blassingame's *Slave Testimony: Two Centuries of Letters, Speeches, Interviews and Autobiographies* (1977); the private letters of Ignatius Sancho, later collected in *Letters of Ignatius Sancho* (1782); or the private letters of Harlem Renaissance writers Arna Bontemps and Langston Hughes, later collected in *Arna Bontemps and Langston Hughes: Letters, 1925–67* (1980), edited by Charles N. Nichols.

Addressed to editors, public figures, or the public at large, the public letter has been limited to topics of racial injustices, inequality, and political or economic protests. See, for instance, Carter G. Woodson's compilation of the public letters of Frederick Douglass, William Wells Brown, and Charlotte Forten in *The Mind of the Negro as Reflected in Letters Written During the Crisis 1800–1860* (1926). Other public letters include James Baldwin's "My Dungeon Shook: Letter to my Nephew on the One Hundred Anniversary of the Emancipation"—a letter that has been reprinted in Baldwin's *Notes of a Native Son* (1955). See also Martin Luther King Jr.'s "Letter from Birmingham Jail" (1963).

There are also collections comprising personal as well as public letters. In addition to Carter G. Woodson's *The Mind of the Negro as Reflected in Letters Written During the Crisis*, see also Dorothy Sterling's edited works *We Are Your Sisters: Black Women in the Nineteenth Century* (1984) and *The Trouble They Seen: Black People Tell the Story of Reconstruction* (1976). See also *To Be an Author: Letters of Charles W. Chesnutt 1899–1905*, ed. Joseph R. McElrath Jr. (1997).

Reference for further reading: Cheryl Lester, "Letters," in Andrews et al., eds. *The Oxford Companion to African American Literature* (1997).

libation A **ritual** that requires pouring small amounts of water on the earth as an inducement for the *loa* (deities) to reside. In African American culture, libation is performed to remember the spirits of deceased loved ones, usually at festivals, ceremonies, and other special occasions.

liberation (See **theme.**)

"lie, the" (See **folktale.**)

literacy (See **theme.**)

literary history/historian (See Criticism and Theory.)

litotes A deliberate understatement of what is said. Examples exist in **slave narratives** that address the actions of practicing Christians and their abuse to slaves. See also Sterling A. Brown's poem "Crossing" (1932).

loud talking A figure of signification. Connotes exactly the opposite of that which it denotes. (See **signifying.**)

lyrics Verse that can be regarded as subjective, emotional, and melodic; a song. Before written lyrics in African American culture, there were **spirituals** that demonstrated verbally subjective, emotional, and melodic qualities found in written lyrics. See, for example, the early lyrics of "Were You There When They Crucified My Lord?":

Were you there when they crucified my Lord?
Were you there when they crucified my Lord?
Oh!—sometime it causes me to tremble, tremble, tremble,
Were you there when they crucified my Lord?
(Gates and McKay 1997:7.)

Dubbed the "poet laureate of the Negro race" (Gates and McKay 1997:884), Paul Laurence Dunbar is known for his ability to express African American life in lyrics. See, for example, "A Negro Love Song" (1895):

Seen my lady home las' night,
   Jump back, honey, jump back.
Hel' huh han' an' sque'z it tight,
   Jump back, honey, jump back
(Gates and McKay 1997:888–89, lines 1–4.)

magara A life force that an individual possesses. In the **blues,** the term is used to mean "the full life" or one's "right to live."
(See **African ontology** and **ecstasy.**)

References for further reading: Janheinz Jahn, *Neo-African Literature: A History of Black Writing* (1968); Sherley Anne Williams, "The Blues Roots of Contemporary Afro-American Poetry" (1979).

magic realism When surrealism and fantasy have influenced writers' depictions of figures and objects in visual art and prose. See the works of Toni Morrison.
(See also **realism.**)

memory (See Criticism and Theory.)

metaphor A figure of speech where a comparison between dissimilar things occurs. A comparison is usually implicit. For example in Martin Luther King Jr.'s "I Have a Dream" speech the metaphors are implicit: "joyous daybreak," "long night," and "beacon light." A comparison is *extended* when the metaphor gets repeated in several lines. For example, in Langston Hughes's "Mother to Son," what gets repeated is that life has not been a "crystal stair" (Gates and McKay 1997:1254–55.)
(See also **proverb.**)

meter The pattern of stressed (') and unstressed (˘) syllables in lines of verse. Any detailed analysis of metrical patterns is called scansion (i.e., displaying stresses, pauses, and rhyme patterns).

metonymy A figure of speech in which some suggestive or attributive word is substituted in order to arrive at an actual meaning (e.g., stage for theater).

middle passage The transatlantic slave trade or the triangular trading route from West Africa to England to the Americas and to the Caribbean. Critics also regard the middle passage as forged bonding of Africans into a common African American culture. See the following literary works: Olaudah Equiano's *The Interesting Narrative of the Life of Olaudah Equiano, or Gustavas Vassa, the African* (1789); Martin R. Delany's *Blake, or the Huts of America* (1859–1861); Alex Haley's *Roots* (1976); and Charles Johnson's *Middle Passage* (1990).

(See also **"the black Atlantic," flying African,** and **Ibo Landing.**)

migration narrative A narrative that shares with the **slave narrative** the migration of African Americans from the South to urban cities in the North, Midwest, and West. Returning **motifs** in the migration narrative are of **ancestors** and of strangers—with the former assisting and the latter hindering the migrant who attempts to negotiate his or her urban landscape or to resist the powers that seek to control. According to Farah Jasmine Griffin in *"Who Set You Flowin'?": The African American Migration Narrative* (1995), in African American literary migration narrative, ancestors are literally "timeless people whose relationships to the characters are benevolent, instructive, and protective" (5). Also, the ancestral presence, as in southern culture, could be in song, food, language or any touchstone that constitutes cultural remembrance. Griffin defines stranger as a northern phenomenon, a literal stranger; one who offers misguidance and/or a new worldview (427). The stranger "exists in a dialectical relationship with the ancestor."

Migration narratives include Paul Laurence Dunbar's *The Spirit of the Gods* (1902); James Weldon Johnson's *The Autobiography of an Ex-Colored Man* (1912); Waters Turpin's *O Canaan!* (1939); William Attaway's *Blood on the Forge* (1941); Chester Himes's *If He Hollers, Let Him Go* (1945); George Wylie Henderson's *Jule* (1946); Dorothy West's *The Living Is Easy* (1948); Paule Marshall's *Brown Girl, Brownstones* (1959), *The Chosen Place, the Timeless People* (1969), *Praisesong for the Widow* (1983), and *Daughters* (1991); Marita Golden's *Migration of the Heart* (1983); and Carlene Hatcher Polite's *The Flagellants* (1967). In works with characters who encounter the stranger and the ancestor, the fate of the character lies with his or her choice of the ancestor or of the stranger: Jean Toomer's *Cane* (1923); Rudolph Fisher's *The Walls of Jericho* (1928); Richard Wright's *Native Son* (1940); Ann Petry's *The Street* (1946); Ralph Ellison's *Invisible Man* (1952); James Baldwin's *Go Tell It On the Mountain* (1953); and Toni Morrison's *Song of Solomon* (1977).
(See also **"safe space"** and **"urban space."**)

mimicry/mimesis The deliberate imitation of gestures, mannerisms, idioms, and language; an imitation of external reality.
(See also **diegesis.**)

minstrelsy Stage entertainment that began in the nineteenth-century on southern plantations. Earliest performers were slaves who offered song, **dance,** jokes, riddles, **sermons,** and musical renditions on various instruments. **Parodies** or stage productions by Euro Americans in burnt cork makeup and exaggerated black dress, speech, songs, customs, and practices followed. After the Civil War, in what would be called the "Coon Shows," African American performers returned to the stage, **signifying** on white minstrel performers. Minstrels ended in the early twentieth-century, but from the shows came "Jim Crow" stereotypes that have become ingrained in the American conscious.
(See also **plantation literature**.)

miscegenation A **theme** of mixing of the races that is used by African American writers when protesting and often when exploring race matters in America. Familiar writers include Harriet Jacobs's *Incidents in the Life of a Slave Girl* (1861); Charles Chesnutt's *The House Behind the Cedars* (1900), James Weldon Johnson's *The Autobiography of an Ex-Colored Man* (1912); Nella Larsen's *Passing* (1929); Chester Himes's *If He Hollers, Let Him Go* (1945); Ann Petry's *The Narrows* (1953); Alice Walker's *Meridian* (1976); Sherley Anne Williams's *Dessa Rose* (1986); and Toni Morrison's *Beloved* (1987).

Reference for further reading: Jonathan D. Little, "Miscegenation," *The Oxford Companion to African American Literature*, edited by Andrews et al. (1997).

moaning (See **folk cries.**)

mock-heroic Satirical prose or **poetry** written in grand style that is of a trivial subject.

modernism A term that denotes avant-garde trends in American literature, beginning in the closing years of the nineteenth century. Rejected by experimentalist writers are most literary conventions. Adopted are more complex and difficult forms and styles, ranging from fragmentary images, complex **allusions,** breaks in chronological developments of time and space, and retreats from cultural values and norms. In *Race, Modernity, Postmodernity* (1996), Lawrence Hogue identifies the African American modernist text and writers in this manner:

Existentialism, secularism, rationalism, and individualism pervade the fiction of the major African American writers, such as Richard Wright, Ralph Ellison, James Baldwin, and Charles Wright. (30)

Critics argue that by definition, modernity pervades Jean Toomer's *Cane* (1923) and Zora Neale Hurston's *Their Eyes Were Watching God* (1937)— texts that are published a number of years before Wright's *Native Son* in 1940. Critic Craig Werner has noted (Andrews et al. 1997:456) that poets Melvin B. Tolson and Robert Hayden, who began their careers in the 1940s, are examples of African American poets that reject the conventions of their times—for example, **proletarian** poetry. Influenced by the "sophisticated modernist compositions" of Langston Hughes and of musicians such as Duke Ellington, Tolson and Hayden pursue "musical modernism" in respectively *Harlem Gallery* (1965) and *The Lion and the Archer* (1948).

Some African American writers simply retreat from modernity. According to Hogue, Toni Morrison "is not concerned ultimately with modern individual experiences on the stage of modern history" (31). In contrast to Richard Wright, Ralph Ellison, and others, Morrison is concerned with the "collective" and with "reintroducing the reading public . . . to an African American racial tradition, the collective African American cultural and historical past" (31).

(See also **Age of Baraka, Age of Wright, existentialism, free verse, postmodernism,** and **stream of consciousness.**)

References for further reading: Houston Baker, *Modernism and the Harlem Renaissance* (1987); Peter Barry, *Beginning Theory: An Introduction to Literary and Cultural Theory,* (1995); Bernard Bell, *The Afro-American Novel and Its Tradition* (1987); W. Lawrence Hogue, *Race, Modernity Postmodernity, A Look at the History and the Literature of People of Color Since the 1960s* (1996); Lorenzo Thomas, *Extraordinary Measures: Afrocentric Modernism and Twentieth-Century American Poetry* (2000); Craig H. Werner, "Early Twentieth Century," in Andrews et al., *The Oxford Companion to African American Literature* (1997).

monologue A lengthy speech uttered by a single person. The monologue is dramatic when the speech (somewhat lyrical) is delivered to a silenced audience. When the speaker is alone on stage, expressing his thoughts and feelings, his speech is called a soliloquy. An example of monologue is with Boy Willie in act one of August Wilson's *The Piano Lesson* (1986).

motif The dominant idea, main **theme,** or recurring theme or idea in a work of literature. Writing in "Alice Walker: The Black Woman Artist as

Wayward," Barbara Christian points to Walker's unique motif in *The Third Life of Grange Copeland* (1970):

> a quilt of recurring motifs which are arranged, examined, and rearranged so that the reader might understand the complex nature of the tension between the power of oppressive societal forces and the possibility for change. Walker's use of recurring economic patterns, much like a quilting process, gives the novel much of its force and uniqueness."

(See also **leitmotif, quilt** and **theme.**)

mulatto Biologically, a racially mixed individual or character—one half Euro American and one half African American. During Reconstruction in the United States, the theme of "tragic mulatto" is introduced in **plantation literature** and in African American literature. At the hands of Euro American and African American writers, the tragic mulatto had a predictable fate (death or marriage; insanity or happy ever after). He or she was usually spiritually and psychologically destructive to the self; and often harbored intraracial prejudices. In order to prosper, the mulatto in fiction and in real life often **passed** for white.

Modern writers such as Zora Neale Hurston in *Their Eyes Were Watching God* (1937) and Ann Petry's *The Street* (1946) have rewritten the stereotypical tragic mulatto **heroine.** Hurston's Janie Crawford and Petry's Lutie Johnson are portrayed as individuals who succeed or fail because of their choices in life, not because of **miscegenation.**

Since the mid-1980s, writers have replaced the tragic mulatto in fiction with the "new cultural mulatto" (Trudier Harris, "New Cultural Mulatto," in Andrews et al., *The Oxford Companion to African American Literature,* 1997:535–36). While racial makeup remains, more or less, the same, all other markers do not exist. The new cultural mulatto is suburban and middle class; well educated; and diverse in language, travel, fashion, and food. Individualism, most often, replaces a collective consciousness, and standards and practices of the larger society, more or less, replace an **African ethos.**

musicals Early musical productions are derived from early **minstrelsy,** the most popular form of musical theater in America in the nineteenth century. Like early minstrel theater, early musical productions draw on stereotypes for humor (see, for instance, Bob Cole's *A Trip to Coontown* [1898] or Will

Marion Cook and Paul Laurence Dunbar's *Clorindy: The Origin of the Cakewalk* [1898], the first African American Broadway production). After the 1970s, musical productions become **satirical** and they allow for self-laughter (see, for instance, Melvin Van Peebles's *Don't Bother Me, I Can't Cope* [1972] and Loftin Mitchell's *Bubbling Brown Sugar* [1976]). The strength of many musical productions has been sacred music—for example, *God's Trombones, Seven Negro Sermons in Verse* (1927) or *Your Arms Too Short to Box With God* (1976). The strength of other musical productions has been secular music—for example, *Sophisticated Ladies* (1981) or *Jelly's Last Jam* (1990). Other productions have been strong because of contemporary music—for example, *Shuffle Alone* (1921); *Porgy and Bess* (1935); and *Carmen Jones* (1943). In the late twentieth century and the early twenty-first century, there has been an increase in musical productions with reliance on secular and sacred music.
(See also **drama, minstrelsy,** and **plantation literature.**)

Mumbo Jumbo According to Clarence Major in *Juba to Jive: A Dictionary of African-American Slang* (1970), the term is derived from *Mama Dyumbo* (Mandingo)—protective spirit of the Khassonkee tribe of Senagal. The term has shifted in meaning from **ancestor** spirit to trick to nonsense.

myth The Greek word *mythos* means "story"; a satisfying story that generally explains creation or how something came to exist.
(See also **folklore; collective unconscious** under Criticism and Theory.)

References for further reading: Jacqueline de Weever, *Mythmaking and Metaphor in Black Women's Fiction* (1991); Joseph Holloway, *Africanisms in American Culture* (1990); Karla Holloway, *Moorings and Metaphors: Figures of Culture and Gender in Black Women's Literature.* (1992).

naming A cultural practice of African origin where parents and grandparents commemorate the birth of their children or grandchildren with names that are given, for instance, after a day of the week or month, or after a special event or personality trait of the newborn. In African American literary criticism, naming is rhetorical. Implicitly or indirectly, the speaker "obscures the addressee" (Geneva Smitherman) while simultaneously **signifying** on the addressee.
(See also **African ontology, pastiche, specifying.**)

narration A form of writing or speaking from a particular **point of view** that relates a series of events in chronological order. Experimentations with formal conventions, or with voice and language will usually signal a modernist influence on narration.

nationalism (See **black nationalism.**)

naturalism From the larger American naturalistic movement (1900–1930), the most celebrated writer is Theodore Dreiser (1871–1945). Like other writers of the 1930s and 1940s such as Frank Norris, Dreiser's social commentary is on the economic determinism and class materialism that condemns American families to hopelessness. Richard Wright, Ann Petry, and Chester Hines are the major writers who form a tradition in the 1940s that is within the larger naturalistic tradition. In the urban settings of Wright's *Native Son* (1940), Ann Petry's *The Street* (1946), and Chester Himes's *If He Hollers, Let Him Go* (1945), documented are economic determinism, violence, racism, and classism that condemn urban African American families to poverty and hopelessness. Petry broadens the critique to include sexism.
(See also **Age of Wright; Chicago Renaissance.**)

necromancy In the tradition of the African **griot** and the **conjurer** in the African American community, the necromancer is subversive of "conventionality" and of "causality." The motivation is often to assert the voice denied and suppressed in the Western world.
(See also **conjurer** and **griot.**)

References for further reading: Bruce Dick and Amritjit Singh, eds., *Conversations with Ishmael Reed* (1995); Chester Fontenot Jr., "Ishmael Reed and the Politics of Aesthetics, Or Shake Hands and Come Out Conjuring" (1978); Joseph Henry, "A MELUS Interview: Ishmael Reed" (1999).

negritude A term coined by Aimé Césaire in *Cahier d'un retour au pays natal (Return to My Native Land)* in 1939. Inspired by the **Harlem Renaissance** writers Countee Cullen, Langston Hughes, Claude McKay, and Sterling Brown, Césaire of Martinque, French West Indies, Leopold Sédar Senghor of Senegal, West Africa, and Leon Damas of Guyana (French Guiana), South America, reject in the 1930s the notion that people of African descent do not have a history or culture prior to colonization. Like

Hughes, Brown and others, Césaire, Senghor, and Damas reclaim an African heritage in their **poetry,** written mostly in French, and against an **African ontology.**

neo-hoodoo aesthetic An approach to African American literary art and writing, where writers use a set of aesthetic values noticeably different from Western aesthetic values. Influenced by the system of **vodun** and advanced by Ishmael Reed in his writings, neo-hoodooism takes into account African components such as **dance,** drum, **nommo, magic realism,** and wood sculptures. The influence of neo-hoodooism is seen in Reed's *Mumbo Jumbo* (1972); Paule Marshall's *The Chosen Place, the Timeless People* (1969); Toni Cade Bambara's *The Salt Eaters* (1980); Toni Morrison's *Tar Baby* (1981); and John Edgar Wideman's *Damballah* (1981).
(See also **Black Arts Movement** and **Obeah.**)

neo-slave narrative Modern or contemporary fiction with slave characters as narrators or subjects. Central to these narratives are **motifs** of power faith, messianic hope, self-reliance, and direct action. See, for instance, Margaret Walker's *Jubilee* (1966); Ernest Gaines's *The Autobiography of Miss Jane Pittman* (1971); Ishmael Reed's *Flight to Canada* (1976); Charles Johnson's *Oxherding Tale* (1982); Sherley Anne Williams's *Dessa Rose* (1986); Louise Meriwether's *Fragments of the Ark* (1994); and Barbara Chase-Riboud's *The President's Daughter* (1994).

New Black Aesthetic Influences by black suburbanites, mostly Ivy League graduates, on African American literature in the late 1980s. The NBA writers are inclusive of traditions that cut across boundaries of race and class as they attempt to express what Greg Tate calls "the complexities of our culture" ("Cult-Nats Meet Freaky Deke"). The writers are more individualistic but still maintain some social and political responsibilities to the community at large. They are culturally eclectic: they are what Trey Ellis calls "young blacks getting back into jazz and the blues," but they attend also "punk concerts" (234). The literature avoids **didacticism**; it reflects aesthetics.

References for further reading: Trey Ellis, "The New Black Aesthetic" (1989); Terry McMillan, introduction to *Breaking Ice: An Anthology of Contemporary African-American Fiction* (1990).

new black poetry (See **poetry.**)

New Criticism A name for criticism introduced in the 1940s by John Crowe Ransom in *The New Criticism* (1941). Attention is given to "close reading" of a work; to intrusive qualities of the work rather than to influences of biography, history, or culture.

new cultural mulatto (See **mulatto.**)

"New Negro, the" Since the early twentieth century, the phrase has represented middle-class African Americans who have challenged and subverted the national attitude about the African American as inferior. The group promotes images of African Americans with middle-class values and middle-class aspirations recognizable in dominate society. During the **Harlem Renaissance** (1917–1935), the New Negro/African American developed a new sense of cultural awareness. Poets, novelists, blues singers, civic and political leaders, and entrepreneurs discovered cultural roots and began to project a racial consciousness of pride, dignity, and self-expression. Alain Locke captured this new racial consciousness via the writings (**essays, poetry,** fiction, social and political analysis) of the young generation of writers in his collection *The New Negro* (1925).

New Renaissance (1950s and 1960s) Used by Arthur P. Davis, in his coedited *Negro Caravan* (1941) and in articles, to identify a literary period that precedes the **Black Arts Movement** and follows the **Chicago Renaissance**. The major writers are Ralph Ellison in *Invisible Man* (1952) and James Baldwin in *Go Tell It On the Mountain* (1953). Both writers are critical of the **School of Wright** and naturalistic **protest literature** that comes out of the Chicago Renaissance. Both Baldwin and Ellison might be said to insist on a focus on craft versus politics.

References for further reading: James Baldwin, "Many Thousand Gone" in *African American Literary Criticism, 1773 to 2000* ed. Ervin (1999); Ralph Ellison, "Richard Wright's Blues."

nommo The African concept is that the word is a life force; the word is creator rather than created. Also, words have power even after they are spoken or written.
(See also **oral tradition.**)

novel, African American, the Reflects traditional conventions of narrative prose (e.g., **characterization, plot, point of view**). Sources of the African American novel include oral forms (e.g., sacred and secular songs, **folktales,** and **spirituals;** abolitionist literature; the Bible; African **myth;** and male and female myths). Experimental sources have been **jazz, blues,** and the **sermon.** Types of African American novels include the following: historical, historical revisionist, **realism, naturalism, protest, magical realism, epistolary, diasporic, passing, migration,** urbanization, lyrical, folk, social criticism/**satire, modern, postmodern,** and **proletarian.** Generally, in the novel, the social, political, psychological, and philosophical conflicts are played out. In the contemporary novel, the individual character remains socially and politically responsible to the community, but seeks also to understand the "self." Emerging in the mid-nineteenth century are recurring **themes:** slavery, freedom, racial uplift, singular achievements, middle-class aspirations and conduct, **passing,** social commitment, solidarity, alienation, disenfranchisement, racism, and the theory of the talented tenth.
(See also **characterization, conflict, denouement, diction, plot, point of view, resolution.**)

References for further reading: Bernard Bell, *The Afro-American Novel and Its Tradition* (1987); Barbara Christian, *Black Women Novelists: The Development of a Tradition, 1892–1976* (1980); Marie Foster, *Southern Black Creative Writers, 1829–1953* (1988); Carol Fairbanks and Eugene Engeldinger, *Black American Fiction: A Bibliography* (1978); Marie Foster, *Southern Black Creative Writers, 1829–1953* (1988); Maryemma Graham, "Novel," in *The Oxford Companion to African American Literature,* eds. Andrews, et al. (1997); Trudier Harris and Thadious Davis, *Dictionary of Literary Biography,* vol. 76, 1988; Helen Houston, *The Afro-American Novel, 1965–1975: A Descriptive Bibliography of Primary and Secondary Materials* (1977); M. Thomas Inge, Maurice Duke, and Jackson Bryer, *Black American Writing, Bibliographical Essays* (1978); Edward Margolies and David Bakish, *Afro-American Fiction 1853–1976: A Guide to Information Sources* (1979); Geraldine Matthews, *Black American Writers, 1773 to 1949: A Bibliography and Union List* (1976); Pat Ryan, *Black Writing in the U.S.A.: A Bibliographic Guide* (1969); Darwin T. Turner, *Afro-American Writers* (1970).

novella Sometimes called a longer short story and sometimes called a short novel. There are basic ingredients and **themes** of both genres. See, for example, Ann Petry's "In Darkness and Confusion" (1947).
(See also **characterization, conflict, denouement, diction, plot, point of view, resolution.**)

Obeah An African witchcraft system of chants and dance and other practices that have been preserved in many of the islands in the Caribbean. The presence of the Obeah is in Ann Petry's short story "Olaf and His Girl Friend" (1945); Toni Cade Bambara's *The Salt Eaters* (1980); Toni Morrison's *Tar Baby* (1981); and John Edgar Wideman's *Damballah* (1981).

"O black and unknown bards" A phrase coined by James Weldon Johnson to define the artistic creators of Negro **spirituals**—the slaves. (See also **bard.**)

Reference for further reading: Lance Jeffers, "On Listening to the Spirituals," 1974.

ode Lyrical **poetry** that is addressed to a person or to an abstract entity and that expresses the thoughts or emotions of the speaker. Marked features include an elaborate stanza structure and a lofty or stateliness in tone and style. For the ode, there are the following: the *regular ode* (strophe and antistrophe are written in one stanza pattern; epode, in another); the *Pindaric* or *irregular ode* (each stanza establishes its own pattern of rhyme scheme, number of lines, and length of lines); and the *Horatian ode* (single repeated stanza form). See Paul Laurence Dunbar's "Ode to Ethiopia" (1893) and "Columbean Ode" (1895) and the numerous odes written by Phillis Wheatley.

omniscient narrator (See **point of view.**)

onomatopoeia The use of words whose sounds echo meaning. In Jean Toomer's "Beehive," the Silver bees are "intently buzzing." In Paul Laurence Dunbar's "Ode to Ethiopia":

> The forests flee before their stroke
> Their hammers ring, their forges smoke

oral tradition Slaves were forbidden by law to learn to read and write. Therefore, their beliefs, customs, and practices—their common culture— were preserved through memory and passed on orally. For the slave, the *word* maintained its African influence—a life force; to speak was to make something come into being.

orality/oracular The voice is central in the delivery of stories and poetic **themes.** Some critics regard the narrative voice in writings by the African American male to be distant. Understanding or meaning is dependent upon visual elements (e.g., appearance and behavior). On the other hand, critics regard the narrative voice in writings by the African American female writers to be intimate; it reflects an inner speech; it claims intimate knowledge and ownership of all narrative dimensions. Meaning in the female text is dependent upon understanding the voice, the language, memory, and the present as well as the past.

(See also **polyphonic.**)

Reference for further reading: Karla Holloway, *Moorings and Metaphors: Figures of Culture and Gender in Black Women's Literature* (1992).

oratory/orature According to Molefi Asanta in *The Afrocentric Idea* (1987), orature is "the comprehensive body of oral discourse on every subject and in every genre of expression produced by people of African descent. It includes **sermons,** lectures, **raps,** the **dozens, poetry,** and **humor.** The voice is **"improv"** with spontaneity and variety—the **soul** of **performance.**

Reference for further reading: Robert Glen, *Black Rhetoric: A Guide to Afro-American Communications*; Zora Neale Hurston, "Characteristics of Negro Expression" (1934) in *The Norton Anthology of African American Literature* ed. Gates and McKay (1997:1019–32).

oxymoron Contradictory words or terms that combine for special effects (e.g., "Wise"/"fool"; "loving"/"hate"; "heavy"/"lightness"; "sick"/"health").

palimpsest narrative A contemporary narrative in slavery. Characters describe modern social relations that are directly conditioned or affected by an incident, event, or story from the times of slavery. Examples of palimpsest narratives include Gayl Jones's *Corregidora* (1975); Octavia Butler's *Kindred* (1979); David Bradley's *The Chaneysville Incident* (1981); Gloria Naylor's *Linden Hills* (1985) and *Mama Day* (1988); J. California Cooper's *In Search of Satisfaction* (1994); Paule Marshall's *The Chosen Place, the Timeless People* (1969), *Praisesong for the Widow* (1983), and *Daughters* (1991).

Reference for further reading: Ashrah Rushdy, "Reading Black, White and Gray in 1968: The Origins of the Contemporary Narrativity in Slavery."

pan-Africanism As revealed by W.E.B. DuBois in "The African Roots of War" (*Atlantic Monthly* 115 (May 15): 707–14), in the aftermath of World War I, expatriates (African Americans, Francophone blacks, Great Britain's Africans and West Indians) united as one African people and vowed global, political, and social struggles to reconnect with a core culture. Together, expatriates and others formed the Pan-African Association.

paradox A contradictory statement with measures of truth. See, for instance, Paul Laurence Dunbar's "Life's Tragedy":

> We count our joys not by the things we have,
> But by what kept us from the perfect thing.
> (*African American Literature: Voices in a Tradition* 1998: 252–53, lines
> 15–16.)

parallelism Involves similar constructions and balances of a series of related words, phrases, or clauses. Commonly present in **poetry,** fiction, songs, and chants, but present also in essays such as James Baldwin's "My Dungeon Shook" (1962):

> [First] as an infant, then as a child, then as a man (14)

Or,

> Let him laugh and I see a cellar . . .
> Let him curse and I remember him . . . .(15)

> (Baldwin, 1962:14–15.)

parenthesis An insertion marked by dashes, commas, or brackets that is used to interrupt a complete sentence.

parody When intentional exaggeration or deliberate distortion occurs in writing for purposes of correction or derision. Less visible are parody narrations that impact a hidden or internal polemic. For example, one might read what Henry Louis Gates calls Sterling Brown's regionalism against Jean Toomer's **lyricism;** Zora Neale Hurston's lyricism against Richard Wright's **naturalism;** Ralph Ellison's **modernism** against Richard Wright's **naturalism;** and Ishmael Reed's **postmodernism** against Wright and Ellison. Read also "A Parody," that concludes *Narrative of the Life of Frederick Douglass, an American Slave, Written by Himself* (1845).
(See also **signifying.**)

passing A historical practice of racial passing into the dominant culture, especially following the end of the Civil War and during Reconstruction. As a **theme,** passing allows writers to focus simultaneously on race, identity, and color in the African American community and in the United States.

Major writers and works that use passing as a theme include, for instance, Frank J. Webb's *The Garies and Their Friends* (1857); Charles Chesnutt's *The House Behind the Cedars* (1900); James Weldon Johnson's *The Autobiography of an Ex-Colored Man* (1912); Walter White's *Flight* (1926); Jessie Fauset in *Plum Bun* (1929); Nella Larsen in *Passing* (1929); and Charles R. Johnson in *Oxherding Tale* (1982).

pastiche When a work is written by pasting together borrowed words, sentences, passages, or rhythmic and harmonic structures of another writer or writers for purposes that range from imitation to revision. A similar practice exists among musicians. Count Basie's *Signify* that alludes to styles of playing between 1920s and 1940s, particularly **ragtime** and boogie-woogie, for the purpose of imitation, is an example of pastiche.

pastoral, African American According to Bernard Bell in *The Afro-American Novel and Its Tradition* (1987), African American pastoral fuses African and Western narrative traditions. Within an African American literary tradition, the term "stresses continuity and change: a reinterpretation of the past in the light of new experiences and a dialectically evolving consciousness" (113–14). Thus, the conventions of the African American pastoral focuses on "the near rather than remote past for paradigms of the good life, celebrat[es] urban as well as rural settings, elevat[es] social outcasts and plain folk to heroic stature and attack[s] the repressive forces of Western civilization, especially social conformity and racism" (114). See, for instance, Claude McKay's *Home to Harlem* (1929) and Zora Neale Hurston's *Jonah's Gourd Vine* (1934).

pathos A term that describes the emotionally moving quality and power within a literary work or a particular passage to evoke, for instance, feelings of compassion or pity and sorrow.
(See also **African ethos.**)

performance A rhetorical style that may be distinctive due to physical magnetism, gestures, and gesticulations but that will have some constants with **rhythm** and syntax: changes of tempo or rhythmic patterns; pauses for effect; sound and tone of voice (e.g., pleasure in sounds and rhythms, regular clustering of tone, intonation, musical and rhythmic wordless sounds, **scatting**); incantatory **repetitions** (see under Criticism and Theory), lan-

guage (i.e., **hyperbole, imagery, puns,** and **rhymes,** functional and orna-
mental).

(See also **dance, folk preacher, grammar of the sermon, "speaking in
tongues," spirituals, toasts,** and **work songs.**)

References for further reading: Kimberly W. Benston, 2000; Fahamisha Patricia Brown,
Performing the Word, African American Poetry as Vernacular Culture (1999); Gale Jackson,
"The Way We Do: A Preliminary Investigation of the African Roots of African American
Performance" (1991).

periphrasis (pe-rif'-e-sis) The use of many words or phrases, especially
when fewer or more simple words and phrases would suffice. See, for example, James Baldwin's "Fifth Avenue, Uptown: A Letter from Harlem"
(1960):

> They do not escape Jim Crow; they merely encounter another, not less
> deadly variety.
> (Baldwin 1961.)

persona Originally, the term denoted a mask or a false face assumed by a
writer in a literary work. Now, the term denotes the person who speaks in a
poem, or the implied author in a fictional work.

personification A figurative term that suggests inanimate objects or ab-
stractions embody human qualities. See, for instance, Maya Angelou's "On
the Pulse of Morning" (1993).

Petrarchan sonnet A verse form, consisting of fourteen lines and made up
of two parts: an octave (the first eight lines that rhyme *abbaabba*) and a
sestet (the remaining six lines that rhyme *cdecde* or *cdcdcd*). Also, there may
be any combinations, minus the **couplet** for the last two lines. In the octave
of "Remember Not" (1931) (Andrews et al. 1997: 1317, line 14), **Harlem Renaissance** writer Helene Johnson vows to love another. In the ending lines
or in the sestet, Johnson resolves "Let Love's beginning expiate Love's end."
See also Harlem Renaissance writer Jean Toomer's "November Cotton
Flower" (1923) (Andrews et al. 1997: 1091).

For examples of poets who have used variations of sonnet forms, see
Paul Laurence Dunbar's "Douglass" (1903) and Gwendolyn Brooks's "The
Rites for Cousin Vit" (1949) (Gates and McKay 1997:903, 1508, 1587).

(See also **Shakespearean sonnet** and **Italian sonnet.**)

piling The coupling of one idea or detail to another to achieve a mounting effect or to build a performance to a **climax**. Like **anadiplosis,** the last word or detail in one line is repeated at the beginning of the next line. See, for instance, "Praise Salute to Shaka the Zula":

He who armed in the forest, who is like a madman,
The madman who is in full view of men
(Okpewho 1992:83.)

places (See **"safe space"** and **"urban space."**)

plantation literature Following the Civil War, Euro American writers used literature, popular magazines, and even newspapers to sentimentalize plantation life and, in other instances, to vilify emancipated slaves. In his essay "Negro Characters as Seen by White Authors," Sterling Brown identifies white writers of the romanticized tradition whose work perpetuated such a tradition: Irwin Russell, Thomas Nelson Page, Joel Chandler Harris, and Thomas Dixon. The stereotypical images of the African American that were created and/or perpetuated by these writers include the following: the contented slave, the wretched freedman, comic Negro, brute Negro, tragic **mulatto,** local color Negro, and the exotic primitive.

In their proslavery literature, writers Russell, Page, and Harris, were always able to justify slavery. Even ex-slaves portrayed as loyal and content knew "their places." Unable to handle freedom (the wretched freedman), they praised slavery, worshiped their masters, and yearned for the return of the old days. (See, for instance, Joel Chandler Harris's *Uncle Remus: His Songs and His Sayings* (1881) and *Gabriel Tolliver* (1902); and Thomas Nelson Page's novels *In Ole Virginia* (1887) and *Red Rock* (1898), poetry collection *Bef' De War,* and stories such as "Marse Chan" and "Meh' Lady."

Slaves who embraced a life of freedom and social progress were vilified in this literature, sometimes called Ku Klux Klan fiction. For instance, in Thomas Dixon's *The Clansman* (1905) or *The Leopard's Spots* (1902), progressive ex-slaves are seen to regress and to become lazy and shiftless and even worse, the men become rapists and murderers.

John P. Kennedy's *Swallow Barn* (1832) is thought to mark the beginning of plantation literature. African American writer Paul Laurence Dunbar appears to capitalize on the popularity of the plantation literature in the nineteenth century (see, for instance, "The Party" [1895] and "The Deserted

Plantation" [1895]). Charles W. Chesnutt, on the other hand, deroman-ticizes plantation life. Through his popular character Uncle Julius, in *The Conjure Woman* (1899), Chesnutt recontextualizes the life and ways of the African Americans in fiction.

playwrights (See **drama.**)

plot A pattern of events and situations in fiction and **drama**. The plot may be described as linear, as tightly knit, or as loosely episodic. Plot movement in African American literary works is often nonlinear. In some works, it is spiraling or forever restarting.
(See also **circular narration, "the cut,"** and **improvisation.**)

plurisignant text A multiplied or layered text that yields multiple as well as **ambiguous** (see under Criticism and Theory) meanings.

References for further reading: Karla Holloway, *Moorings and Metaphors: Figures of Culture and Gender in Black Women's Literature* (1992); Claudia Tate, *Domestic Allegories of Political Desire, The Black Heroine's Text at the Turn of the Century,* 1992.

poetic license The writer's imaginative and linguistic freedom to invent words, change the natural word order, omit punctuation, and/or misspell words in order to emphasize mood and meaning. See, for instance, Ishmael Reed's "Beware: Do Not Read this Poem" (1976); Gwendolyn Brooks's "The Bean Eaters" (1950); and Robert Hayden "Runagate Runagate" (1962).

poetry A form of literary art that is recognizable by its language, meter, rhyme, and stanza patterns (e.g., **free verse, blank verse,** rhymed lines). African American poetry is referred to as the **"furious flower"**—a phrase introduced by Pulitzer Prize winner of poetry, Gwendolyn Brooks in "Second Sermon on the Warpland" (1968). The implication is that as the "furious flower," African American poetry is of two significant intertwining developments: radical and aesthetic. Prior to the twentieth century, African American poetry is called imitative of various traditional forms (**hymn, elegy, sonnet,** etc.). During the twentieth century, particularly beginning with the **Harlem Renaissance,** African American poetry begins to reflect experimentations with cultural forms such as **spirituals, blues, work songs,** and **ballads.** A historical/cultural purpose of African American poetry has been to uplift the race, to function as "fists" and "daggers" (in the 1960s and 1970s), and to help writers (contemporary writers) to understand themselves. Recurring **themes** from the 1700s to present include the following: religious devotedness, patriotism, slavery, liberation, freedom, justice, equality, **protest,** ancestral past, hope, violence, **heroes** and **heroines,** and self-determination.

References for further reading: Dorothy Chapman, *Index to Black Poetry* (1974); Frank Deodine and William French, *Black American Poetry Since 1949: A Preliminary Checklist* (1971); Joanne Gabbin, "Poetry," in *The Oxford Companion to African American Literature,* eds. Andrews et al. (1997); Stephen Henderson, *Understanding the New Black Poetry: Black Speech and Black Music as Poetic References* (1973); Mary Hopkins, *Black American Poetry: A Selected Bibliography* (1985); R. Baxter Miller, *Langston Hughes and Gwendolyn Brooks: A Reference Guide* (1979); Dorothy Porter, *North American Negro Poets: A Bibliographical Checklist of Their Writings, 1760–1944* (1945); Eugene B. Redmond, *Drumvoices: The Mission of Afro-American Poetry* (1976).

poetry slam A performative art that has its start in the 1990s. Like jazz performers that competed with each to earn recognition as best solo before an audience, poets vie to deliver the best performance of a poem.

point of view Events in a story may be presented from the vantage point (or point of view) of a first-person narrator or a third-person narrator. First-person point of view is restricted; third-person point of view can come from a character or an "all knowing" or omniscient narrator.

polyphonic/polyrhythmic/polyrhythms The term is used in music and in literary criticism to denote multiplicity. In music, at least two or more, and usually more, rhythms are going on alongside the listener's own beat. According to Mikhail Bakhtin in *Problems of Dostoievski's Poetics* (1929), in literary art, characters that are not controlled by their authors are allowed to speak "a plurality of independent and unmerged voices and consciousness." Bakhtin calls this practice **dialogic** or polyphonic. Female critics such as Mae Henderson, Barbara Christian, and Karla Holloway, who have theorized about the linguistic construction of novels by African American women writers, note a distinction in how the voice is controlled in literary works by African American male and female writers. In *Moorings and Metaphors: Figures of Culture and Gender in Black Women's Literature* (1992), Holloway writes: "[T]exts by black males often isolate the word. . . . Black male writers' texts claim the power of creative authorship but do not seem to share the word with the reader, or among the characters. . . . Instead, the word is carefully controlled and its power is meagerly shared" (7). With African American women writers, Holloway insists, "Black women writers seem to concentrate on shared ways of saying" (7). In particular, African American women writers and their characters "create, tell, and talk back." (See also **orality.**)

postcolonialism The term entails interdisciplinary studies (e.g., anthropological, historical, literary, and cultural) of writers from countries that were once colonies of European powers. Influenced by Edward Said's *Orientalism* (1978), postcolonial critics struggle with, among others, **representation** (see under Criticism and Theory), the third world as the Other, **binary oppositions,** and objectivity—that is, with attempts to move beyond constructions by the West. In addition, critics seek to recover marginalized "subaltern voices" and to put in **context** the effects of dominant colonial powers on identity, nationhood, and a cultural core.
(See also **deconstruction.**)

References for further reading: Peter Barry, *Beginning Theory: An Introduction to Literary and Cultural Theory* (1995); Kamau Brathwaite, *Roots* (1993); Sarah Harasym, *The Post-Colonial Critic* (1990); Vincent B. Leitch et al., *The Norton Anthology of Theory and Criticism* (2001);

postmodernism A term that denotes style and aesthetics, starting, more or less, in the 1960s in America. With regard to literature, postmodernism resembles modernism by way of **themes** such as fragmentation, asceticism, and abstract forms, but then, again, postmodernism is not modernism. Distinctions of modernism and postmodernism are provided by Peter Barry in *Beginning Theory, An Introduction to Literary and Cultural Theory* (1995).

With modernism, lament, pessimism, and despair follow fragmentation; in postmodernism, celebration follows fragmentation. With modernism, minimalism and sparse and distinctions of "high" and "popular" art follow asceticism; in postmodernism, distinctions between "high" and "popular" art are rejected. Furthermore, excess, gaudiness and "bad taste" might well become a mixture of qualities. With modernism, there is the blurring of distinctions between genres and the discontinuous or fragmented narrative form influenced by abstract forms such as Cubism, Dadaism, Surrealism, and Futurism; in postmodernism, the past and the modeled genre are revisited, but with irony. Furthermore, there is the mixing of literary conventions, and there are references made between one text and another, using inter-textual elements in literature such as **parody, pastiche,** and **allusion** (81–85).

According to Bernard Bell, writing in *The Afro-American Novel and Its Tradition,* postmodern sensibilities in the African American text

were shaped and misshaped by modern jazz, rock music, drugs, war in Vietnam, political assassinations, black power and women's rights movements, civil rights and antiwar demonstrations, campus sit-ins and building take-overs. . . . To proclaim the death of art's traditional claims to truth and to herald the birth of a new sensibility, postmodernists employ fantasy, parody, burlesque, and irony. [B]lack modernists and postmodernist[s] . . . are definitely influenced by the traditions of Western literature and committed to the freedom of hybrid narrative forms. But because the legacy of institutional racism and sexism that shaped and continues to shape their consciousness fosters ambivalence about their culture, and because the struggle for social justice continues, most modern and postmodern Afro-American novelists . . . are not inclined to neglect moral and social issues in their narratives. . . . Unlike their white contemporaries, black American postmodernists are not merely rejecting the arrogance and anachronism of Western forms and conventions, but also rediscovering and reaffirming the power and wisdom of their own folk tradition: Afro-American ways of seeing, knowing, and expressing reality, especially black speech, music, and religion. (283–84)

Familiar African American postmodern writers include Ishmael Reed, Clarence Major, John Edgar Wideman, and Leon Forrest to name a few. (See also **modernism.**)

References for further reading: Peter Barry, *Beginning Theory: An Introduction to Literary and Cultural Theory* (1995); Bernard Bell, *The Afro-American Novel and Its Tradition* (1987); Jean-Francois Lyotard, *The Postmodern Conditions: A Report on Knowledge* (1979).

poststructuralism A term that denotes the study of textuality. For the poststructuralists Jacques Derrida and Paul de Man—in their reactions to

structuralism—meaning is inherently unstable because of the linguistic, rhetorical, and **intertextual** properties of language that undermine, deconstruct, and defer meaning.

References for further reading: Peter Barry, *Beginning Theory: An Introduction to Literary and Cultural Theory* (1995); Vincent B. Leitch et al., *The Norton Anthology of Theory and Criticism* (2001).

practical criticism A criticism that is influenced by I. A. Richards (see *Practical Criticism: A Study of Literary Judgment* [1929]). The position is that literature is read closely for its intrinsic qualities without any other information on the author or the work.

Reference for further reading: Vincent B. Leitch et al., *The Norton Anthology of Theory and Criticism* (2001).

praise song Words of praise. Reverence. See, for instance, Pharaoh Akhenaton's reverence for the sun, "The Hymn to the Aton" (1350 B.C.; translated by John A. Wilson).

proletarian novel The narrative focuses on the economic plight of the working-class African American. Propagandistic protest is the novel's end function. Almost any of the novels from the school of Wright (e.g., the **Chicago Renaissance**) that are set in urban America would classify as proletarian, particularly Richard Wright's *Native Son* (1940) and Ann Petry's *The Street* (1946).
(See also **protest literature.**)

propaganda Between 1895 and 1954, creative and critical writers of African American literature debated endlessly about how to **represent** the African American in literary art. To quote an activist of the late 1800s, Victoria Matthews, the role of the writer and the function of the literature was to "undermine and utterly drive out the traditional Negro in dialect—the subordinate, the servant as type representing the race" ("Value of Race Literature" in *With Pen and Voice: A Critical Anthology of Nineteenth-Century African-American Women*, edited by Shirley Wilson Logan (1995:126–48). The writer and works were for "uplifting the race." Those writers who were willing to sacrifice **verisimilitude** for social or political end were called propagandists. Creative writer, literary critic, and sociologist W.E.B. DuBois, writing in "Criteria of Negro Art" (1926), was clear on his position:

I stand in utter shamelessness and say that whatever art I have for writing has been used always for propaganda for gaining the right of black folk to love and enjoy
(Ervin, ed. 1999:42).

DuBois complicates his position, however, when he cautions writers to avoid defamation of characters of others in order to maintain their allegiance: "I do care when propaganda is confined to one side while the other is stripped and silent" (42).

Alain Locke, philosopher, literary critic, and editor of *The New Negro* (1925), accepts propaganda as a literary tool of persuasion, but with censorship. Writing in "Art or Propaganda?" (1928), Locke contends:

Propaganda at least nurtures some form of serious social discussion, and social discussion (is) necessary, is still necessary. . . . Propaganda itself is preferable to shallow truckling imitation. . . . Beauty [however] . . . will be more effective than sermons. (50)

While Locke is an influential advocate of propaganda in literature, he envisions future writers having the right to choose art or propaganda, and importantly when choosing the former to create **"art of the people."**
(See also **didactic literature.**)

References for further reading: Sterling A. Brown, "Our Literary Audience" (1999); W.E.B. DuBois, "Criteria of Negro Art" (1926); Alain Locke, "Art or Propaganda?" (1928); Victoria Earle Matthews, "The Value of Race Literature: An Address" (1895).

prosody A study of meter, rhythm, rhyme, stanza, or patterns of intonation.
(See also **performance.**)

prosthesis (pros'-the'-sis) An orthographical scheme of words that involve adding a syllable in front of a word (e.g., *beloved* for *loved*) to accommodate the poetic diction in verse or prose.
(See also **apocope** and **aphaeresis.**)

protagonist The main character in prose, **drama,** or film who is opposed by the antagonist.

protest literature A tradition, beginning in African American literature as early as 1773, that indicts the American society for its racial hatred, oppression, and maltreatment of underprivileged groups; for its hypocrisy of the **American Dream**. In the 1950s and 1960s, African American writers such as Ralph Ellison and James Baldwin reassess the function of protest literature. For instance, Ralph Ellison, writing in *Shadow and Act* (1964), objects to the literature's "lack of craftsmanship and provincialism" (xix). James Baldwin, writing in several essays in *Notes of a Native Son* (1955), questions the literature's humanistic and aesthetic ends:

> The failure of the protest novel lies in its rejection of human beings, the denial of his beauty.
> (Baldwin, "Everybody's Protest Novel," 1949:17.)

> What the [protest] novel reflects is the isolation of the Negro within his own group. . . . [a] climate of anarchy and unmotivated and unapprehended disaster and it is this climate, common to most Negro protest novels, which has led us all to believe that in Negro life there exists no tradition, no field of manners, no possibility of ritual or intercourse.
> (Baldwin, "Many Thousand Gone," 1951:27–28.)

Writers of the 1960s (of the **Black Arts Movement**) eschew **protest literature**. According to Larry Neal, author of "The Black Arts Movement," implicit in the protest literature "is an appeal to white morality." Critics such as Larry Neal, Amiri Baraka, Addison Gayle, and others wanted the literature to appeal specifically to African Americans.

There are other critics who suggest that *all* literature is protest. According to Ann Petry, writing in "The Novel as Social Criticism" (1950), the minute a writer begins to question the status quo he is writing social criticism or protest.

References for further reading: James Baldwin, "Everybody's Protest Novel" and "Many Thousand Gone," in *African American Literary Criticism, 1773 to 2000* ed. Ervin (1999); Dickson B. Bruce Jr., "Protest Literature," in *The Oxford Companion to African American Literature* eds. Andrews et al. (1997); Ann Petry, "The Novel as Social Criticism," *African American Literary Criticism, 1773 to 2000* ed. Ervin (1999); Faith Berry, ed. *Good Morning, Revolution: Uncollected Writings of Langston Hughes* (1992).

proverb A flexible folk form of antiquity that is used primarily to impart truth and values. As pointed out by Arthur P. Davis, Sterling Brown, and Ulysses Lee, editors of *Negro Caravan* (1941), the pithy sayings appear also in traditional **spirituals, blues,** and **ballads.**

From a spiritual:

> Better look out, sister, how you walk on de cross
> yo' foot might slip and yo' soul git lost

From the blues:

> Every shut-eye ain't sleep, every good-bye ain't gone

Or:

> You never miss de water till de well goes dry
> You'll never miss yo' baby till she says good-bye

From a ballad:

> Never drive a stranger from yo do'
> He may be yo' best friend; you never know

Also, there are **Gullah** proverbs that are close (and perhaps closer) in **context** to African proverbs. One characteristic, according to Muriel Miller Branch in *The Water Brought Us: The Story of the Gullah-Speaking People* (1995), is the **metaphor** used to relate real-life situations:

> Take no more on your head than you can kick off with your toes.
> Every grin teeth don't mean laugh.
> Every shut eye don't mean sleep.
> Feed you with the corn and choke you with the cob.
> Sad we got to be burn fore we learn.
> Heart don't mean every thing mouth say.
> Man p'ont, but God disap'pint (Man's plans are subject to the
>   changes that God places upon them). (64)

psychoanalysis The critic of psychoanalytic criticism, among others, pays close attention to the following: the unconscious motives, desires, and feelings of the author and characters; the psychic **context** of a literary work at the expense of social and/or historical contexts; and the elusiveness of the language and/or signs. Writing in *Psychoanalysis and Black Novels: Desire and the Protocols of Race* (1998), Claudia Tate envisions a similar psychoanalytical approach to literary art by African American writers:

> A racially contextualized model of psychoanalysis . . . can help us analyze black textuality by identifying the discourse of desire generating the text. Such a model . . . can advance our understanding of racialized

behavior in other social settings as well. . . . I am asking black literary criticism to consider the roles of the narrator and protagonist in constructing various racial dilemmas and also suggesting that we probe such conflicts within and beyond their attribution to race. (17)

To achieve such an end, Tate concludes,

I . . . consid[er] a black text as a partly self-conscious fantasy. This conceptual framework facilitates our speculating about the author's [about the character's] inscription of pleasure as well as pain in the text. While we cannot gain direct access to the inner world of authors, we can detect and analyze the traces of emotional meaning left behind in print. (17)

References for further reading: Peter Barry, *Beginning Theory: An Introduction to Literary and Cultural Theory* (1995); Hortense J. Spillers. "All The Things You Could Be By Now If Sigmund Freud's Wife Was Your Mother," in *African American Literary Theory: A Reader,* edited by Napier, Winston (2000); Claudia Tate, *Psychoanalysis and Black Novels: Desire and the Protocols of Race* (1998).

pulp fiction A term for formulaic writing aimed at the masses, particularly urban and working-class readers. Categories that fall under the genre include the following: crime, mystery, thriller, adventure, romance, and some **speculative fiction**. See, for instance, John E. Bruce's *The Black Sleuth* (1907–1909); Joe Nazel's *Wolves of Summer* (1984) and *Delta Crossing* (1984); Donald Goines's *Daddy Cool* (1974); Robert Beck's (a.k.a. Iceberg Slim's) *Pimp: The Story of My Life* (1967) and *Trick Baby* (1967). See also romance series such as Hollywood House's *Heartline Romance* and Pinnacle Books' *Arabesque.*

pun Wordplay that is also characteristic of **signification**.

queer theory and criticism In 1991, Charles Nero published the seminal essay "Toward a Black Gay Aesthetic: Signifying in Contemporary Black Gay Literature," which promoted methods of critical analysis used by other critics in the African American letters. The intent was to move criticism of gay literature beyond causative approaches. Nero encouraged **signifying** because of its parameters such as linguistics and structure, and because at its core there are shared social, historical, and cultural knowledge among communicators within the tradition. In other words, Nero and other gay writers sought methods that had been used by critics before them to communicate visibility and validity (i.e., **signfying, indirection, parody, deconstruction** and **intertextuality**—all of which allow writers to challenge and revise attitudes). In addition to visibility and validity, other motifs in later twentieth century queer criticism include **migration** and **passing**.

References for further reading: Thelma Golden, ed. *Black Male: Representations of Masculinity in Contemporary American Art* (1994); Winston Napier, ed. *African American Literary Theory: A Reader* (2000); Charles Nero, "Toward a Black Gay Aesthetic: Signifying in Contemporary Black Gay Literature" (1999); Emmanuel S. Nelson, ed. *Critical Essays: Gay and Lesbian Writers of Color* (1993).

quilt (See **motif** and **symbols/symbolism.**)

race Although both race and ethnicity are generally deemed social constructs that at their foundational meanings name pronounced and less-pronounced phenotypic differences among humans, race is more often assessed as the more dubious construction, while the construct of ethnicity is seen as a more legitimate way to name phenotypic differences among humans. Consider how anthropologist Ashley Montagu in *Man's Most Dangerous Myth: The Fallacy of Race* (1997) distinguishes between race and ethnicity:

> [I]n biological usage a race has been conceived as a subdivision of a species that inherits the physical characteristics serving to distinguish it from other populations of the species. In the genetic sense a race has been defined as a population that differs in the incidence of certain genes from other populations, one or more genes of which it is exchanging or is potentially capable of exchanging across whatever boundaries (usually geographical) that may separate them. (53)

To his definition of race, which he replaces with the term "extended group," Montagu defines ethnic group, which he sees as a subset of the larger extended group:

> An ethnic group represents part of a population in process of undergoing genetic and socially, genetically unrelated, cultural differentiation; it is a group of individuals capable of hybridizing genetically and culturally with other groups to produce further genetic and cultural differentiation. (49)

However, in *Racial and Ethnic Groups* (1993), Richard T. Schaeffer does not patently define ethnicity as a subdivision of race, nor does he explore the constructions of nation and the performativeness of culture when he defines an ethnic group as one "set apart from others because of its national origin or distinctive cultural patterns" (34). Likewise, Schaeffer's definition of race at best implicitly challenges race as a product of social construction; indeed, a racial group, according to Schaeffer, "is socially set apart from others because of obvious physical differences" (35).

References for further reading: Eric J. Sundquist, *To Wake the Nations: Race in the Making of American Literature* (1993); Cornel West, *Race Matters* (1993).

"racial mountain" A phrase coined by Langston Hughes in his essay "The Negro Artist and the Racial Mountain" (1926). According to Hughes, because of social, political, and cultural obstacles faced by artists of color, the mountain becomes metaphorical; it is that which artists must overcome in order to discover themselves and their own aesthetic positions.

ragtime According to William Barlow in *Looking Up at Down: The Emergence of Blues Culture* (1989), ragtime emerged in the Mississippi Valley. It is an age-old West African practice of separating the melody from the basic time scheme, which is done by positioning notes slightly ahead of or behind the ground beat. The effect produces a pattern of simple cross-rhythms. A predecessor of **jazz** is ragtime. Direct references to ragtime appear in James Weldon Johnson's *Autobiography of an Ex-Colored Man* (1912); Paul Laurence Dunbar's *The Sport of the Gods* (1902); and Ann Petry's "Has Anybody Seen Miss Dora Dean?" (1958).

rap According to Tricia Rose writing in *Black Noise* (1994),

> Rap lyrics are a critical part of a rappers' identity, strongly suggesting the importance of authorship and individuality in rap music—yet sampling as it is used by rap artists indicates the importance of collective identities and group histories. There are hundreds of shared phrases and slang words in rap lyrics, yet a given rap text is the personal and emotive voice of the rapper. . . . Rap lyrics . . . articulate a distinct oral past. (95)

Like **jazz** musicians in a jazz session that vie to perform the best solo, rappers extend the **performance,** calling it "cutting contest." According to

Mtume ya Salaam writing in "The Aesthetics of Rap" (1995), when evaluating rap

> Critics of rap must consider the same elements commonly found in good poetry—simile, metaphor, and alliteration as well as creative expression, originality, and conveyance of emotion. . . . All of the great rappers, like all of the great singers/instrumentalists in other genres, have an intangible sound that distinguishes them from other rappers. Like a fingerprint, this individual sound helps any knowledgeable rap fan identify the better rappers. . . . What makes this possible is the concept of "sound"—an artist's non-quantifiable, identifying characteristics. (448)

(See also **Age of Baraka, alliteration, bard, Black Arts Movement, griot, Hip-hop culture, last poets, metaphor, performance, simile,** and **"the spoken word."**)

References for further reading: Tricia Rose, *Black Noise: Rap Music and Black Culture in Contemporary American Music/Culture* (1994); Mtume ya Salaam, "The Aesthetics of Rap" (1999).

reader-response criticism   The reader is an active agent in producing meaning in a work. To arrive at meaning (which is created by the reader), he or she determines how to approach the work; how to construct his or her own identity in the work; and how to make sense of other experiences in the work.

References for further reading: Stanley Fish, *Is There a Text in This Class? The Authority of Interpretive Communities* (1980); Vincent B. Leitch et al., *The Norton Anthology of Theory and Criticism* (2001).

realism   In literature, the portrayal of everyday life as it is represented in reality—without idealism or sentimentalism. Traditionally, the term is credited to African American novels of the 1960s—for example, Gordon Parks's *Learning Tree* (1963); Louise Meriwether's *Daddy Was a Number Runner* (1970); and Cecil Brown's *Life and Loves of Mr. Jiveass Nigger* (1969). But, existing are even earlier authors of realism literature: Charles W. Chesnutt's *The Marrow of Tradition* (1901); Paul Laurence Dunbar's *The Sport of the Gods* (1902); Arna Bontemps's "A Summer Tragedy" (1932); Richard Wright's *Uncle Tom's Children* (1938), *Native Son* (1940), "Big Boy Leaves Home," and "The Man Who Was Almost a Man"; and Ann Petry's

The Street (1946). In *The Afro-American Novel and Its Tradition* (1987), Bernard Bell defines "folk realism" as "everyday life of ordinary churchgoing black folk in a particular environment and social rituals" (128). Literary works include Langston Hughes's *Not Without Laughter* (1930); Countee Cullen's *One Way Ticket to Heaven* (1931). Bell defines "poetic realism" as "call[ing] attention to the problematics of reality and language while simultaneously insisting that reality is shaped more by consciousness than consciousness is by reality" (269). Literary works include Toni Morrison's *The Bluest Eye* (1970), *Sula* (1973), and *Song of Solomon* (1977). Bell defines "neorealism" as "pragmatic; responding to modernism's alienation" (246). Literary writers include John O. Killens, John Williams, Alice Walker, Ernest Gaines, and Margaret Walker.
(See also **verisimilitude.**)

Reconstruction and postmodernism period (1976 to present) Starting in the 1970s, contemporary critics promote what literary critic Houston Baker Jr. calls "sound theoretical frameworks" (in "Generational Shift and the Recent Criticism of Afro-American Literature" 1981:80) and creative writers produce what author Terry McMillan calls literary art that is "entertaining . . . informative, thought-provoking . . . [and] uplifting" (*Breaking Ice: An Anthology of Contemporary African-American Fiction* 1990:xxi). The title of Greg Tate's essay captures the essence of contemporary literature: "Cult-Nats Meet Freaky Deke" (1986:5). In other words, the contemporary writer has become culturally eclectic. While socially and politically responsible to the African American community, the contemporary writer pulls also from the "complexities" of African American culture—wherever that takes him or her. According to Trey Ellis in "The New Black Aesthetic [NBA]" (1989), icons for the NBA might include "postmodernist writers Ishmael Reed, Clarence Majors, Toni Morrison, and John Edgar Wideman; [the post 1960s] George Clinton with his spaced-out funk band Parliament/Funkadelic [or] jazz, blues and [punk rock]" (234).

Unlike past creative writers who debated, without any resolutions, the contemporary writers agree on the function of contemporary literature: art over propaganda; craft over politics. Contemporary writers are encouraged, however, by John Edgar Wideman to preserve and express an identity through folk culture: "our songs, Dreams, dances, styles of walk and talk, dressing, cooking, sport, our heroes, and heroines" (Preface, *Breaking Ice: An Anthology of Contemporary African-American Fiction* ed. McMillan,

1990:vii). But Wideman says avoid past efforts by writers to prescribe African American literature into some "ideologically sound, privileged category" (ix). Rather, Wideman instructs the writers:

If what a writer wants is freedom of expression, then somehow that larger goal must be addressed implicitly/explicitly. A story should somehow contain clues that align it with tradition and critique tradition, [and] establishes the new space it requires, demands, appropriates. (viii)

In other words, the writer is encouraged to "min[e] territory that maximizes the possibility of free, original expression" (ix).

Reconstruction, reaction, and realism period (1865–1917) Emerging after the Civil War is a growing African American middle class that is intellectual, literary, community-oriented, civic-minded, and economically progressive. Emerging also during these years are a Jim Crow system and a fraternal white supremacy group (i.e., Ku Klux Klan) that physically displace the African American in the South. The outcome is disenfranchisement among African Americans. Furthermore, there are southern Euro American writers who perpetuate stereotypes of African American slave life and character in popular **plantation literature**. An immediate response from the African American literary world is to create literature that would change dominant attitudes during Reconstruction about the African American race (see, for example, Frances Harper's novels *Minnie's Sacrifice, Sowing and Reaping,* and *Trial and Triumph,* written between 1868 and 1888; and *Iola LeRoy* (1892). Abandoning the folk culture, middle-class African Americans draw on Victorian ideals (family, civic organizations, women's clubs, fraternities) in their further attempts to show Euro Americans that African Americans possessed similar aspirations, tastes, and values.

The question of how to empower the disenfranchised African American is raised by two powerful influential race leaders during these years: Booker T. Washington and W.E.B. DuBois. Responding in, for example, his "Atlanta Exposition Address" that is delivered in 1895 in Atlanta before the Cotton States and International Exposition, Booker T. Washington proposes "economic advancement" for African Americans via technical school training. Washington fails to call for civil rights or equality under the Constitution or for integration in the **South**. In fact, Washington holds the position that African Americans are responsible for the African American "problem." Instead of legal action of some sort to improve equality, Washington prefers keeping "peace" among the races. (See Washington's *Up From Slavery*, 1901.)

Opposing Washington is W.E.B. DuBois—critic, educator, editor, and sociologist—who advocates equal rights and fairness for African Americans. Unlike Washington who promotes technical training for ex-slaves, DuBois promotes a liberal arts education. Unwilling to blame African Americans for the racism, violence, and other social problems in the South, DuBois chooses to explore race relations in America and the "souls" of African Americans. From his important work *The Souls of Black Folk* (1903), he introduces terms such as **double consciousness,** the **color line,** and **the veil**.

Realist writers of the period include Charles Chesnutt and Paul Laurence Dunbar. Both are unwilling to romanticize the African American middle class or to ignore the disenfranchisement of African Americans in the late 1880s. Responding to the Jim Crow system, to the supremacist groups, and to plantation literature, Chesnutt in *The Marrow of Tradition* (1901) and Dunbar in *The Sport of the Gods* (1902) are realistic and subversive. (See also **plantation literature** and **Fisk Jubilee Singers.**)

Reference for further reading: William L. Andrews, ed. *The African-American Novel in the Age of Reaction: Three Classics,* 1992.

Renaissances and radicalism period (1917–1953) Following the two World Wars, there are two literary movements that mark artistic, social, and cultural awakenings among African Americans: the **Harlem Renaissance** (1917–1935) and the **Chicago Renaissance** (1935–1953/54). Both movements are energized by the Great **Migration**—the influx of African Americans from the South to urban cities—and the new dissenting voices among the masses that are willing to challenge the Jim Crow system, by the middle class seeking integration, and by the younger generation seeking self-expression. Architects of the Harlem Renaissance such as Charles S. Johnson, James Weldon Johnson, W.E.B. DuBois, and Alain Locke propose creating art that is imitative of Euro American middle-class life for the sole purpose of demonstrating an intellectual parity and the middle-class aspirations of African Americans. For as James W. Johnson contends, "The status of the Negro in the United States is more a question of national mental attitude toward the race than of actual condition" (Preface, *The Book of American Negro Poetry* 1921:9). "While the more conservative spokespersons [DuBois and James Weldon Johnson] agree to promote propaganda (versus art) to **represent** the African Americans in general, a younger generation of writers

[Langston Hughes, Countee Cullen, Zora Neale Hurston, Jean Toomer, Rudolph Fisher, Sterling Brown, and others] choose to represent African Americans that are, to quote Hughes, "beautiful . . . and ugly too" (Hughes, "The Negro Artist and the Racial Mountain," 1926). To promote a sense of self-expression in their art, the younger writers proposed experimenting in their writings with cultural forms such as **spirituals, blues, work songs, ballads,** and **blues-ballad.**

Like the younger generation of Harlem Renaissance writers, major writers of the Chicago Renaissance (Richard Wright, Margaret Walker, Ann Petry, and Chester Himes) promote self-expression. Like the Harlem Renaissance writers, the Chicago Renaissance writers pull effortlessly from the culture to inform their literature. While the younger Harlem writers of the 1920s give voice to rural and urban African America, working-class African Americans occupy the novels of the writers of the 1940s.

Among the Harlem Renaissance writers, poets Langston Hughes, Claude McKay, and Fenton Johnson might be regarded as protest writers. In particular, they protest against the double standards with regard to the **American Dream, miscegenation,** and racism. As Hughes, writing in "Let America Be America" (1936), contends "America never was America to me / And yet I say America must be" (Rampersad 1995:189–91). For similar reasons, the novels of the 1940s will interchangeably reflect **protest.** Because of their deterministic approaches to urban life, and because of their criticism of classism, racism, and sexism, the works of Wright, Himes, and Petry may be classified as **naturalistic** and as **proletarian.**

Among the masses in the 1920s, Marcus Garvey rises as spokesperson in his involvement with the Universal Negro Improvement Association. The grassroots organization responds to the Jim Crow system by publically organizing to return masses of African Americans to Africa.
(See also **black aesthetics, modernism, realism.**)

repetition (See Criticism and Theory.)

representation (See Criticism and Theory.)

resolution The events that follow the outcome of the **climax** in a plot; the "falling action" in a plot.
(See also **denouement.**)

rhetorical question A question that is asked without the expectations of receiving an answer. However, based on the **context** in which the question is asked, the rhetorical device may be used as an act of persuasion. Examples of the rhetorical question used as subtle persuasion appear in the spiritual "Were you there when they crucified my Lord?" In literature, there are the following works:

Olaudah Equiano's *The Interesting Narrative of the Life of Olaudah Equiano, or Gustavas Vassa, the African* (1789):

> O, ye nominal Christians! Might not an African ask you—Learned you this from your God, who says unto you, Do unto all men as you would men should do unto you?
> (Hill et al. 1997:136.)

Harriet Jacob's *Incidents in the Life of a Slave Girl* (1861):

> What cares my owners for that? He was merely a piece of property.
> (Gates and McKay 1997:213.)

Ann Petry's *The Street* (1946):

> Instead she'd cleaned another woman's house and looked after another woman's child while her own marriage went to pot; breaking up into so many little pieces it couldn't be put back together again, couldn't even be patched into a vague resemblance of its former self. . . . Yet what else could she have done? (30)

rhyme A device that brings unity to a poem and intensifies its meaning. Echoed are accented vowel sounds that can be associated with the sense of music (i.e., **rhythm** and beat).

rhyme scheme The pattern of rhyme in a stanza. A different letter of the alphabet is used for each new rhyme: As in Angelina Weld Grimke's "For the Candle Light" (1927) a small letter *a* represents the first rhyme; a small letter *b* represents the second rhyme, and so on:

The sky was blue, so blue, that day	(*a*)
And each daisy white, so white,	(*b*)
Oh! I knew that no more could rain fall gray,	(*a*)
And night again be night.	(*b*)

rhythm and blues, the "Race music" of the late 1940s that incorporates urban **blues, jazz,** and **gospel** is called rhythm and blues or R&B. Like blues, rhythm and blues has a social message. Like gospel, it projects the emotional fervor of gospel songs, field cries, and hollers (see **folk cries**). Also merged are song and **sermon** (i.e., alternating reality) with **performance** and **ritual**. Like jazz, rhythm and blues incorporates **call and response, riff,** a vocal line, and emphasis on **rhythm** and beat. Pioneers of rhythm and blues include, to name a few, Dinah Washington, Louis Jordan, Ray Charles, Fats Domino, B. B. King, Chuck Berry, Bill Haley, Sam Cooke, Otis Redding, Sam and Dave, Rufus and Carla Thomas, Booker T. and the MGs, Isaac Hayes, Percy Sledge, Joe Tex, Wilson Pickett, Johnny Taylor, Curtis Mayfield, Aretha Franklin, and James Brown.

References for further reading: William Barlow, *Looking Up at Down: The Emergence of Blues Culture* (1989); Eileen Southern, *The Music of Black America: A History* (1997).

riff A term borrowed from jazz musicians that denotes **improvisational** soloing by horn players and the borrowing of techniques used by blues vocalists such as vibrato, pitch variations, tremolo, and slurring and sliding notes.

References for further reading: William Barlow, *Looking Up at Down: The Emergence of Blues Culture* (1989); and Eileen Southern, *The Music of Black America: A History* (1997).

ring shout A sacred **ritual dance** that is accompanied by drum and **performed** in a **circular,** counterclockwise direction. Participants are rhythmically shuffling their feet and shaking their hands. Outside of the circle, others clap, sing, and gesticulate. Overall, there is ecstatic participation and **ecstasy** sought. The ritual has been abandoned largely throughout the southern United States at the request of African American ministers who felt the ritual was a conflict with Christianity. After the Civil War, however, the dance was found to still exist on the coasts of South Carolina and Georgia. An inherent form of African art and spiritual outpouring, the ritual continues to symbolize community integration, particularly by African descendents (**Gullah**-speaking people) on the coasts of South Carolina and Georgia and people in the Caribbean. Presented in Paule Marshall's *Praisesong for the Widow* (1983), which is set on the coast of the United States and in the Caribbean, is the ring shout.

Reference for further reading: Muriel Miller Branch, *The Water Brought Us: The Story of the Gullah-Speaking People* 1995.

rites de passage (See **secret societies.**)

ritual (See **cathartic release, the dozens, "laying on the hands," Obeah, ring shout, secret societies, signifying,** and **"speaking in tongues."**)

roman à clef A novel with identifiable fictional characters from real life. See Wallace Thurman's *Infants of the Spring* (1932) and John A. Williams's *The Man Who Cried I Am* (1967).

romance (See **pulp fiction.**)

rootlessness (See **ancestors.**)

"safe space" (See **"urban space."**)

satire/satirical A literary mode of writing that points out the vices or shortcomings of individuals, institutions, or societies via ridicule or censure, usually for corrective purposes. Major satirists include Wallace Thurman, Rudolph Fisher, Zora Neale Hurston, Langston Hughes, George S. Schuyler, Douglas Turner Ward, John O. Killens, Ben Caldwell, Sam Greenlee, and Ishmael Reed.

References for further reading: Daryl Dance, *Honey Hush! An Anthology of African American Women's Humor,* 1998; Darryl Dickson-Carr, *African American Satire: The Sacredly Profane Novel.* 2001; Femi Euba, *Archetypes, Imprecators, and Victims of Fate: Origins and Development of Satire in Black Drama,* 1989.

saturation A term coined by Stephen E. Henderson in *Understanding the New Black Poetry: Black Speech and Black Music as Poetic References* (1973) to denote a perception, a quality, and a condition of the **theme** and structure. Echoing romanticist John Keats, Henderson, writing in "Progress Report on a Theory of Black Poetry" (1975), says the term suggests a "standard of intuition for judging the successful reading of Black poetic structure" (Napier 2000:109–10). Furthermore, he says, "one must not consider the poem [or literary work] in isolation, but in relationship to the reader/audience or to the wider context—the Black experience" (Napier 2000:104). (See also **context.**)

scansion (See **meter.**)

scat The **blues** and **jazz** vocalists keep the **rhythm** going often by trying to imitate verbally the sounds of musical instruments.

science fiction (See **speculative fiction.**)

secret societies In traditional West Africa, the secret societies Poro (or Beri) for males and Sande (or Bundu) for females were means of initiating young members of a community into adulthood and impressing upon the initiates their sacred duty to Poro and Sande and to the community. This is a mandatory and uniform initiation process that caused adolescents to be isolated from the community for a year and to participate in what might be called "bush schools." Both males and females were familiarized with tribal history and lore, and they were schooled in social conduct and behavior befitting their sex and station. They were educated also to know their life's work. For females, this meant a social introduction to ideal womanhood or the responsibilities of women as mothers and wives or as homemakers and caregivers. For males, this meant a social introduction to ideal manhood or the responsibilities of men as protectors, builders, farmers, and hunters.

The social and political ends of the secret societies were to deter deviant social behavior and arbitrary power. The other functions were to promote collective societal goals, solidarity, and social cohesion in the community. According to Margaret Creel in *A Peculiar People: Slave Religion and Community Culture Among the Gullah* (1988), the traditional African concept is that Poro and Sande are institutions "made by God." In a special (and sacred) place where initiations take place, sometimes called "the sacred grove," spirits have particular roles or functions, as well. Hidden behind masks, the ancestral spirits explain, for instance, life and death. And as protectors, the ancestral spirits are said to be concerned with the well-being of family and society at large. Water and bush spirits emphasize special knowledge and punishment.

In the coastal Sea Islands of South Carolina and Georgia, remnants of the secret society have survived. According to Muriel Miller Branch, writing in *The Water Brought Us: The Story of the Gullah-Speaking People* (1993), "The African initiation ceremonies in which the young were required to go into the bush to be instructed by the older members of their tribe" were combined with "European practices and instructions in the catechism, a book of questions and answers about the scriptures and Christianity" (35). What emerged was "the lengthy process of *seeking* before being accepted into the fellowship of a church" (35) (and indirectly, the community). Resembling the African Poro and Sande, "The seeker is matched with a 'leader,' a 'spiritual teacher,' or 'spiritual mother' who guides the seeker through the seeking experience" (36).

In keeping with African tradition, the seeker is required to remove himself (herself) from the rest of the world, including family and friends. He or she spends time alone in meditation and prayer, usually in the backyard or often in the woods at night. The seeker gives up everything while praying. Upon examination of the initiate (or the seeker), if satisfied, the spiritual leader or spiritual teacher teaches the seeker the catechism. A number of southern churches with a large population of adolescents are returning to initiation ceremonies that are reminiscent of the Poro and Sande societies.

semiotics A science of signs; a subbranch of **structuralism.**

sermon The first **poetry** of the African in America. It is oral and improvisational and it is marked with cadences and rhythm. As a historical text, the sermon has helped the African American community to adapt to changing external circumstances. As a speech act, is has historicized the experiences of African Americans in the United States and revised reality for the sole purpose of physical and spiritual survival. According to Dolan Hubbard in *The Sermon and the African American Literary Imagination* (1994), "black writers are attracted to the sermon because it empowers blackness. It is central to the way in which a black identity is produced and reproduced when the preacher and community in unison engage in the emancipation of the self" (146).

When returning to the sermon, African American writers employ literary/cultural modes not only reminiscent of the **folk preacher** but also of musicians (e.g., **orality, repetition** under Criticism and Theory, **improvisation, call and response, syncopation, adorned metaphor, rhythm,** and **ritual**). According to Hubbard, "Like the preacher (and the musician), writers [also] extend and revise the nature of reality" (146) for the African American audience. As a cultural marker, the sermon has influenced writings of Frances Harper, Jean Toomer, Zora Neale Hurston, Langston Hughes, Richard Wright, Ishmael Reed, Leon Forrest, Alice Walker, Ernest Gaines, Toni Morrison, Gloria Naylor, Julius Lester, and C. Eric Lincoln.

Sermonic rhetoric—biblical **allusions,** cadences and **rhythms**—are present in, for example, James Baldwin's *Go Tell It On the Mountain* (1953) or in the contemporary Jill Scott song "A Long Walk."
(See also **grammar of the sermon.**)

Reference for further reading: James Weldon Johnson, introduction to *God's Trombones: Seven Negro Sermons in Verse* (1927).

sermonic rhetoric (See **sermon.**)

setting The locale of a story or play that is best determined by asking where does the story or play take place? When does the story or play take place?

sexuality (See **queer criticism** and **feminism.**)

References for further reading: Rudolph P. Byrd and Beverly Guy-Sheftall, *Traps: African American Men on Gender and Sexuality* 2001; Haki R. Madhubuti, *Black Men: Obsolete, Single, Dangerous?* 1990; Mary Helen Washington, *Black-Eyed Susans and Midnight Birds: Stories by and About Black Women* (1989).

shadow (See **collective unconscious** under Criticism and Theory.)

Shakespearean sonnet A verse form that consists of fourteen lines and is usually in **iambic pentameters**. Made up of three quatrains (each of which explores a **theme**) and a concluding **couplet** (which offers **resolution**). Existing are varied **rhyme schemes,** such as *abab, cdcd, efef, gg;* or *abba, cddc, effe, gg.* For an example of the former rhyme scheme, see Claude McKay's "If We Must Die" (1919); and "My Mother" (1921) (Gates and McKay 1997:984, 986). For an example of the latter rhyme scheme, see Gwendolyn Brooks's "A Lovely Love" (1960; Gates and McKay 1997:1593).

short story A genre that has elements that are found in the novel (e.g., **theme, setting, plot, character**), but the genre is a brief narrative in prose. The pyramid of plot construction moves from complication, **climax, resolution** to **denouement.** Before the 1960s, characters are commonly subversive. After the 1960s, characters become aggressive and/or experimental. Recurring themes in the African American short story include the struggle to survive with what DuBois calls "beauty," "truth," and "justice," reverse humiliations and relationships (DeBois, "Criteria of Negro Art," 1926). Structural influences are traceable to the **sermon, folktale, spirituals,** and **blues.**

(See also **characterization, conflict, denouement, diction, plot, point of view,** and **resolution.**)

References for further reading: Peter Bruck, ed., *The American Short Story: A Collection of Critical Essays* (1977); John Henrik Clarke, ed. *Black American Short Stories: A Century of the Best* (1993); Wolfgang Karrer and Barbara Puschlmann-Nolenz, eds. *The African American Short Story, 1970 to 1990: A Collection of Critical Essays* (1995); Clarence Major. *Calling the Wind: Twentieth-Century African-American Short Stories* (1993); Bill Mullen, ed. *Revolutionary Tales*, 1995; John C. Shields, "The Short Story" (1997); Preston Yancy. *The Afro-American Short Story: A Comprehensive Annotated Index with Selected Commentaries* (1986).

shouts (See **ecstasy, magara, ring shouts.**)

"shucking and jiving" (See **lies** and **soul.**)

sign (See **semiotics, signification,** and **signifying.**)

signification The term denotes implicit criticism, or referential interpretations. Like **signifying,** there is **indirection** or subtle circumlocution; a punning or play of words. According to Henry Louis Gates in *Figures in Black: Words, Signs and the Racial Self* (1987), Ralph Ellison in *Invisible Man* (1952) provides implicit criticism of Richard Wright's literary structure and protagonist in *Native Son* (1940).
(See also **parody, pastiche,** and **signifying.**)

signifying/signification (See Criticism and Theory.)

simile Unlike the metaphor, where implicit and advanced comparisons exist, the simile is recognized by the writer's use of "like" or "as." According to Zora Neale Hurston in "Characteristics of Negro Expression" (1934), in the African American community, the will to adorn everyday speech with simile and **metaphor** is a notable characteristic of African American culture. Hurston contends that the African American's greatest contribution to the language is the simile. Examples of the simile adorning the language exist in early **spirituals** such as "Sometimes I Feel like a Motherless Child":

> Sometimes I feel like a motherless child
> Sometimes I feel like a motherless child
> Sometimes I feel like a motherless child
> Such a long long way from home

In **sermons** of the oral tradition:

His voice . . . got so low it sounded like a roll of thunder

or

She stood in front of the alter, shaking like a freshly caught trout.

Examples of writers and works that rely on simile include the following: Claude McKay's poem "If We Must Die" (1919):

If we must die, let it not be like hogs
Haunted and penned in an inglorious spot
(Gates and McKay, 1997:984.)

Maya Angelou, writing in her autobiography *I Know Why the Caged Bird Sings* (1970), employs simile and metaphor:

It looked like an unopened present from a stranger. Opening the front door was like pulling the ribbon off the unexpected gift. (13)

Nathan McCall's autobiographical *Makes Me Wanna Holler* (1995):

Compared to my divorce, doing time in prison was like a day at the beach. (379)

skaz A term of Russian formalism used to identify texts that resemble oral narratives; a term that means "to tell." Gayl Jones, writing in *Liberating Voices: Oral Tradition in African American Literature* (1991), suggests the term sounds like a combination of "skat" and "jazz" and might be a paradigm of the African American **oral tradition**.

slang According to Geneva Smitherman, writing in *Talkin and Testifyin: The Language of Black America* (1977), slang is "a highly specialized vocabulary used only by a certain group" (43). Slang is also the vocabulary of **soul** and cool talk. According to Clarence Major, writing in *Juba to Jive: A Dictionary of African-American Slang* (1970), slang is "the most alive aspect of our language" (xxvii). Like Smitherman, Major cautions that slang "is not colloquialism; it is not dialect, not argot, not jargon or cant. Black slang is composed of or involves the use of redundancies, jive rhyme, nonsense, fad expressions, nicknames, corruptions, onomatopoeia, mispronunciations, and clipped forms" (xxx).

slave narrative A subgenre of the African American **autobiography,** written by former slaves, starting as early as 1760. Major **themes** are the inhumanity of the slave system—as experienced by the authors of the narratives—and antislavery activism. Women authors add as a theme the trials of black womanhood in slavery. One may also find in the genre influences of the oral tradition: the **trickster** motif, extensive literary and biblical **allusions,** and the **picaresque** perspective (or flight from bondage to freedom). The most referenced slave narratives include the following: Harriet Jacob's *Incidents in the Life of a Slave Girl* (1861) and Frederick Douglass's *Narrative of the Life of Frederick Douglass, an American Slave, Written by Himself* (1845). Thematic influences of the slave narrative find their way into antebellum works such as Booker T. Washington's *Up From Slavery* (1901) and Richard Wright's *Black Boy* (1945).

References for further reading: William L. Andrews, *To Tell a Free Story: The First Century of Afro-American Autobiography 1760–1865* (1986); Frances Smith Foster, *Witnessing Slavery: The Development of Ante-bellum Slave Narratives* (1994) and *Written by Herself* (1993); and John Sekora and Darwin T. Turner, eds., *The Art of Slave Narrative: Original Essays in Criticism and Theory* (1982).

sociological novel (See **naturalism** and **protest literature.**)

soliloquy (See **monologue.**)

sonnet (See **Italian sonnet, Petrarchan sonnet,** and **Shakespearean sonnet.**)

"sorrow songs" Coined by W.E.B. DuBois in *The Souls of Black Folk* (1903) to denote "the soul of the black slave [which] spoke to men" in "sorrow songs" (250) or the **spirituals.**

soul A black lifestyle. The black wisdom of the race. Virtuoso elegance. Lyrical. Also **slang** for patient and hip.

References for further reading: Daryl Cumber Dance, *Shuckin' and Jivin': Folklore from Contemporary Black America* (1978); Clarence Major, *Juba to Jive: A Dictionary of African-American Slang* (1970).

sounding A term that denotes exploitation of the unexpected and quick verbal surprise.

(See also **signifying** under Criticism and Theory.)

sounds (See **ideophones, onomatopoeia,** and **riff.**)

South, the The site or place of African American tradition and of tragi-comic relationships for African Americans and Euro Americans; a symbol of oppression, pain, and suffering, particularly during slavery and Recon-struction; the home of legacies and ancestral mentors; a **context** of beauty and values for **sorrow songs, blues,** and seculars. See, for example, Ernest Gaines's *The Autobiography of Miss Jane Pittman* (1971); Raymond Andrews's *Appalachee Red* (1978); Reginald McKnight's *I Get on the Bus* (1990); and Lewis Edward's *Ten Seconds* (1991).
(See also **folklore, migration narrative, "urban space."**)

Reference for further reading: John Killens and Jerry W. Ward Jr., *Black Southern Voices: An Anthology* (1992).

South Side Writers, the A literary group of artists from Chicago's southside that organized in 1936. According to Margaret Walker, writing in *Richard Wright, Daemonic Genius* (1988), its members held collectively many of the ideas and opinions expressed by Richard Wright in "Blueprint for Negro Writing" (1937). The essay called for writers to create values by which black people could live and die (111). Members of the group included Richard Wright, Margaret Walker, Frank Marshall Davis, Theodore Ward, Fern Gayden, and later Margaret Esse Danner and Gwendolyn Brooks. Many would go on to establish themselves as first-rate writers, doing what Wright called for in his essay, "lift[ing] the level of consciousness higher" (111).

speakerly text A mode of narration that reflects a development of self-consciousness in a character who is neither the novel's protagonist nor the text's disembodied narrator—but a blend of both; an emergent and a merging moment of consciousness.
(See also **free indirect discourse, signification** and **signifying,** and **skaz.**)

"speaking in tongues" According to Mae Henderson in "Speaking in Tongues" (1989) in African American culture, the phrase connotes the ability to speak in and through the spirit. In African American letters, "speaking in tongues" denotes what Henderson calls "a plurality of voices" as well as a "multiplicity of discourses," within a work, particularly works by African

American women writers. Henderson uses also the term *glossolalia* to suggest "**ecstatic**, rapturous, inspired speech[,] based on intimacy and identification between the individual and God" (352–53). She suggests that in community settings the term might be called "the particular, private, closed, and privileged [speech] between the congregant and the divinity" (352). (See also **heteroglossia**.)

Reference for further reading: Mae Henderson, "Speaking in Tongues: Dialogics, Dialectics, and the Black Woman Writer's Literary Tradition," in *African American Literary Theory: A Reader*, edited by Napier (2000).

specifying A verbal **ritual** of "name-calling" that is embodied in oral and fictional writings.

Reference for further reading: Susan Willis, *Specifying: Black Women Writing the American Experience* (1990).

speculative fiction The term speculative is inclusive of science fiction, fantasy, utopian and dystopian fiction, supernatural, and fabulation. The shared premise of these subgenres is the presentation of a changed, distorted, or alternated reality. Major writers of speculative fiction include Octavia E. Butler in *Wild Seed* (1980), *Dawn* (1987), *Kindred* (1979), and *Survival* (1978); Samuel R. Delany in *The Jewels of Apton* (1962), *Babel* (1966), *The Fall of the Towers* (a trilogy, 1963–1965); and Steven Barnes in *Streetlethal* (1983), *Gorgon Child* (1989), and *Fire Dance* (1993).

Reference for further reading: Sandra Y. Govan, "Speculative Fiction" (1997).

"spirit possession" A trancelike state guided by a life force. (See also **ecstasy** and **magara**.)

"spirit-writing" According to Harryette Mullen in "African Signs and Spirit Writing" (Napier 2000:623–42), the phrase "spirit-writing" denotes "a reliance on visions, dreams, inner voices, and possession of the Holy Spirit, empowering one to speak and write" (Napier 2000:683). Defined also as "spiritual communicators with the divine"; a "submission to trance and in the spirit, [which] taps unseen potencies, deriving from The Holy Spirit" (Napier 2000:636). Furthermore, emphasis is on the "gift of literacy due to divine instruction" (Napier 2000:237). See, for instance, *Gifts of Power: The Writings of Rebecca Jackson, Black Visionary, Shaker Eldress*, ed. Jean McMahon Humez (1981). See also writings of Jarena Lee, Toni Cade Bambara,

Randell Kenan, Ishmael Reed, Toni Morrison, Gloria Naylor, Nzotake Shange, Alice Walker, Octavia Butler, Nathaniel Mackey, and Adrienne Kennedy.

spirituals Dating back to the beginning of slavery in the 1600s, the spirituals are sometimes called **epics,** folk literature, the precursor to the **blues,** signal songs, and **sorrow songs.** As an epic, there are biblical **heroes** who serve as **race** prophets and who demonstrate perseverance, acceptance of a higher authority, and eventually triumph over slavery. As folk literature, the spirituals are cultural paradigms of good and evil, of justice and injustice, and of sin and retribution. The verse structure of *aab* (see, for instance "Deep River" or "Sometimes I Feel Like a Motherless Child") becomes also the verse structure of the blues. Elements of the oral tradition are found also in the spirituals: **call and response,** topical experiences, and **rhythm.** As signal songs, the spirituals were used to carry messages to members of the shared community that were not understood by the overseers. The messages were often about escape by following the Big Dipper (e.g., "Follow the Drinking Gourd"). Other messages signaled slaves to meet collectively (e.g., "Steal Away"). As sorrow songs, the spirituals reflected sorrow and joy as they called for deliverance of the slaves from oppression and exile and the reflected promises of redemption from hardships and suffering.
(See also **oral tradition.**)

spirituality A definition emerges when the following terms are read together: **African ontology, conjuring, "spirit writing," "the spoken word," ecstasy, magara, "speaking in tongues," hoodoo, voodoo/vodun, "saturation," "rituals," "safe space," secret societies, ring shouts, grammar of the sermon, spirituals, blues.**

"spoken word, the" The term implies that speech takes precedence over writing; that the unwritten has no final version; and that the creative process in **context** is an ongoing one. According to Karla Holloway in *Moorings and Metaphors: Figures of Culture and Gender in Black Women's Literature* (1992), African American women writers "nurture the spoken word within their texts" (26). Look for repetitions of words and then determine the memory or sociocultural history of the words. The word is creator rather than created; it is cultural property.
(See also **def-jam poetry, Hip-hop culture,** and **rap.**)

stanza A pattern of specific lines, **meter,** and **rhyme schemes;** a unit or verse in a poem. Stanza forms are identifiable by lines. For instance, the **couplet** consists of a pair of rhymed lines. The tercet is a stanza of three lines. The quatrain is a stanza of four lines. The most common stanza is the quatrain (see, for instance, Arna Bontemps's "A Black Man Talks of Reaping," 1926). Variations of stanza forms will appear in **free verse.** See, for instance, Alice Walker's poem "For My Sister Molly Who in the Fifties," 1973.

stereotypes (See **plantation literature.**)

storytelling A symbolic pattern of action and words, imparting a moral lesson. Like the **sermon,** storytelling is a performative act and during the **performance** the speaker comments on history and may reconstruct reality. Promoted also is an interdependent relationship between speaker and the African or African American society. The storyteller is like an oral archive of the culture's customs, beliefs, values, and practices. The structure or form of the story allows the speaker (or storyteller) to comment on how things are, and how they ought to be in the community. In an African tradition, storytelling is more than simply the use of words. Included may be song, **dance,** mime, drums and/or other instruments. Between the storyteller and audience, there is also **call and response.**

stranger (See **migration narrative.**)

stream of consciousness Coined by William James in *Principles of Psychology* (1890) to denote "the flow of inner experience." In literary criticism, the term denotes the character's flow of inner thoughts, feelings, and other mental processes without the apparent intervention of the narrator. See, for instance, John Edgar Wideman's *A Glance Away* (1967), *Hurry Home* (1970), and *Sent for You Yesterday* (1983); and the writings of Toni Morrison and Alice Walker.

structuralism (See **signifying/signification** under Criticism and Theory.)

style A writer's signature: his or her characteristic diction, sentence structure, and use of word schemes (e.g., **parallelism, antithesis, parenthesis, anastrophe, ellipsis, asyndeton, alliteration, assonance, anaphora,**

epistrophe, epanalepsis, **climax, anadiplosis, antimetabole, chiasmus**) and figurative speech (**metaphor, simile, synecdoche, metonymy, puns, periphrasis, personification, hyperbole, litotes, rhetorical question, irony, onomatopoeia, oxymoron**). Among others, style may range from formal to informal, serious to humorous, or lyrical to journalistic.

subjective correlative The term is introduced by Stephen E. Henderson in the introduction to *Understanding the New Black Poetry: Black Speech and Black Music as Poetic References* (1973). A technique used by poets and novelists of the 1960s and 1970s to stir subjective feelings in their writings. By the end of the twentieth century, some rappers are employing the term to express emotions or to stir subjective feelings. In particular, poets and novelists incorporate lines from traditional **spirituals, blues,** or **rhythm and blues** to create a certain **context** or subjective mood understood or experienced by the audience. Their lines or lyrics also evoke "a particularized [memory or] emotional response" (Henderson 1973:59). For instance, the poet's line "Still are we motherless children" evokes the poignant subjective feeling stirred by the lyrics of the familiar spiritual "Sometimes I Feel Like a Motherless Child."

In *Brothers and Keepers* (1984), novelist John Edgar Wideman evokes feelings of communal and family solidarity on a Sunday morning when he writes:

> Reach out and touch. Sam Cooke and the Soul Stirrers, the Harmonizing Four, James Cleveland, the Davis Sisters, the Swan Silvertones. I dug out my favorite albums and lined them up against the stereo cabinet. A cut or two from each one would be my Sunday morning service. Deejaying the songs got me off my backside, forced me out of the chair where I'd been sitting staring at the ceiling. With good gospel tunes rocking the house I could open the curtains and face the snow. (7)

In contrast to T. S. Eliot's *Objective Correlative* (see Eliot's "Hamlet and His Problems" [1919]), which is a way of expressing emotions in literature via a set of objects, a situation, a chain of events, the African American writer returns to black music and black speech as poetic references—to the **memory** and the "assumed emotional response" captured in the musical line or words.

Reference for further reading: Joanne Gabbin, *Sterling A. Brown: Building the Black Aesthetic Tradition* (1985).

subversive (See **indirection, modernism, signifying,** and **trickster.**)

symbols/symbolism Anything that stands for or represents something else—for example, the patchwork quilt in Alice Walker's "Everyday Use" represents heritage and **ancestors**. The Pan-Africanist's red, black, and green flag is symbolic: the red is for the blood that might be shed for liberty; the black is for black people; and the green is for the land and the acquisition of land. Symbolism appears early in African American letters through discussions of the **spirituals**—for example, "the mighty river" or "Jerusalem" as heavenly places of solace and retribution.

synchronicity (See **diachronic and synchronic.**)

syncopation A rhetorical and musical technique that functions similarly for writers, preachers, and musicians. As a technique, syncopation is the crowding in of many syllables (or notes) or the lengthening out of a few to fill one metrical foot.

synecdoche The transference of meaning, especially as the part will stand for the whole. See, for instance Paul Laurence Dunbar's "Ode to Ethiopia" (1893) where the part "Mother Africa" stands for the whole *Africa.*

tale (See **folktale.**)

"tale-within-a-tale" (See **framed narrative.**)

"talented tenth, the" A term used to define middle-class professionals, schools, and colleges that were once charged with **"uplifting the race."** In *The Souls of Black Folk* (1903), DuBois identifies some of the current schools that were charged with uplifting the race in the 1900s: Fisk University, Hampton University, Howard University, Morehouse College, Spelman College, and Atlanta University.

talking book, the A trope; a figurative act; a "voice in the text" that talks to other texts. According to Henry Louis Gates Jr., the trope has been popularized by the literary works of Ishmael Reed.
(See also **signifying/signification** under Criticism and Theory.)

testifyin/testifying According to Geneva Smitherman, writing in *Talkin and Testifyin: The Language of Black America* (1977), the term means a verbal witness by one who represents efficacy, truth, and power of shared experience. Examples of the **ritual** can be observed during church services, especially on Sunday mornings and on New Year's Eve. An example of testifyin in the secular world would be Aretha Franklin's song "Dr. FeelGood."

theater/theatre (See **drama.**)

"theatre of the absurd" (See **the absurd.**)

theme The dominating idea stated indirectly in a literary work. It is also the central idea that provides insight into human behavior and life. Recurring themes in African American literature include journey, liberation, freedom, endurance, invisibility, literacy, the **American Dream,** hope, homeplace, heritage, migration, struggle, escape, and survival. Contemporary writers are less predictable when it comes to theme. The theme may range from any of the above to love, death, family, integrity, insanity, childhood innocence and experience, friendships, and heterosexual or homosexual relationships. (See also **leitmotif.**)

Third World (See **diasporic literature** and **postcolonialism.**)

toasts A creative narrative that is used to pay tribute to the "superbad." It is a loose and episodic structure that employs rhetorical embellishment and imaginative **imagery.** The **hero** of the toasts is defiant, fearless, rebellious, and full of braggadocio about **sexuality** and **heroism** (see, for instance, Frankee and Albert of the popular song "Frankie and Johnnie" or heroes of "Stag-o-Lee" and "The Signifying Monkey"). A less known hero appearing in a toast is Dolemite who "[a]t the age of one . . . was drinking whiskey and gin / At the age of two . . . was eating the bottles it came in" (Bruce Jackson, *"Get Your Ass in the Water and Swim Like Me: Narrative Poetry from Black Oral Tradition* 1974:58, lines 11–12). African American writers influenced by the toasts include Sterling Brown in "Slim in Hell" (*The Last Ride of Wild Bill and Eleven Narrative Poems* 1975:40) and Walter Mosley in his portrayal of Mouse in *Devil in a Blue Dress* (1990). See also Iceberg Slim's *Pimp: The Story of My Life* (1967); Julius Lester's collection *Black Folktales* (1967); and toasts collected in *Call and Response: The Riverside Anthology of African American Literature,* ed. by Hill et al. (1997:813–18).

tone The term refers to the writer's attitude, manner, mood, and moral outlook in a work—all of which can be determined by identifying, for instance, the writer's choice of words, patterns of words, and phrases or expressions.

tradition The term denotes an inherited past or records of how a particular people have lived in the world. Immediate clues exist in literary art forms such as aphorisms, literature, speech, and music, and in **folklore,** customs, and other conventions.
(See also **oral tradition.**)

Reference for further reading: Trudier Harris, "The Meaning of a Tradition," in *The New Cavalcade* (1991).

tragedy A form of **drama** concerned with the ordinary man or woman. Within this dramatic form, most **heroes** and **heroines** are tragic and worthy of pity—not because of some error in judgment but most often because of their experiences (e.g., social injustice and/or economic inequality) within an unjust and unequal society: Amiri Baraka's (LeRoi Jones's) *Dutchman* (1964) or *The Slave* (1964); Ed Bullins's *Goin' a Buffalo* (1968); Mary Burill's *Aftermath* (1919); Alice Childress's *Florence* (1948) or *Trouble in Mind* (1955); Charles Fuller's *A Soldier's Play* (1984); Shirley Graham *It's Morning* (1940) or *Dust the Earth* (1938); Lorraine Hansberry's *A Raisin in the Sun* (1959); Theodore Ward's production *Big White Fog* (1938); August Wilson's *Ma Rainy's Black Bottom* (1982); and Richard Wright's production *Native Son* (1986). See also the short story "A Summer Tragedy" (1928) by Arna Bontemps and the poem "Strange Legacies" (*Crisis* 40 (August 1928):242) by Sterling Brown.

From the plots of these works, there arises most often cries of anguish and terror, protest and rage, and warnings of violence and bloodshed—directed most often toward perpetrators of social injustices or economic disparity. On some occasions, through music or other forms of an African American **oral tradition,** writers attempt to recenter spiritually a displaced or unfulfilled character. See, particularly, C. J. Memphis in Charles Fuller's *A Soldier's Play,* or Marentha in August Wilson's *The Piano Lesson* (1986).
(See also **mulatto.**)

trickster A folk **hero** who is disempowered yet he triumphs over his adversary, using his superior wit and guile. Central to the tale is the trickster who demonstrates will and ingenuity or the aptness "to get ovah." The trickster is usually an animal with human personalities. In the African American community, the trickster has survived as **Brer Rabbit** and in popular slave **folktales** as **John de Conquerer**. In the Caribbean, the animal trickster, the Spider, has survived, as well.

In contemporary African American lore, characteristics of the indestructible trickster can be found in the boll weevil, an enemy to the cotton industry and to the South. African American characters pull from African American lore to create trickster figures. See, for instance, Charles Chesnutt's Uncle Julius in the collection *The Conjure Woman* (1899). See also Cecil Brown's Efan in *The Life and Loves of Jiveass Nigger* (1969).

References for further reading: Ralph Ellison, "Change the Joke and Slip the Yoke," in *Shadow and Act* (1964); Ropo Sekoni, *Folk Poetics: A Sociosemiotic Study of Yoruba Trickster Tales* (1994).

"two-ness" (See **double consciousness.**)

ubi sunt A **motif** in, for instance, **Black Arts** poetry where the persona questions the **hero** or **heroine** as to what has happened.

Umbra Workshop, the The first post–Civil Rights era literary group that, in a radical sense, experimented with and established a distinct African American voice within the literary establishment. Based in Manhattan's Lower East Side, the Umbra Workshop helped to increase readership among African Americans of African American literature. Similar groups such as the Free Lance Group of Cleveland and the Dasein Group of Washington, D.C., also experimented with language, structure, and form in black **poetry**. According to Craig Werner, Umbra, Free Lance, and Dasein link writers from the **Chicago Renaissance** of the 1940s, the universalist modernist of the 1950s (James Baldwin, Ralph Ellison, Robert Hayden, and Melvin B. Tolson), and the **Black Arts Movement** of the 1960s.

underground railroad Organized escape routes and schemes (e.g., hidden rooms) that were devised to assist slaves in their flight from the **South** to northern cities such as New York and Boston, and even to provinces of Canada. Abolitionists who organized and oversaw the escapes were, among others, Quakers. The slave Harriet Tubman who guided a multitude of slaves to the North and Canada has become mythologized as the "Moses" of her race. Literary works that use the underground railroad as **motif** include: *Harriet Tubman, Conductor on the Underground Railroad* (1964) by Ann Petry; *Dessa Rose* (1986) by Sherley Anne Williams; and *Beloved* (1987) by Toni Morrison.

understatement (See **litotes.**)

Up South A term to connote that a northern city has the racial bigotry usually associated with the South.

"urban space" A term that is understood in conjunction with **"safe space."** Both terms point to ways in which ex-slaves attempted to maintain control of the spiritual self when faced with displacement and dislocation in the North. To maintain a sense of self-identity and self-worth and to resist his assigned place in society by Euro Americans (see the **great chain of being**), the ex-slave (the former southerner) demonstrated will and ingenuity through his music (**spirituals, work songs, field cries**); speech (**ballads,** folk **sermons,** and **folktales**); and **dance.** In the South, be it in the home, in the fields, or in the master's house, the music, **trickster** tales, field cries, sermons, and other oral traditions became "safe spaces" where the slave "got ovah" or felt self-control in spite of his reality.

When the ex-slave migrated to the North, again, he had to contend with the control of Euro Americans via segregation, racism, discriminations, and, of course, the detrimental forces of urbanization. While the ex-slave brought with him **traditions** that had helped him to maintain a sense of spiritual wholeness in the **South,** the North proved a greater challenge. As Farah Jasmine Griffin points out in her discussions of the **migration narrative** in *"Who Set You Flowin'?" The African-American Migration Narrative* (1995), the misguided and weak among the ex-slaves were vulnerable. Other means of maintaining control of one's self-identity and self-worth in urban America were needed. The "urban spaces" became **gospel songs, jazz,** and **blues**. Also, there were barber shops, beauty shops, pool halls, dance halls, kitchenettes, churches, and even street corners.

Reference for further reading: bell hooks, "Homeplace: A Site of Resistance," in *Yearning: Race, Gender, and Cultural Politics* (1990).

"veil, the" (See **double consciousness.**)

verbal rituals (See **grammar of the sermon, lies, signifying, testifyin,** and **toasts.**)

verisimilitude A term that denotes an appearance of truth or reality in a literary work.

vernacular The everyday language of the African American; patterns and rhythms of an African American way of life. A continuum of communal language practices; the mother tongue.

voice (See **oracular.**)

voodoo/vodun Misunderstood in Western culture, voodoo/vodun is defined almost always as witchcraft and superstitious beliefs and practices. But, as Robert Farris Thompson writes in *Flash of the Spirit: African and Afro-American Art and Philosophy* (1984), "Vodun, first elaborated in Haiti. . . , is a vibrant, sophisticated synthesis of the traditional religion of Dahomey, Yorubaland, and Kongo with an infusion of Roman Catholicism" (163). The religion promotes civility, peace, and reconciliation (called Rada) and it uses charms for healing and for attacking evil forces (called Petro). The use of charms has been elaborated in African American communities, particularly communities in South Carolina and New Orleans.

"We wear the mask" A phrase that suggests a performative act of subversion and survival. The phrase has been popularized by the underprivileged in the **trickster** tales and by Paul Laurence Dunbar's "We Wear the Mask" (1895). As Dunbar summarizes:

> We wear the mask that grins and lies,
> It hides our cheeks and shades our eyes,
> (Gates and McKay 1997:896.)

Like many African performances, "wearing the mask" allows African Americans, particularly prior to the 1960s, to grin and lie in the presence of their adversaries or oppressors in order to "get ovah."

womanism/womanist A theory in continuum about audacious African American women committed to the survival and wholeness of entire people, female and male.

(See also **Africana womanism.**)

References for further reading: Tuzyline Jita Allan, *Womanist and Feminist Aesthetics: A Comparative Review* (1995); Carol Marsh-Lockett, "Womanism" (1997); Alice Walker, *In Search of Our Mothers' Gardens: Womanist Prose* (1983); Sherley Anne Williams, "Some Implication of Womanist Theory" (2000).

"word, the" (See **nommo.**)

work songs Secular songs that were sung by African Americans to the rhythm of work. During slavery this work included working in the fields and in the domiciles of the plantations; after slavery, the work included working on levees, chain gangs, lumber camps, railroads, or wherever African Americans were involved in manual labor. Like most African American folk literature, work songs are built on an African foundation: **improvisational** and communal—that is, spontaneous and collective. Too, the work songs are of an **antiphonal** structure (stanzaic with chorus or **call and response**). A popular belief among slaveholders and even others, long after slavery, has been that the work songs increased productivity among the workers, but, to the contrary, work songs like most of the early secular and sacred art, expressed resignation or resistance to forced labor or to oppressive work conditions. On other occasions, the songs expressed personal emotions among the creators to recent events; resentment against injustices; and yearnings for freedom or for loved ones. Unlike other literary art forms such as the **blues** (although the work song is a forerunner to the rural blues), work songs did not rely on **irony** or double meaning. The songs were straightforward.

Sterling A. Brown has been the most notable poet to experiment with the structure of the work song in his poetry. See, for instance, Brown's "Southern Road" (1931):

> Swing dat hammer—hunh—
> Steady bo';
> Swing dat hammer—hunh—
> Steady bo';
> Ain't no rush, bebby
> Long ways to go.
> (James Weldon Johnson, ed. (1922) 1931:250–51.)

"worrying the line" A structural **blues** form used by writers, particularly poets, for emphasis or effect or to underscore an **interjection** that is a bit of wisdom. As pointed out by Stephen E. Henderson, like the musician, writers worry the line via changes in stress and pitch—that is, changes in the word order, additional or exclamatory phrases, or repetition of phrases within the line itself. See, for example, Langston Hughes, who strives to emphasize the themes of truth and loneliness in "Young Gal's Blues":

> I'm gonna walk to the graveyard
> 'Hind ma friend, Miss Cora Lee
> *Hind ma* dear friend Cora Lee
> Cause when I'm dead some
> Body'll have to walk behind me (Emphasis added.)
> (Hughes 1974:148.)

See also Sterling Brown's interjection of wisdom in "New Steps" (*Southern Roads* 1932:92):

> Good times, seems like, ain't fuh las'—
> Nebber *de real* good times, dey ain't—(Emphasis added.)

References for further reading: Stephen E. Henderson, "Worrying the Line: Notes on Black American Poetry" (1988); Sherley Anne Williams, "The Blues Roots of Contemporary Afro-American Poetry" (1979).

Yoruba The language and people of southwestern Nigeria associated with forms of verbal art in the African American community.

Criticism and Theory

Ambiguity

Writing in *The Journey Back: Issues in Black Literature and Criticism* (1980), Houston Baker Jr. raises interest in ambiguity as a term for critical study in African American letters. Echoing William Empson, who contends that "words connote as much as they denote in terms of meaning" (*Seven Types of Ambiguity* 1930), Baker contends that in African American literary texts, there are "semantic levels" of meaning. He insists that when readers take African American literature at face value, they risk not getting to its "communicative context."

To illustrate his point, Baker cites a critical review of Charles W. Chesnutt's *The Conjure Woman* (1899) in the *Atlantic* appearing the same year. Based on the review, Chesnutt's work "seemed guaranteed of [the] success . . . that had earlier greeted one of [his] stories [from the book]" (157). That story was "The Goophered Grapevine" (1899) and as Baker tells, "it had been praised [earlier] by white readers" (157) (the audience of black text in the 1800s). What Chesnutt's white reviewers praised or failed to praise is what helps to raise questions of ambiguity in African American letters. According to Baker with regard to the reviews:

> Chesnutt's short stor[ies] seemed [to his white readers] simply another effort in a long line of works deducted to a portrait of blacks as amiable, childlike creatures devoted to strumming and humming all day on the plantation. (157)

Baker's question is "Have readers taken Chesnutt's stories at face value?" In other words, have they assigned a value by their own limiting attitudes and patterns of judgment? But, more important, are they uninformed of the fact that

> If blacks "entered" the English language with values and concepts **anti-thetical** to those of the white externality surrounding them, then their vocabulary is less important than the underlying codes, or semantic fields, that governed meaning [?] (157)

What Baker is suggesting is that readers who move "exclusively within the boundaries of their own semantic categories" risk taking "the words of the black work or verbal art at face value, or worse, at a value assigned by their own limiting attitudes and patterns of judgment" (157).

To demonstrate how meaning could have been enhanced, Baker rereads Chesnutt, paying close attention to "semantic levels of black culture":

> In African American culture, a forceful and powerful figure is the **conjurer**. Former slaves, as they were in Chesnutt's *The Conjure Woman,* constructed with the assistance of the conjurer, a psychological defense against serfdom. Such a role of the conjurer and such an attitude of resistance by the slaves are important to understanding the Chesnutt stories. (158)

In other words, Chesnutt's "linguistic clues" that govern "an appropriate reading" or that enhance the "communicative context" of stories in *The Conjure Woman* have not been recognized.

Baker's commentary on ambiguity seems to point beyond the 1800s to suggest that even in the twenty-first century, the reader that is not conscious of the "lexical and conceptual fields" in African American literary texts is "ill-prepared" to understand African American literature.

Discussions of ambiguity as a term for critical study in African American letters have existed prior to Baker's *The Journey Back.* Ralph Ellison in the 1950s, Amiri Baraka in the 1960s, and Toni Morrison in the 1980s have called for more attention to the "lexical and conceptual fields" that permeate African American literary texts, or at least to pay attention to the "semantic levels of black culture." Discussions of ambiguity as a term for critical study continue in the 1990s with critics such as Karla Holloway in *Moorings and Metaphors: Figures of Culture and Gender in Black Women's Literature* (1992). The point is that ambiguity as a critical term in African American letters is documented.

In "The Art of Fiction: An Interview" (1955), Ellison voices his concerns in this manner:

Q. Have the critics given you any constructive help in your writing, or changed in any way your aims in fiction?

A. No, except that I have a better idea of how the critics react, of *what they see and fail to see, of how their sense of life differs with mine and mine with theirs. In some instances they were nice for the wrong reasons.* In the United States and I don't want this to sound like an apology for my own failures—*some reviewers did not see what was before them.* (Emphasis added.) (176)

In his essay "expressive language" (1963), LeRoi Jones/Amiri Baraka writes:

[F]or every item in the world, there are a *multiplicity of definitions* that fit. And *every word we use could mean something else. And at the same time. The culture fixes the use, and usage. And in "pluralistic" America, one should always listen very closely when he is being talked to. The speaker might mean something completely different from what we think we're hearing.* (200)(Emphasis added.)

In "Rootedness: The Ancestor as Foundation" (1980), Toni Morrison reveals:

There is something very special and very identifiable about [African American literature] and it is my struggle to find that *elusive but identifiable style. . . .* My general disappointment in some of the criticism that my work has received has nothing to do with approval. It has something to do with the vocabulary used in order to describe these things. *I don't like to find my books condemned as bad or praised as good when that condemnation or that praise is based on criteria from other paradigms. I would much prefer that they were discussed or embraced based on the success of their accomplishment within the culture out of which I write.* (200) (Emphasis added.)

Writing in *Moorings and Metaphors* (1992), Holloway extends discussions of the "multiplicity of meaning" or the "elusive" style in African American literature. Focusing on African and African American women writers, Holloway thinks that words in novels by women of color are not "ambivalent" but "displaced" because of shifting narrative structure. While her terminology to define ambiguity shifts somewhat, she adds, nonetheless, to the critical discussion of why it behooves the reader not to always read African American literature at face value:

> The narrative-structure in [women writers'] works *force the words within the texts to represent (re)memories in/or events and ideas that revise and multiply meanings. A result of this revision is that what seems to be ambivalence is actually a sign of displacement....* [These works] are *shifting, shape-changing texts.* (56) (Emphasis added.)

Implied by Baker, Ellison, Baraka, Morrison, and Holloway is that much may go "unseen" by analysts who are ill-prepared for the ambiguity of language (and structure) in African American literature.

Influence

In *The Folk Roots of Contemporary Afro-American Poetry* (1974) and later in *The Afro-American Novel and Its Tradition* (1987), Bernard Bell describes African American literary art as "hybrid .. [,] derived from the sedimented indigenous roots of black American folklore and literary genres of the Western world (1987:xii). Within this definition, Bell suggests that influence-study in African American letters could range from African American **myth** and **folklore** to Western art forms.

Prior to the 1970s, influence-study in African American letters is more or less accomplished thematically, symbolically, and/or metaphorically. By the late 1970s, however, influence-study becomes informed by African American culture and Western critical thought such as **structuralism** (the study of rhetorical parallels, echoes, patterns, reflections, and contrasts) and **post-structuralism** (the study of the "text read against itself" or deconstruction). In *From Behind the Veil: A Study of Afro-American Narrative* (1991), Robert Stepto becomes one of the earliest critics of African American literature to devote chapters to what might be called influence-study in African American letters. Focusing on **intertextuality** (the nonthematic manner by which texts . . . respond to other texts), he explains his interest:

> [A] major tradition in African American narratives is an intertextual one in which each generation defines its literary task in terms of earlier writers and in terms of a "pregeneric myth" or the quest for freedom and literacy or "intimacy," with writers and texts outside the normal boundaries of nonliterary structures. (16)

In *Figures in Black: Words, Signs, and Racial Self* (1987), Henry Louis Gates returns to influence-study in African American letters. Like Stepto, Gates seeks paradigms within and outside the boundaries of African American literary criticism. Echoing Harold Bloom's "Anxiety of Influence"—that is, the usurpation of male precursor by another male writer in order to establish independence and autonomy—Gates is interested in the *refiguration* or the *revision* of precursory texts by African American male writers. Like Stepto, Gates relies on intertextual sensibilities in order to discover how in relationships between African American male precursors and protégés, the latter comes to "a new way of seeing." In his study, Gates focuses on Richard Wright's *Native Son* (1940) and *Black Boy* (1945) and Ralph Ellison's *Invisible Man* (1952). From his analysis, Gates reveals the following:

> Ellison in his fiction signifies upon Wright by parodying Wrights' literary structures through repetition and difference. . . . The play of language . . . starts with the titles: Wright's *Native Son* and *Black Boy*, connoting race, self and presence. Ellison tropes with *Invisible Man*, invisibility an ironic response, of absence, to the would-be presence of "blacks" and "natives" . . . Wright's protagonist, voiceless to the last, Ellison signifies upon with a nameless protagonist. Ellison's protagonist is nothing voice, [but] it is he [not the author as in *Native Son*] who shapes, edits, and narrates his own tale (246).

(See also **parody, repetition** under Criticism and Theory, **invisibility.**) Continuing, Gates writes,

> By explicitly repeating and reversing key figures of Wright's fiction . . . Ellison expose[s] Wright's naturalism as merely a hardened conventional representation of "the Negro problem" and perhaps part of "the Negro problem" itself. . . . Ellison record[s] *a new way of seeing and defining both a new manner of representation and its relation to the concept.* (246)(Emphasis added.)

Gates's unveiling of his study of influence among male writers is more detailed than is presented here, but the point to be made is that because of his study of Wright as precursory figure and Ellison as protégé, he (Gates) is able to illustrate the importance of influence as a term for critical study in African American letters. His study anticipates questions for future studies. For example, if as "revisionary" protégé, Ellison negates the influences of Wright and **naturalism** and clears imaginative space for himself, are there other examples of an "anxiety of influence" in African American literary studies? How has usurpation of precursory figures by protégés influenced the African American literary tradition? Influenced the African American literary canon?

Influence-study of female precursory figures and female protégés exists most noticeably in Michael Awkward's *Inspiriting Influence: Tradition, Revision, and Afro-American Women's Novels* (1989) and Ann duCille's *The Coupling Convention: Sex, Text and Tradition in Black Women's Fiction* (1993). While these critics agree on the "unique" tradition of African American women writers and the presence of precursory figures, they do not agree on who the literary models are.

Coined by Michael Awkward in the introduction to his work of the same title, "Inspiriting Influence" is a term that suggests intertextual responses between female writers and their literary texts. But, rather than usurpation of a ancestor or competition between women writers, "inspiriting influence" suggests a tradition of "nurturance and dependence" among African American women writers. Michael Awkward, along with Ann duCille, argues convincingly that "the [African American] female precursor represents ... a literary forebear whose texts are celebrated even as they are revised" (7) by other African American women writers. Furthermore, Awkward, along with duCille, recognizes the tradition out of which African American women work to be "a unique bond, an energetic exploration for and embrasure of [African American] female precursorial figures" (7). Yet, when it comes to identifying a female precursor or female precursors of this tradition, the critics begin to disagree.

Awkward, along with a number of other critics, points to Zora Neale Hurston as precursory ancestor to women writers:

> Hurston's position as initiator of an Afro-American woman's tradition in novels can be seen in subsequent Afro-American women writers' refigurations of Hurston's complex delineation of black female unity in *Their Eyes Were Watching God* in their novels' content and form. (8)

Critic duCille disagrees that Hurston is "the model" of influence and imitation, especially for an entire tradition of women writers. She takes Awkward to task on his decision to assign to Hurston such a distinction:

> Zora Neale Hurston did not give birth to herself, unread and unassisted by literary models and inspiriting influences. Hurston, too, passed through a birth canal that reaches back ... not only through folklore

and slave narratives and blues rhythms, but through the fiction of such precursors as Frances Harper and Pauline Hopkins, as well as that of her contemporaries Jessie Fauset, Nella Larsen, Alice Dunbar Nelson and Marita Bonner. . . . If this sisterhood [among African American women writers] indeed "inspirits" works of art that configure into a tradition, what are the origins of that sisterhood? Who are Hurston's inspiriting sisters? Who are Hurston's literary precursors? (82)

In the twenty-first century, influence-study as a term of critical study in African American letters continues. If, as Bernard Bell contends, African American literature is "hybrid" due to its "indigenous roots of black American folklore and literary genres of the Western world," then the ubiquitous term lends itself to ongoing discussions of authors, past and present texts, the canon, and traditions.

Literary History

In 1970, in the essay "Afro-American Literary Critics: An Introduction," Darwin T. Turner rendered a dismal conclusion about the visibility of the African American critic: "If . . . one wanted . . . silence. . . , ask for the names of black literary critics" (54). Much has changed since 1970 to make the names of critics who study African American literary texts prominent household names. But, when it comes to identifying literary historians or cultural historians in African American letters, there may still be the issue of visibility. Turner's definition of literary historian (used interchangeably with cultural historian) is one who "applauds[s] more than . . . appraise[s], for his [or her] purpose [is] to record literary achievement and to encourage additional activity [in the canon and in the criticism]" (62). In his study of literary critics prior to 1970, Turner offered these explanations for the lack of visibility:

> [B]lack critics failed to make America see them, to say nothing of reading or hearing their words. [In the Eighteenth and Nineteenth Centuries] . . . [t]he best-known critics of Afro-American literature [were] white (54).

In the twenty-first century, the best-known critics of African American literature are African American and Euro American. But the least known among them are the literary or cultural historians (black or white).

In the Norton critical edition of Harriet Jacobs's *Incidents in the Life of a Slave Girl* (2001), editors Nellie McKay and Frances Smith Foster return discussions to the "silenced" or the invisibility of the literary or cultural historian. McKay and Foster's approach is indirect, but their desire to acknowledge the historian in African American letters does not go unnoticed. For example, the editors pay tribute to Jean Fagin Yellin for her "painstaking archival research," "meticulous work," and "patience" in determining in the 1980s the author of *Incidents* (xiii). In their efforts to recognize the preliminary work of literary or cultural historians in general, McKay and Foster keep before the reader significant questions for consideration: Why does historical research matter? What is the role of the literary or cultural historian in shaping the African American literary canon? What is the function of the literary or cultural historian in African American letters?

In an unpublished speech delivered at the PreScholars in the Humanities Symposium, held in Atlanta in March of 2002, Frances Smith Foster responds to some of these questions. She impresses upon her audience that the vital role of the literary or cultural historian is to influence the quality of scholarship in African American letters. Foster emphasizes that because of the work of literary or cultural historians (uncovering personal correspondence, articles in newspapers, journals, and magazines usually packed away in archives; interviews; maps; and various other documents), critics and scholars in the academy as well as others outside the academy are without question free "to engage texts with wide-ranging critical curiosity" or even to authenticate a literary canon.

Foster goes on to hypothesize about the continued "silence" (or **invisibility**) of the literary or cultural historian in African American letters:

> My point here is that if [literary and cultural historians] do not do the work of rediscovering, reinterpreting and revisioning our pasts, someone else will and those someones may not be as capable, as conscientious, as ultimately concerned with getting it right.

To underscore this concern for a more visible literary or cultural historian, Foster paraphrases Toni Morrison from *The Bluest Eye* (1970):

> [Others] substituted good grammar for intellect; [others] switched habits to simulate maturity; [others] rearranged lies and called it truth, seeing in the new pattern of an old idea the Revelation and the word. (159)

Like Darwin Turner, Nellie McKay, and others, Frances Foster considers "scholars and readers everywhere" to be "indebted" to literary or cultural historians for their archival work and presence in arts and letters. As she concludes, she challenges the audience:

> Think for a moment at the research you have done on Harriet Jacobs. Virtually none of it was possible twenty years ago. Imminent scholars once proclaimed that *Incidents in the Life of a Slave Girl* was a novel by an Euro-American woman named Lydia Maria Child. Jean Fagin Yellin found the documents that proved them wrong. . . . [In addition] [u]ntil recently, Frances Harper was known primarily as an "anti-Slavery poet". . . . And as late as 1986, an authoritative history of African American literature stated that between the Civil War and 1886, there were no novels published by African Americans. What we have learned about Frances E. W. Harper's life and literature has not only revised what we thought we knew about her canon but also our notions of the African American literary canon and our cultural history in general.

Here Foster is referring to her own discoveries in the 1990s of three novels that were actually published by Harper between 1869 and 1876: *Minnie's Sacrifice, Sowing and Reaping,* and *Trial and Triumph.*

In the twenty-first century, most literary or cultural historians function as literary critics and theorists in African American letters. See, for instance, the edited works of Gates such as *The Schomburg Library of Nineteenth-Century Black Women Writers* (1988); *Invisible Poets: Afro-Americans of the Nineteenth Century* (1989), edited by Joan Rita Sherman; *Wines in the Wilderness: Plays by African American Women from the Harlem Renaissance to the Present* (1990) and *Their Place on the Stage: Black Women Playwrights in America* (1988), both edited by Elizabeth Brown-Guillory; *Black Women Playwrights* (1998), edited by Carole Marsh-Lockett; and forgotten novelists that appear in Bernard Bell's chronicle *The Afro-American Novel and Its Tradition* (1987). One should also add to the list the following: Henry Louis Gates's discoveries of *Our Nig* (1859) by Harriet Wilson and *The Bondswoman's Narrative* (1859) by Hannah Crafts; William Andrews's Web site on slave narratives (wandrews@email.unc.edu); and, again, Frances Foster's discovery in 1990s of Frances Harper's novels *Minnie's Sacrifice, Sowing and Reaping,* and *Trial and Triumph.*

In the new millennium, the charge will be to discuss more at length why historical research matters?

Reference for further reading: Darwin T. Turner, "Afro-American Literary Critics: An Introduction" (1970).

Memory

African captives who were brought to America as slaves in the 1600s were unwilling to accept America's conjectured stereotypes of the African as uncivilized inhabitant or as barbarian of "a dark continent." In her article "The Slave Ship Dance" (in *Black Imagination and the Middle Passage,* ed. Maria Diedrich, Henry Louis Gates Jr., and Carl Petersen, 1999:33–46), Geneviève Fabre cites slaves' earliest attempts to hold on to their true identity through "memory" of a culture (or cultures) and of a heritage that spoke differently of their self-worth.

According to Fabré, when brought to the decks of the slave ships, many African captives chose not to remain in captivity. They leapt into the Atlantic Ocean to their deaths. For many reasons, other African slaves elected to bring "shape and meaning to their experiences." They elected to find ways to create a defense against psychological "control and manipulations." Fabré cites one of many cruel realities of the **middle passage:**

> [on the decks of slave ships] African captives were encouraged or forced to dance and sometimes "whipped" into cheerfulness (34).

According to Fabre, forced dancing became not only a means of forced "cheerfulness" but also one of the earliest "sites of memory" and "of [figurative] escape" by Africans. Citing Olaudah Equiano in *The Interesting Narrative of the Life of Olaudah Equiano, or Gustavus Vassa, the African* (1789), Fabre validates Africans' determination, even while in the belly of slave ships, to nurture the spiritual self:

> Slaves (e.g., shipmates and African countrymen) took silent vows either to find a way back home [e.g., death] or to cultivate ties to sustain new communities. (34)

Put another way, the slave ship dance marks one of the earliest steps taken by slaves to create "new communities" via the "still vivid memories" of Africa. Within these "new communities," cultural memory has been "kept and reactivated" via dances, songs, **folktales,** rituals, customs, and practices. To quote Fabre:

> In the slave ship dance, *the basic principles of many performances to come were set [in memory]:* the blending and interplay of dance, song, and music; the call-and-response pattern between dance and music,

between voice and instrument, body, and song. (40) (Emphasis added.)

Writers of African American literature implore "memory" in their writings in order "to cement [the] new communities." The writers include, to name a few, Zora Neale Hurston, Toni Morrison, John Edgar Wideman, Alice Walker, Gloria Naylor, Paule Marshall, Sherley Anne Williams, and Randell Kenan. As illustrated in novels by these writers, memory (or re-memory) is a form of oral culture. People, music, and dance are information. The former has become a speaking document; the latter are oral documents. Discussions of "memory" as creative process are ongoing. According to Melvin Dixon, it is "memory contribut[ing] to the process of cultural recovery" (18–19).

References for further reading: Geneviève Fabre, "The Slave Ship Dance," in *Black Imagination and the Middle Passage* eds. Diedrich et al. (1999); Melvin Dixon, "The Black Writer's Use of Memory," in *History and Memory in African-American Culture* ed. Fabre and O'Meally (1994); and Karla F. C. Holloway, *Moorings and Metaphors: Figures of Culture and Gender in Black Women's Literature* (1992).

Repetition

In 1999, in a literary workshop sponsored by the journal *Callaloo* at Morehouse College, a southern male college in Atlanta, Georgia, distinguished guest novelist John Edgar Wideman asked students to pretend they were editors of an African American literary journal. He wanted the students to decide whether to accept or to reject a story that was being submitted. With characters that were unidentifiable by race and with a setting that was even less familiar in this story, Wideman proceeded to read it. Finally, a student responded that as editor, he would accept the story, for the narrator had used repetition and **improvisation** throughout the story like a **jazz** musician.

According to James A. Snead in the article "Repetition as a figure of black culture" (1984), the term repetition "finds its most characteristic shape in **performance**—for example, "rhythm in music, dance and/[or] language." Snead points to James Brown as an example of a brilliant musical practitioner of repetition:

The format of the Brown "cut" and repetition is similar to that of African drumming: after the band has been "cookin" in a given key and tempo, a cue, either verbal ("Get down" or "Mayfield"—the sax player's name—or "Watch it now") or musical (a brief series of rapid, percussive drum and horn accents), then directs the music to a new level where it stays with more "cookin"—or perhaps a solo—*until a repetition of cues then "cuts" back to the primary tempo.* (216) (Emphasis added.)

Snead points also to the black church as a place that has centered the manifestations of repetition through the nonlinear "circulation and flow" of "music and language." Repetition, through music and language can be cited also in the **sermon** on the "Blackness of Blackness" in Ralph Ellison's *Invisible Man* (1952); in the circularity of fiction, song, and **poetry** in Jean Toomer's *Cane* (1923); in the final song of "Jake," the only son of Solomon in Toni Morrison's *Song of Solomon* (1977); and in the folk poems and other repeated uses of **folklore** in Leon Forrest's *There Is a Tree More Ancient than Eden* (1973) and Ishmael Reed's *Mumbo Jumbo* (1972), *The Free-Lance Pallbearer* (1967) and *Flight to Canada* (1976).

What Wideman was seeking and heard from his audience was that what makes a work African American is not simply African American characters in an African American setting. Rather as implied by the student who spoke, there are cultural markers. In Wideman's narrative, the cultural markers included a rupture or a seemingly unmotivated break (or "cut") with a series of utterances, already in progress and, then, a willed return to prior utterances. In short, the words and phrases when delivered repeatedly signaled repetition—call and response, cyclicality—in the work-in-progress and signaled characteristics of African American text.

Reference for further reading: James A. Snead, "Repetition as a figure of black culture," in *African American Literary Criticism, 1773 to 2000* ed. Ervin (1999).

Representation

As early as the nineteenth century, there have been discussions of representation as a term for critical study in African American letters. As suggested by Henry Louis Gates in *The Signifying Monkey* (1988), concerns of representation have meant concerns about "reality imitated in a text" (172)—that is, How to portray the African American in literary art? What are the proper manners of representation?

For Critic W. S. Scarborough, writing in "The Negro in Fiction" (*The Anglo-American Magazine* [1899]), the manner was to gain sympathy for African Americans by presenting African American characters as human beings much like their white and middle class counterparts—that is, as aspiring middle class individuals:

> Let the Negro writer of fiction make of his pen and brain all-compelling forces to treat of that which he well knows, best knows, and give it to the world with all the imaginative power possible, with all the magic touch of an artist. Let him portray the Negro's love and hates, his hopes and fears, his ambitions, his whole life, in such a way that the world will weep and laugh over the pages. (67)

Moreover, for Scarborough, the writer was

> [to] find the touch that makes all nature kin, forgetting completely that they the hero and heroine are God's bronze images, but knowing only men and women with joys and sorrows that belong *alike to the whole human family*. (67) (Emphasis added.)

A more familiar creative writer of the nineteenth century, Frances Watkins Harper joins the discussion. She is in favor of portraying "feelings that [were] general." In a letter written in 1861 to Thomas Hamilton, the editor of *The Anglo-African Magazine*, Harper instructs writers: "We must write less of issues that are particular and more of feelings that are general" (Gates Jr., *The Signifying Monkey: A Theory of Afro-American Literary Criticism*, 276n4). The critics and creative writers of the nineteenth century are agreeing to representations of the African American "alike the whole human family."

When creative and critical writers gather in Harlem in the early twentieth century, stances on representation shift. According to Hazel Carby, writing in "The Quicksands of Representative, Rethinking Black Cultural Politics" (Carby 1987):

> Before World War I, the overwhelming majority of blacks were in the South, at a vast physical and metaphorical distance from those intellectuals who represented the interests of the race. After the war, black intellectuals had to confront the black masses on the streets of their cities and responded in a variety of ways. (164)

In short, after World War I and following the migration of African Americans to the urban cities, there was no longer a unitary "people" who could be represented. Writers and critics had to respond in a variety of ways to the various classes of African Americans.

Those critics and writers who saw representation as unchanged in the

1920s included, for instance, W.E.B. DuBois and George Schuyler. As DuBois states in "The Criteria of Negro Art" (1926), the end remains to gain "sympathy and human interest" from mainstream America.

Addressing writers in his article, "Instructions for Contributors," published in *The Saturday Evening Quill* (1929), George Schuyler is more explicit about the manner of representation. At length, he writes

> Stories must be full of human interest. Short, simple words. No attempt to parade erudition to the bewilderment of the reader. No colloquialisms such as "nigger," "darky," "coon," etc. Plenty of dialogue, and language that is realistic.
>
> We will not accept any stories that are depressing, saddening, or gloomy. Our people have enough troubles without reading about any. We want them to be interested, cheered, and buoyed up; comforted, gladdened, and made to laugh.
>
> Nothing that casts the least reflection on contemporary moral or sex standards will be allowed. Keep away from the erotic! Contributions must be clean and wholesome.
>
> Everything must be written in that intimate manner that wins the reader's confidence at once and makes him or her feel that what is written is being spoken exclusively to that particular reader.
>
> No attempt should be made to be obviously artistic. Be artistic, of course, but "put it over" on the reader so he or she will be unaware of it.
>
> Stories must be swiftly moving, gripping the interest and sweeping on to a climax. The heroine should always be beautiful and desirable, sincere and virtuous. The hero should be of the he-man type, but not stiff, stereotyped, or vulgar. The villain should obviously be a villain and of the deepest-dyed variety: crafty, unscrupulous, suave, and resourceful. Above all, however, these characters must live and breathe, and be just ordinary folks such as the reader has met. The heroine should be of the brown-skin type.
>
> All matter should deal exclusively with Negro life. Nothing will be permitted that is likely to engender ill feelings between blacks and whites. The color problem is bad enough without adding any fuel to the fire. (20)

(Schuyler 1929)

When Schuyler's criteria of African American art and representation of African American characters are read against other notable critics and writers of the Harlem Renaissance such as Langston Hughes and critics and writers of the Chicago Renaissance such as Richard Wright and Ann Petry, he suggests representation in print in the 1920s, 1930s, and 1940s is prescriptive. Challenges seem inevitable.

Writing in "The Negro Artist and the Racial Mountain" (1926), Hughes seems to capture the opposition to the more conservative Schuyler and DuBois. As Hughes contends, **heroines** were not to be portrayed always as "beautiful," "desirable," "sincere," "virtuous," and of "the brown-skin type." And **heroes** were not to be portrayed always as "just ordinary folk. . . . such as the reader has met." Hughes insists the African American character is "beautiful" and "ugly too" and should be portrayed as such. Furthermore, Hughes insists "[the African American] artist must be free to choose what he does," including the use of "low-down fol[k]" as subjects (45–48).

The discussion of representation continues among critical and creative writers of the 1930s, 1940s, and 1950s. Writing in "Blueprint for Negro Writing" (1937:200), Richard Wright warns against "a sort of conspicuous ornamentation" that was being called for by DuBois, Schuyler, and others. Like Hughes, Wright opposes using literature as a manner of "plead[ing] with white America for [sympathy] and justice." As spelled out in "How Bigger Was Born" (1940), Wright insists on representation that is "so hard and deep" that readers are forced to face reality—and "without the consolation of tears" (454; reprinted in *Native Son* by Richard Wright. New York: Perennial Classics, 1998.)

For Ann Petry, a peer of Richard Wright's, the writer must allow characters "[to] battle with themselves to save their [own] souls" because "[t]heir defeat or their victory [should be]. . . their own." While in her essay "The Novel as Social Criticism" (1950) Petry agrees with critics and writers that wish to use literature to help audiences "[to] know and understand" African American life—for example, that these were the character's thoughts, dreams, faith, difficulties and triumphs, she disagrees with those writers and critics who urge others to manipulate the characters in order to promote a political or social end. Petry insists:

> Once the novelist begins to manipulate his characters to serve the interests of his theme [or some social or political end] they [the characters] lose whatever vitality they had when their creator first thought about them. (97)

In the 1960s and 1970s, writers and critics begin to challenge previous notions of representation and of an African American literary aesthetics. For example, Carolyn F. Gerald, writing in "The Black Writer and His Role"

(1969), encourages writers and critics of the 1960s and 1970s "[to] reject white attempts at portraying black reality" (133). Larry Neal, writing in "The Black Arts Movement" is even more emphatic: "[The] art [will speak] directly to the needs and aspirations of Black America" (122). The writers and critics of the 1960s and 1970s are adamant also about how to represent the African American in literature. According to Gerald, the African American would not be represented "by proxy and in someone else's image" (131), but by familiar symbols and icons from the African American community. Neal insists further that "[i]n order to perform this task, the Black Arts Movement [was] propose[ing] a radical reordering of the Western cultural aesthetic"—for example, "separate symbolism, mythology, critique, and iconology" (122).

In the late twentieth century, John Edgar Wideman, who seems mindful of prior discussions of and debates over representation, places the term into a new light in African American letters. In the preface to *Breaking Ice: An Anthology of Contemporary African American Fiction* (1990), Wideman writes at length:

> Vernacular language is not enough. Integration is not enough, unless one views mathematical, proportioned [R]epresentation as a goal instead of a step. If what a writer wants is freedom of expression, then, somehow that larger goal must be addressed implicitly/explicitly in our fictions. A story should somehow contain clues that align it with tradition and critique tradition, establish the new space it requires, demands, appropriates, hint at how it may bring forth other things like itself, where these others have, will, and are coming from.... [Finally,] We must continue inventing our stories, sustaining, not sacrificing, the double consciousness that is a necessity for any writing with the ambition of forging its own place. (306)

Echoing Hughes, Wright, Neal, and others Wideman insists on pulling from the culture when representing the people and art:

> Folk culture preserves and expresses an identity, a history, a self-evaluation apart from those destructive, incarcerating images proliferated by the mainline culture. Consciously and unconsciously we've integrated these resources of folk culture into our writing. Our songs, dreams, dances, styles of walk and talk, dressing, cooking, sport, our

heroes and heroines provide a record of how a particular group has lived in the world, in it, but not of it. (305)

Unlike most of the critics and writers of the 1960s and 1970s, Wideman is against "admitting stories [and characters] into some ideologically sound, privileged category." Rather, he advocates "seeking conditions, mining territory that maximizes the possibility of free, original expression" (306).

The contemporary writers of the 1980s and 1990s inherit the wisdom and the lessons learned from prior writings of "privileged category." According to Terry McMillan, writing in the introduction to *Breaking Ice: An Anthology of Contemporary African-American Fiction* (1990), "contemporary writers [are] no longer shocked by racism" as were those of the Harlem Renaissance, nor [are they] "preoccupied with it" as were those of the Black Arts Movement (309). While still socially and politically responsible for uplifting the community, the contemporary writer is governed less "by proxy" and more by individual choices. As Terry McMillan explains:

These days, our work is often as entertaining as it is informative, thought-provoking as it is uplifting. Some of us would like to think that the experiences of our characters are "universal," and yet sometimes a situation could only happen if the color of your character's skin is black. (310)

Furthermore, McMillan reveals that the mindset of the African American writer seems no longer "to be representative of the whole." Rather, she seems to echo Hughes's [African Americans are "beautiful" and "ugly too"]:

Let's face it, there are some trifling men and women that some of us have come across, so much so that we have to write down the effect they had on us. On the other hand, there are also some kind, loving, tender, gentle, successful, and supportive folks in our lives, who also find their way into our work. (310)

In *Breaking Ice*, a familiar work of contemporary literature published in the last decade before the new millennium, critical and creative writers expand discussions of representation. While the medium remains literature, the manner of representation changes. As McMillan concludes, "If anything, we're tying to make sense of ourselves to ourselves" (310).

Reference for further reading: bell hooks, "Revolutionary Attitudes" (1992); Frances Smith Foster, 1993; Thelma Golden, 1984.

Signifying/Signification

As suggested by the title of his book *The Signifying Monkey, A Theory of Afro-American Literary Criticism* (1988), Henry Louis Gates is interested in a theoretical approach to African American literature. Gates seeks a technique or paradigms of analytical interpretation of African American texts. He pulls from within African American culture, and he pulls from other disciplines in other cultures to shape his theory, as well. For example, Gates returns to the **Yoruba** oral tradition to define the repeated "play of language" in African American literary art. As well, he seeks instructions from Western culture—for example, Ferdinand de Saussure's **poststructuralist** theory of signification that is rooted in linguistics. Functioning like an anthropologist and a poststructuralist, Gates establishes a traceable lineage between the African mythological figure **Esu-Elegbara** and the Signifying Monkey (an African American cultural equivalent to **Esu**). At length, in *The Signifying Monkey,* he explains:

> Signifyin(g) as a rhetorical strategy emanates directly from the Signifying Monkey tales (54). . . . I [am arguing] for a consideration of a line of descent for the Signifying Monkey from his Pan-African cousin, Esu-Elegbara. I [am doing] so not because I have unearthed archeological evidence of a transmission process, but because of their functional equivalency as figures of rhetorical strategies and of interpretation. Esu . . . is the Yoruba figure of writing within an oral system. Like Esu, the Signifying Monkey exists, or is figured, in a densely structured discursive universe, one absolutely dependent on the play of differences. The poetry in which the Monkey's antics unfold is a signifying system: in marked contrast to the supposed transparency of normal speech, the poetry of these tales turns upon the free play of language itself, upon the displacement of meanings, precisely because it draws attention to its rhetorical structures and strategies and thereby draws attention to the forces of the signifier. (53)

Here lies Gate's contribution to African American letters: signifying as a critical term of study.

As suggested by Gates in the lengthy passage that follows, signification is a mode of evaluative discourse. In particular, Gates's focus is on the rhetorical trope signifyin(g), which is culturally **"double-voiced"** and which includes the process of **repetition** and revision or **intertextuality** with **differ-**

ence—identifiable via "the play of language" or an encoded intention to say one thing but to mean quite another. As Gates writes,

> Scholars have for some time commented on the peculiar use of the word Signifyin(g) in black discourse. Though sharing some connotations with the standard English-language word (e.g., identical spelling of Signification and the homonym Signification as a mode of discourse as signifier)..., Signifyin(g) has rather unique definitions in black discourse (53). Epitomized by Esu's depictions in sculpture as possessing two mouths ... Signifyin(g) is the figure of the double-voiced (xxv).

Relying also on linguistical studies of the characteristics of signifyin(g) or signifying by African American linguists Claudia Mitchell-Kernan and Geneva Smitherman, and relying on the extended range of meanings of the rhetorical term (e.g., duality, **indirection, irony, sounding, capping, the dirty dozens**), Gates introduces as critical paradigms the following: "double-voiced," the **"talking book,"** and the **"speakerly text."** For clarification, the theorist defines the "talking book" as

> [A] tropological revision ... in which a specific trope is repeated with difference between two or more texts. (xxv)

He defines "speakerly text" in this manner:

> Represented ... is **free indirect** discourse ... with shifts in [the] levels of diction drawn upon to reflect a certain development of self-consciousness in a hybrid character, a character who is neither the novel's protagonist nor the text's disembodied narrator, but a blend of both, an emergent and merging moment of consciousness (xxv–xxvi).

Writing in *The Oxford Companion to African American Literature*, eds. Andrews et al., 1997), Theodore O. Mason Jr. enters discussions of signifyin(g) as a critical term in African American letters. He refers to the term as the "context of African American culture," for it (signifying) "says without explicitly saying, critiques without actually critiquing; and insults without really insulting" (665).

In 1926, in "The Negro Artist and the Racial Mountain," Langston Hughes wrote of his expectations of criticism in African American letters:

> [W]e have an honest American Negro literature, already with us. And within the next decade [next several decades] I expect to see the work

of a growing school . . . [that] model[s] the beauty of dark faces with
. . . technique[s]. (47)

Are Claudia Mitchell-Kernan, Geneva Smitherman, Henry Louis Gates, and
others, the earliest pupils of a school of criticism and/or theory in African
American letters that Hughes foresaw? Is signifyin(g) one of the techniques
that Hughes anticipated would become a critical term of discussion in African American letters?

Collective Unconscious

In the following passage from Toni Morrison's *Sula* (1973), does the narrator
evoke one or more of the archetypes designated as persona, anima/animus,
or shadow when attempting to explain Sula's psychic makeup?

> In a way [Sula's] strangeness, her naivete, her craving *for the other half
> of her equation* was the consequence of an *idle imagination.* Had she
> paints, or clay, or knew the discipline of the dance, or strings; had she
> anything to engage her tremendous curiosity and her gift for meta-
> phor, she might have exchanged the restlessness and preoccupation
> with whim for an activity that provided her with all she yearned for.
> And like any artist with no art form, she became dangerous. (121) (Em-
> phasis added.)

Does Morrison's quotation "the other half of her equation" evoke a Jungian
reading of the text? Does her quotation call to mind Jung's persona (i.e., the
social mask) and the terms anima/animus? As if the human psyche were a
coin, the image on one side is the anima/animus (i.e., the life force, the
soul); on the other side is the persona. Jung's theory of individuation requires both sides of the equation (Guerin et al., 1979:181).

In an attempt to explain Jung's theory of individuation (as gathered
from Guerin et al.):

> The persona is the character's mask that he shows to the world; it is
> any social personality—a personality that is sometimes quite different
> from his true self. In the female psyche, the archetype is called the ani-
> mus, the male psyche, anima. The anima/animus is a kind of mediator
> between the ego (the conscious will or thinking self) and the uncon-
> scious or inner world of the individual. (181)

According to Jung, "to achieve psychological maturity," the individual must have a flexible, viable persona that can be brought into harmonious relation with the other components of his or her psychic make up (the anima/animus) (181). Has Sula's persona proved inadequate in mediating between her ego and the unconscious or inner world?

Next, in the following passage from **Sula,** has the narrator evoked a character type on the community (in African American literature, the community/chorus may function as a character) that projects the Shadow archetype, or what psychologists would call the "latent disposition" or the projection of one's "dark side" onto another?

> Those with husbands had folded themselves into starched coffins, their sides bursting with other people's skinned dreams and bony regrets. Those without men were like sour-tipped needles featuring one constant empty eye.... [Sula] was pariah, then, and knew it. Knew that they *despised her* and believed that they *framed* their hatred as disgust. (122) (Emphasis added.)

In the final pages of *Sula*, does Nel's holler and her experiences thereafter symbolize a death and rebirth—that is, a fundamental pattern of an archetype in myth criticism? Or, is Nel projecting? (a familiar activity of interest to the psychologist):

> Sula? [Nel] whispered. . . . All that time, all that time, I thought I was missing Jude. . . . We was girls together. . . . O Lord, Sula. . . . girl, girl, girlgirlgirl. (174)

In African American letters, critics do not appear to have explored—in book-length—the African American literary imagination and archetypes designated as persona, anima/animus, and shadow. Are exceptions the archetypal sensibilities found in discussions of "racial memory" by Ralph Ellison in "The Art of Fiction: An Interview" (1955); Stephen E. Henderson in *Understanding the New Black Poetry: Black Speech and Black Music as Poetic References* (1973); and Sherley Anne Williams in "The Blues Roots of Contemporary Afro-American Poetry" (1979)?

Carl G. Jung (1875–1961) is the Swiss psychologist most associated with the collective unconscious as a term of study. In "On the Relation of Analytical Psychology to Poetic Art" (see the 1922 essay in *The Norton Anthology of Theory and Criticism* [2001], ed. Vincent Leitch et al.), Jung regards foundational facts of human existence to be archetypal: birth, love, tribal life, et cetera. The recurrence of fundamental facts about human existence [during a birth, death, ritual, etc.] may be called archetypal; when experienced universally, the term is collective unconscious. When provoked, fundamental facts in the unconscious [about love, death, tribal life, etc.] may recur in folklore, dreams, rituals, et cetera (987–1000).

Does Ellison, speaking in "The Art of Fiction: An Interview," allude to the collective unconscious and the African American?

Folklore . . . offers the first drawings of any group's character. It preserves mainly those situations [that] have repeated themselves again and again in the history of any given group. It describes those rites, manners, customs, and so forth, which insure the good life, or destroy it; and *it describes those boundaries of feeling, thought, and action [that] that particular group has found to be the limitations of the human condition. It projects this wisdom in symbols [that] express the groups will to survive; it embodies those values by which the group lives and dies. These drawings may be crude but they are nonetheless profound in that they represent the group's attempt to humanize the world.* (172)(Emphasis added.)

Jung refers to the collective unconscious as "racial memory." He defines archetypes as "a priori, inborn form[s] of intuition." According to Jung in "On the Relation of Analytical Psychology to Poetic Art," the impact of archetype on a group—be it in the form of immediate experience or an expressed thought or spoken word—"stirs us," or "summons up voices," and it "transmutes our personal destiny into the destiny of mankind" (1001). Are Henderson and Williams, in their discussions of the term "mascon"—i.e., "a massive concentration of black experiential energy"—alluding to archetypal sensibility? Williams contends

Often the mascons are not really images in the literary sense of the word, rather they are verbal expressions [e.g., "home," "the streets," "Trane," or "keep on pushing on"] *which evoke a powerful response in the listener because of their direct relationship to concepts and events in the collective experience.* (Emphasis added.)

(Sherley Anne Williams, "The Blues Roots of Contemporary Afro-American Poetry" 1979, in Ervin 1999:179–91.)
Is William [influenced by Henderson's term mascon] referencing the collective unconscious?

For the critic in the twenty-first century who wishes to extend classification and interpretation of African American literary art, one challenge is myth criticism, particularly the collective unconscious as a term of critical study in African American letters.

Reference for further reading: Frantz Fanon, "The Negro and Psychopathology," *Black Skin, White Masks*. New York: Grove Press, 1967:141–209; Stephen Henderson, *Understanding the New Black Poetry: Black Speech and Black Music as Poetic References*, 1973.

Appendix 1

Outlines of Literary History: African American, African, and Anglophone Caribbean

African American	African	Anglophone Caribbean

The Colonial Period (1745–1831)

African American	African	Anglophone Caribbean
Jupiter Hammon (1711–1806c)	*Epic of Soundiata or Sunjata* (recorded 1959; published in 1960 by Niane)	
Lucy Terry (1730–1821)		
Olaudah Equiano (1745–1797)		
Phillis Wheatley (1753c–1784)	*Epic of Son-Jara* (1123)	
David Walker (1785–1830)	*The Epic of Askia Mohammed Ruler of the Songhay* (1493–1528)	
George Moses Horton (1797c–1883c)	*Mwindo Epic* (recorded 1956; published in 1969 by Daniel Biebuyck)	
Sojourner Truth (1797–1883)		
Marie W. Stewart (1803–1879)		
Martin R. Delany (1812–1885)		
Harriet Jacobs (1813–1897)	*Epic of Jeki la Njambe of the Duala* (recorded c1880; published by Ralph Austen)	
William Wells Brown (1814c–1884)		
Victor Se'Jour (1817–1874)	*Epic of Lianja of the Mongo* (published in 1949 by E. Boelaert)	
Frederick Douglass (1818–1894)		
James Whitfield (1822–1871)	*Epic of Ozidi Sage of the Ijo* (recorded 1963; published in 1991 by J. Bekederemo)	
Frances Watkins Harper (1825–1911)	*Emperor Shaka the Great: A Zula Epic* (1795–1828)	
Harriet Wilson (1828c–1863c)		

1657		Richard Ligon, *True and Exact History*
1700s		Frances Williams, *Integerrimo et fortissimo viro, Georgio Holdano*
1731		Samuel Keimer, *Verses Lately Composed at a Gentleman's House in the Country*

1738	Anton Wilhelm Amo, *Tractatus de arte sobrie et accurate philosophandi*
1746	Lucy Terry, *Bars Flight*
1760	Jupiter Hammon, *An Evening Thought: Salvation by Christ with Penitential Cries*; Britton Hammon, *Narrative of the Uncommon Sufferings and Surprizing Deliverance of*; Briton Hammon, *A Negro Man*
1770	Albert Ukawsaw Gronniosaw, *A Narrative of the Most Remarkable Particulars in the Life of James Albert Ukawsaw Gronniosaw, An African Prince, Written by Himself*
1773	Phillis Wheatley, *Poems on Various Subjects, Religious and Moral*
1782	Ignatius Sancho, *Letters*
1785	John Marrant, *A Narrative of the Lord's Wonderful Dealings with John Marrant, a Black (Now Going to Preach the Gospel in Nova-Scotia) Born in New-York, in North-America*
1787	Ottobah Cugoano, *Thoughts and Sentiments on the Evil and Wicked Traffic of the Slavery and Commerce of the Human Species, Humbly Submitted to the Inhabitants of Great-Britain, by Ottobah Cugoano, a Native of Africa*

(continued)

	African American	African	Anglophone Caribbean
1789		Olaudah Equiano, *The Interesting Narrative of the Life of Olaudah Equiano, or Gustavus Vassa, the African*	
1828		Roger, J. F. *Fables Senegalaises recueillies dans l'OuoLof* [Senegalese fables collected from the Wolof]	
1829	David Walker, *Appeal*; George Moses Horton, *Hope of Liberty*		
The Anti-Slavery Period (1831–1864)			
	Charlotte Grimke (1837–1914)		
	Albery A. Whitman (1851–1902)		
	Booker T. Washington (1856–1915)		
	Charles W. Chestnutt (1858–1932)		
	Anna Julie Cooper (1858–1964)		
	Pauline Hopkins (1859–1930)		
	Ida B. Wells-Barnett (1862–1931)		
1831	Marie W. Stewart, *Religion and the Pure Principles of Morality, the Sure Foundation on Which We Must Build*		
1832		Gaddiel Robert Acquaah, *Ababaawa na atwer* (folktales)	
1833		Dawalu Bukele, *Val Scripts*	M. J. Chapman, *Barbados and Other Poems*

Year			
1834	Matthew Gregory Lewis, *Journal of a West Indian Proprietor*		
1835	J. W. Orderson, *The Fair Barbadian and Faithful Black*		
1837			Victor Se'Jours, *The Mulatto*
1838	E. L. Joseph, *History of Trinidad*		
1842	J. W. Orderson, *Creoliana*		
1843		Samuel Crowther, *Vocabulary of the Yoruba Language*	
1845	M. J. Chapman, *Jephttah's Daughter*		Frederick Douglass, *The Narrative of the Life of Frederick Douglass, An American Slave*
1846		Kali Bara, *Book of Rora* (autobiography and aphorisms)	
1847			William Wells Brown, *Narrative of William W. Brown*
1849		*Yoruba Primer* by Ajayi (aka Samuel Crowther)	
1850		Danial Olorunfemi Fagunwa, *Ogboju ode Ninu Igbo Irun-Male* (folktales)	Sojourner Truth, *Narrative of Sojourner Truth: Northern Slave*; Hannah Crafts, *The Bondswoman's Narrative*
1853			William W. Brown, *Clotel, or the President's Daughter*; J.W. Whitfield, *America and Other Poems*
1854		James White, (trans.) *Christian Hymn*; Koelle, S. W. *African Literature; or Proverbs, Tales, Fables, and Historical Fragments in the Kanuri or Bornu Language*	Frances E. W. Harper, *Poems on Miscellaneous Subjects*

(continued)

	African American	African	Anglophone Caribbean
1855	Frederick Douglass, *My Bondage and My Freedom*; William W. Brown, *Sketches of Places and People Abroad*		
1858	William W. Brown, *My Escape*; Martin Delany, *Blake, or the Huts of America*		
1859	Harriet Wilson, *Our Nig*	Henry Townsend, *Iwe Irohin* (a news sheet)	
1861	Harriet Jacobs, *Incidents in the Life of a Slave Girl*; Frances Harper, *The Two Offers*	C. F. Schlenker, *A Collection of Temne Traditions, Fables, and Proverbs, with an English Translation, with a Temne-English Vocabulary*	

The Reconstruction, Reaction, and Realism Period (1864–1917)

W.E.B. DuBois (1868–1963)
James D. Corrothers (1869–1917)
James Weldon Johnson (1871–1938)
Paul Laurence Dunbar (1872–1906)
Sutton Griggs (1872–1933)
Alice Moore Dunbar-Nelson (1875–1935)
William Stanley Braithwaite (1878–1962)
Angelina Weld Grimke (1880–1958)
Jessie Fauset (1884–1961)
Georgia Douglas Johnson (1886–1966)
Alain Locke (1886–1954)
Marcus Garvey (1887–1940)
Fenton Johnson (1888–1958)

Claude McKay (1889–1948)
Zora Neale Hurston (1891–1960)
Nella Larsen (1893–1964)
Jean Toomer (1894–1967)
George Schuyler (1895–1977)
Rudolph Fisher (1897–1934)
Melvin B. Tolson (1898–1966)
Marita Bonner (1899–1971)
Sterling A. Brown (1901–1989)
Arna Bontemps (1902–1973)
Langston Hughes (1902–1967)
Wallace Thurman (1902–1934)
Countee Cullen (1903–1946)
Arthur P. Davis (1904–1996)
Nick Aaron Ford (1904–1982)
Therman B. O'Daniel (1904–1982)
Frank Marshall Davis (1905–1987)
Saunders Redding (1906–1988)
Dorothy West (1907–1998)
Ann Petry (1908–1997)
Richard Wright(1908–1960)
Blyden Jackson (1910–2000)
Hugh M. Gloster (1911–2002)
Robert Hayden (1913–1982)
Ralph Ellison (1914–1994)
Margaret Walker (1915–1998)
Richard Barksdale (1915–1993)

(continued)

Appendix 1—*Continued*

	African American	African	Anglophone Caribbean
1865		R.F. Burton, *Wit and Wisdom from West Africa; or, a Book of proverbial philosophy; idioms, enigmas, and iconisms*	
1868	Mrs. Elizabeth Keckley, *Behind the Scenes, Or Thirty Years A Slave, And Four Years in the White House*	H. Callaway, *Nursery tales, traditions, and histories of Zulus*	
1870	Frances Harper, *Sketches of Southern Life*	J. C. Taylor, *Ibo Hymns*	
1877	James Whitfield, *Not a Man and Yet a Man*		
1879		Christaller, J. G. *Three Thousand Six Hundred Ghanaian Proverbs (From the Asanta and Fante Language)*	William Hosack, *The Isle of Streams* (The Jamaica Hermit)
1881	Frederick Douglass, *Life and Times of Frederick Douglass*		
1882			Lucy L. Clifford, *Anytime Stories*
1883			Egbert Martin, *Poetical Works*; Rev. P. Giddings, *Quid Rides (Why Do You Laugh?)*; R. H. Trowbridge, *Gossip of the Caribbees*
1884	James Whitfield, *The Rape of Florida*		
1885			

Year			
1890		A. B. Ellis, *The Ewe-Speaking Peoples of the Slave Coast of West Africa*	
1892	Anna Cooper, *A Voice from the South*; Frances Harper, *Iola Leroy*		
1893	Paul Laurence Dunbar, *Oak and Ivy*		
1894		A. B. Ellis, *The Yoruba-Speaking Peoples of the Slave Coast of West Africa*	R. H. Trowbridge, *The Children of Men*
1895	Alice Moore Dunbar-Nelson, *Violets and Other Tales*; Paul Dunbar, *Majors and Minors*; Ida Wells, *A Red Record*		R. H. Trowbridge, *For the Vagabond Hour and Aurora Hill Poems and Serious Reflections in Prose*
1896	Paul Dunbar, *Lyrics of Lowly Life*		
1897		John Mensah Sarbah, *Fanti Customary Laws: A Brief Introduction to the Principles of the Native Laws and Customs of the Fanti and Akan Districts of the Gold Coast, with a Report of Some Cases There-on Decided in the Law Courts*	
1898	Will Marion Cook and Paul Dunbar, *Clorindy, Origins of the Cakewalk*; Joseph Cotter, *Links of Friendship*; Paul Dunbar, *Folks from Dixie* and *The Uncalled*		
1899	Charles Chesnutt, *The Conjure Woman* and *The Wife of His Youth*; Paul Dunbar, *Lyrics of the Hearthside*		

(continued)

Appendix 1—*Continued*

	African American	African	Anglophone Caribbean
1900	Charles Chesnutt, *The House Behind the Cedars*; Paul Dunbar, *The Love of Landry*; Pauline Hopkins, *Contending Forces*		
1901	Booker Washington, *Up From Slavery*; Charles Chesnutt, *The Marrow of Tradition*; Paul Dunbar, *The Fanatics*		
1902	Paul Dunbar, *The Sport of the Gods*		
1903	W.E.B. DuBois, *The Souls of Black Folk*; Paul Dunbar, *Lyrics of Love and Laughter*, *In Old Plantation Tales*	Cronise, Florence M., and Henry W. Ward, *Cunnie Rabbit, Mr. Spider and the Other Beef: West African Folk Tales*	Edward Corde, *Overheard*; Tom Redcam, *Becka's Buckra Baby*
1904	William S. Braithwaite, *Lyrics of Life and Love*; Paul Dunbar, *The Heart of Happy Hollow*		Tropica, *The Island of Sunshine*
1905	Sutton Griggs, *The Hindered Hand*		
1906	Joseph Cotter, *Caleb, the Degenerate*	Thomas Mofolo, *Moeti oa Bochabella* (*The Pilgrim for East*)	
1908	W. S. Braithwaite, *The House of Falling Leaves with Other Poems*	Thomas Mofolo, *Chaka*	Alexander Bailey, *The Poems of Alexander Hamilton Bailey*; Cathcart Dunlop, *The Homeguide*
1909		Henry Ndawa, *U Hambo Luk A Gboboka* (*A Journey toward Conversion*); *Iwe kike Ekerin Li Ede Yoruba* (anthology)	

1911	DuBois, *The Quest of the Silver Fleece*	Claude McKay, *Songs of Jamaica*
1912	James W. Johnson, *The Autobiography of an Ex-Colored man*; Claude McKay, *Songs of Jamaica and Constab Ballads*	H. G. Dehisser, *Jane: A Story of Jamaica*
1913	Dunbar, *Complete Poems*; Fenton Johnson, *A Little Dreaming*	J. J. Adaye, *Bere Adu*
1914		R. H. Nassau, *Where Animals Talk: West African Folklore Tales*
1915	Fenton Johnson, *Vision of the Dusk*	Charles Lynch, *Gladys Klyme, and More Harmony*; A. J. Rock, *Passage Road*

The Renaissances and Radicalism Period (1916–1954)

John O. Killens (1916–1987)
Gwendolyn Brooks (1917–2000)
Alice Childress (1920–1994)
George Kent (1920–1982)
Hoyt Fuller (1923–1981)
James Baldwin (1924–1987)
Stephen Henderson (1925–1996)
Bob Kaufman (1925–1986)
Malcolm X (1925–1965)
M. L. King Jr. (1929–1968)
Lorraine Hansberry (1930–1965)
Etheridge Knight (1931–1991)

(continued)

	African American	African	Anglophone Caribbean
	Darwin T. Turner (1931–1991) Addison Gayle Jr. (1931–1991) Calvin Hernton (1932–2001) Henry Dumas (1934–1968) Audre Lorde (1934–1992) June Jordan (1936–2002) Leon Forrest (1937–1997) Larry Neal (1937–1981) George Bass (1938–1990) Toni Cade Bambara (1939–1995) John Sekora (1939–1997) Sherley Anne Williams (1944–1999) Barbara Christian (1944–2000) Claudia Tate (1946–2002) Melvin Dixon (1950–1992)		
1916	Angelina Grimke, *Rachel*; Fenton Johnson, *Songs of the Soil*	R. S. Rattray, *Ashanti Proverbs*	Cathcart Dunlop, *Undersongs: Lines of Communication*
1917	James Johnson, *Fifty Years and Other Poems*	W. H. Barker and C. Sinclair, *West African Folk-tales*	Joel Rogers, *From Superman to Man*
1918	Georgia Douglas, *The Heart of a Woman and Other Poems*		Joseph Harlequin, *Lyrics and Other Poems*
1920	DuBois, *Darkwater*; Fenton Johnson, *Tales of Darkest America*; Claude McKay, *Spring in the New Hampshire and Other Poems*; James W.	Gaddiel Robert Acquaah, *Fanta Classical Poems*; N. Curtis, *Songs and Tales from The Dark Continent*	A. Richmond Wheeler, *Desert Musings: Verse*

Year			
1921	Johnson, The Book of American Negro Poetry; Sissle and Blake, Shuffle Along	Duro Ladipo, History of the Yorubas; Samuel Johnson, History of The Yorubas from the Earliest Times to the Beginning of the British Protectorate	
1922	Georgia D. Johnson, Bronze; Claude McKay, Harlem Shadows		
1923	Jean Toomer, Cane		
1924	DuBois, The Gifts of Black Folks; Fauset, There Is Confusion	A. Werner, African Mythology	Martha Beckwith, Jamaica Anansi Stories
1925	Countee Cullen, Color; J. W. Johnson, The Book of American Negro Spirituals; Alain Locke, The New Negro; Walter White, Fire in the Flint		Alfred Mendes, Wages of Sin; Barbara Zencraft, Native Soil
1926	Hughes, The Weary Blues; Walter White, Flight; Eric Walround, Tropic Death		Eric Walround, Tropic Death; Adolphe Roberts, The Haunting Hand
1927	Cullen, Caroling the Dusk, The Ballad of the Brown Girl, and Copper Sun; Hughes, Fine Clothes to the Jew; J. W. Johnson, God's Trombones	Akwakwo Ogugu Igbo (a reader)	
1928	Marita Bonner, The Purple Flower; DuBois, Dark Princess; Rudolph Fisher, The Walls of Jericho; Georgia D. Johnson, An Autumn Love Cycle; Nella Larsen, Quicksand		Claude McKay, Home to Harlem; Adolphe Roberts, Pan and Peacock

(continued)

Appendix 1—*Continued*

	African American	African	Anglophone Caribbean
1929	Cullen, *The Black Christ and Other Poems*; Fauset, *Plum Bun*; McKay, *Banjo* and *Home to Harlem*; Wallace Thurman, *The Blacker the Berry*		Basil McFarlane, *Voices from Summerland*; Adolphe Roberts, *The Mind Reader*
1930	Hughes, *Not Without Laughter*; J. W. Johnson, *Black Manhatten*	Gaddiel Robert Acquaah, *Akyekyewere* (poetry); R. S. Rattray, *Akan-Ashanti Folktales*	Gordon Rogers, *The Postcard*; H. A. Thorne, *Poems and Essays of West Indies*
1931	Arna Bontemps, *God Sends Sunday*; Fauset, *The Chinaberry Tree*; George Schuyler, *Black No More*; Toomer, *Essentials*		Lena Kent, *The Hills of St. Andres*; Henry McFarland, *Experiences of a Heart, Its Joys. Its Sorrows*
1932	Sterling Brown, *Southern Road*; Cullen, *One Way to Heaven*; Rudolph Fisher, *The Conjure Man Dies*; McKay, *Gingertown*; Thurman, *Infants of the Spring* and *The Interne*	Gaddiel Robert Acquaah, *Ababaawa na atwer* (folktales)	Claude McKay, *Gingertown*
1933	Fauset, *Comedy American Style*; J. W. Johnson, *Along the Way*;		Lena Kent, *Dews on the Branch*; K.C. Lewis, *Floraspe*; McKay, *Banana Bottom*
1934	Hughes, *The Ways of White Folks*; Zora Neale Hurston, *Jonah's Gourd Vine*	P. M. Desewu, *Mise gli loo (folktales)*	Gordon Bell, *Wayside Sketches*; Alf Mendes, *PitchLake*
1935	Arna Bontemps, *Black Thunder*; Cullen, *The Medea and Some Poems*;	E. N. Amaku, *Ufok-uto-iko-Efịkl kini kini* (poetry); Emmanuel	Henry Bennett, *Thirteen Poems and Seven*; Alf Mendes, *Black Fauns*;

	George Wylie Henderson, *Ollie Miss*; Hughes, *Mulatto*; Hurston, *Mules and Men*	J. Osew, *Nana Agyeman hwehwe* (drama)	Adolphe Roberts, *The Top Floor Killer*
1936	Bontemps, *Black Thunder*; Locke, *Negro Art: Past and Present*		C.L.R. James, *Minty Alley*
1937	Hurston, *Their Eyes Were Watching God*; Walter Turpin, *These Low Grounds*	Kwasi Fiawoo, *Toko Atolia* (*The Fifth Landing*)	Edgar Mittelholzer, *Creole Chips*; Alfred Cruickshank, *Poems in All Moods*; Anna Sealy, *Poems*
1938	Hurston, *Tell My Horse*; Wright, *Uncle Tom's Children*	E. N. Amaku, *Equaro* (poetry); Clement Anderson Akrofi, *Twi Spelling Book*	C.L.R. James, *The Black Jacobins*; Mavis Carter, *Barbados in Verse*
1939	Hurston, *Moses, Man of the Mountain*; Turpin, *O, Canaan!*		Roger Mais, *And Most of All Men*; Aime Cesaire, *Return to My Native Land*
1940	DuBois, *Dusk of Dawn*; Hayden, *Heartshape in the Dust Poems*; Hughes, *The Big Sea*; McKay, *Harlem*; Wright, *Native Son*	Gaddiel Robert Acquaah, *Mfantse mbebusem* (proverb)	Willoughby Moore, *Barbados*; Adolphe Roberts, *The Caribbean: Sea of Destiny*
1941	William Attaway, *Blood on the Forge*; Wright, *Twelve Million Black Voices*	Joseph Boakye Danquah, *Nyankonsen* (fables of the Celestial)	Mittelholzer, *Colonial Artist in Wartime: A Poem*; William Arthur, *Whispers in the Dawn*
1942	Hurston, *Dust Tracks on a Road*; Margaret Walker, *For My People*		Roger Mais, *Another Ghost in Arcady*; Louise Bennett, *Verses in American Dialect*
1943		Joseph Boakye Danquah, *The Third Woman* (drama)	

(continued)

	African American	African	Anglophone Caribbean
1944	Tolson, *Rendezvous with America*		Undine Giuseppi, *These Things are Life*; Frank Collymore, *30 Poems*
1945	Bontemps, *They Seek a City*; Gwendolyn Brooks, *A Street in Bronzeville*; Himes, *If He Hollers, Let Him Go*; Wright, *Black Boy*	Hubert Ogunde, *Strike and Hunger* (drama); C. K. Nyomi, *Wodzi Xola na mi* (drama); Leopold Sedar Senghor, *Songs of the Shadow*	Frank Collymore, *Beneath the Casuarinas*; H. A. Vaughan, *Sandy Land and Other Poems*
1946	Ann Petry, *The Street*		
1947	Himes, *Lonely Crusade*; Petry, *Country Place*	Cyprian Ekwensi, *When Love Whispers*; Birago Diop, *The Tales of Amadou*; E. K. Amegashie, *Vovogi* (folktales) and *Togbi Mawuena II*; Adekanmi Oye-dele, *Ayie Ree!*; Gaddiel Robert Acquaah, *Mfantse amambra* (customs)	M. P. Alladin, *3 One-Act Plays*
1948	Hayden, *The Lion and the Archer*; Zora Neale Hurston, *Seraph on the Sewanee*; Dorothy West, *The Living Is Easy*		Dereck Walcott, *25 Poems*
1949	Brooks, *Annie Allen*	J. H. Kwabena, *Nketia Akanfoo anansesem nghoma* (folktales)	Basil McFarlane, *A Treasury of Jamaican Poetry*; V. S. Reid, *New Day*; Walcott, *Epitaph for the Young: A Poem in XII Cantos*
1950		E. O. Koranteng, *Mpuaasa ntiamoa* (drama); Thomas Yao Kani, *Asikayo, Akanfoo Nnuane titire ne abasem* (folktales); William Anderson, *Jonah*; Clement Anderson Akroje, *Akanfoo Amammere* (wisdom)	

1951	Hughes, *Montage of a Dream Deferred*	Safori Fianko, *Twifo amamuisem* (customs); J. H. Kwebena Nketia, *Ananwoma* (drama)	Forde, *Canes by the Roadside*; Walcott, *Henri Christophe*
1952	Ralph Ellison, *Invisible Man*	E. E. Okon, *Unam obon enyenekpaobon* (drama); *Sidibe* (drama); J. H. Kwebena Neketia, *Kwabena Amoa and Anwonsem* (poetry); Lily Baeta, *Da togli nam* (folktales); Amos Tutuola, *The Palm-Wine Drunkard and His Dead Palm-Wine Tapster in the Dead's Town*	Frantz Fanon, *Black Skin, White Masks*; Louis Simpson, *The Arrivistes: Poems*
1953	James Baldwin, *Go Tell It on the Mountain*; Brooks, *Maud Martha*; Petry, *The Narrows*; Tolson, *Libretto for the Republic of Liberia*; Wright, *The Outsider*		George Lamming, *In the Castle of My Skin*; Walcott, *Poems, Wine of the Country*; Samuel Selvon, *A Brighter Sun*; Phillip Sherlock, *Ten Poems*

The Cultural Assertion Period (1954–1975)

1954	Himes, *Third Generation*; John Killens, *Youngblood*	Camara Laye, *The Radiance of the King*; Amos Tutuola, *My Life in the Bush of Ghosts*; Ekwensi Cyprian, *People of the City*	Lamming, *The Emigrants*; Walcott, *The Sea of Dauphin*
1955	Baldwin, *Notes of a Native Son*; Alice Childress, *Trouble in Mind*; Hayden, *Figures of Time*; Himes, *Cast the First Stone* and *The Primitive*	Amos Tutuola, *Simbi and the Satyr of the Dark Jungle*	Selvon, *An Island Is a World*; John Hearne, *Voices Under the Window*; W. S. Arthur, *No Idle Winds*; Collymore, *Notes for Glossary of Barbadian Dialect*

(continued)

	African American	African	Anglophone Caribbean
1956	Baldwin, *Giovanni's Room*; Brooks, *Bronzeville Boys and Girls*	Daryll Ford, *Efik Traders of Old Calabar* (diary); Adebayo Faleti, *Eda KoL'Aropin* (poetry); Emmanuel J. Osen, *Asantehene Osee Tutu* (drama)	Henry McFarlene, *Passing Through: Poems*; Nellie Olson, *Pondered Poems*
1957		Olumbe Bassie, *An Anthology of West African Verse*	V. S. Nailpaul, *The Mystic Masseur*; Walcott, *Ione*
1958	Wright, *The Long Dream*	Prince Modupeh, *I Was a Savage* [Reissued as *A Royal African* in 1969]; Chinua Achebe, *Things Fall Apart*; Birago Diop, *The New Tale of Amadou Koumba*; Amos Tutuola, *The Brave African Huntress*; Wole Soyinka, *The Swamp Dwellers*; Chief Joseph Folohan Odunjo, *Agbalowomeeri* (drama); Adeboye Babalola, *Pasen Sina* (drama); Clement Anderson Akrofi, *Twi Mmebusem: Twi Proverbs, with English Translations and Comments*; Joseph Oduro, *Seantee: A Novel in Asante: Twi*	Jan Carew, *Black Midas*; Lamming, *Of Age and Innocence*; Naipaul, *The Suffrage of Elvira*; Walcott, *Drums and Colors*; Andrew Salkey, *A Quality of Violence*
1959	Hansberry, *A Raisin in the Sun*; Hughes, *Selected Poems*; Paul Marshall, *Brown Girl, Brownstone*	Wole Soyinka, *The Lion and The Jewel* (drama); Joseph Ghartey, *TwerNyame* (drama); Kwasi Fiawoo, *Fia yi dziehe* (drama)	
1960	Brooks, *The Bean Eaters*; Williams, *Angry Ones*	Chinua Achebe, *No Longer at Ease*; Birago Diop, *Lures and Lights*; Wole	Lamming, *Season of Adventure*; Wilson Harris, *Palace of The Peacock*;

1961	Hughes, *The Best of Simple* and *Ask Your Mama: Twelve Moods for Jazz*; Himes, *Pinktoes*; LeRoi Jones (Amiri Baraka), *Preface to a Twenty Volume Suicide Note*; Marshall, *Soul Clap Hands and Sing*; Williams, *Night Song*; Wright, *Eight Men*	Soyinka, *The Trials of Brother Jero*; Robert Asare Tabi, *Me nko me yam* (drama) Onuora Nzekwu, *Wand of Noble Wood*; Joseph Akinyele, *Omoyajowo, Itan Adegbesan* (detective); E. O. Koranteng, *Osabarima* (drama); Chief Joseph Folohan Odunjo, *Akojono ewi aladun* (drama)	Naipaul, *Miguel Street* Harris, *The Far Journey of Oudin*; Naipaul, *A House for Mr. Biswas*
1962	Baldwin, *Another Country*; Hayden, *Ballad of Remembrance*	Chinua Achebe, *The Sacrificial Egg and Other Stories*; James Matthews, *Azikwelwa Stories*; Efua Theodora Sutherland, *Foriwa*; Amos Tutuola, *The Feather Woman of the Jungle*; Daniel K. Abbia, *Ndzemba ahyese* (folktales); Cyprian Ekwensi, *Burning Grass*; Onuora Nzekwu, *Blade Among the Boys*	Sylvia Wynter, *Hills Hebron*; Rhonda McKenzie, *Jamaican Pocomanra and Others*; Carew, *The Last Barbarian*; Hendricks/Lindo, *Anthology of Jamaican Literature*
1963	Baraka, *The Dead Lecturer*; Brooks, *Selected Poems*; Martin Luther King Jr., *I Have a Dream* and *Letter from Birmingham Jail*; Williams, *Sissie* and *And Then We Heard the Thunder*; Wright, *Lawd Today*	Birago Diop, *Tales and Commentaries*; James Matthews, *Commentaries*; *Mary, Bill, Cyril, John and Joseph*; Leopold Sedar Senghor, *Nocturnes*; Moore and Beier, *Penguin Modern African Poetry*	C.L.R. James, *Breaking a Boundary*; Naipaul, *Mr. Stone and the Knight's Companion*; Harris, *The Secret Ladder*

(continued)

	African American	African	Anglophone Caribbean
1964	Baldwin, *Blues for Mr Charlie*; Baraka, *Dutchman; Ellison, Shadow and Act*; Gaines, Catherine Carmier; Adrienne Kennedy, *Funnyhouse of a Negro*	Gabrial Okara, *The Voice*; Chinua Achebe, *Arrow of God*; Mongo Beti, *Mission to Kala*; Ngugi wa Thiong'o, *Weep Not, Child*; Winful E. Archie, *Akan Awensen* (poetry); Joseph Kwasi Brantuo, *Asetena mu Awonsem* (Poems of Everyday Life, with English Translation)	Harris, *Heartland*; Walcott, *Selected Poems*; Austin Clarke, *The Survivors of the Crossing*; H. Patterson, *The Children of Sisyphus*; Ismith Khan, *The Obeah Man*
1965	Baldwin, *Going to Meet the Man*; Alex Haley, *Autobiography of Malcolm X*; Hansberry, *The Sign in Sidney Brustein's Window*; Himes, *Cotton Comes to Harlem*; Bob Kaufman, *Solitudes Crowded with Loneliness*; A. B. Spellman, *The Beautiful Days*; Tolson, *Harlem Gallery*	Ama Ata Aidoo, *The Dilemma of a Ghost*; Abioseh Nicol, *The Truly Married Woman and Other Stories and Two African Tales*; Wole Soyinka, *Before the Blackout, The Detainee, and The Interpreter*; Ngugi wa Thiong'o, *The River Between*	Carew, *Green Writer*; Harris, *The Eye of the Scarecrow*; Earl Lovelace, *While Gods are Falling*; Walcott, *The Castaway and Other Poems*
1966	Baraka, "Black Art" and *Home: Social Essays*; June Jordan, *Who Look at Me*; Margaret Walker, *Jubilee*	Chinua Achebe, *A Man of the People*; Flora Nwapa, *Efuru*; Mbella Sonne Dipoko, *A Few Nights and Days*; Obotunde Ijimere [Ulli Beier and Duro Lapido], *Woyengi. In The Imprisonment of Obatala and Other Plays*; Elechi Amadi, *The Concubine*; Ulli Beier, *The Origin of Life and Death: African Creation Myths*	Walcott, *Malcochon: Or, Six in the Rain*; J. B. Emtage, *Brown Sugar*; A. N. Forde, *The Passing Cloud*; Mervyn Morris, *Poems*; Washington King, *New Modern Poems*

Year			
1967	Baraka, *The Toilet*; Gaines, *Of Love and Dust*; Nikki Giovanni, *Black Feeling, Black Talk*; Bob Kaufman, *Golden Sardine*; Haki Madhubuti, *Think Black*; Ishmael Reed, *The Free-Lance Pall-Bearers*; Williams, *The Man Who Cried I Am*; Jay Wright, *Death as History*	Amos Tutuola, *Ajaiyi and His Inherited Poverty*; Amu Djo- leto, *The Strange Man*; Sarif Easmon, *The Burnt-Out Man*; Soyinka, *Idanre and Other Poems* and *Kongi's Harvest*; Efua Theodora Sutherland, *Edufa*; Ngugi wa Thiong'o, *A Grain of Wheat*	Alma Norma, *Ballads of Jamaica*; Dathorne, *Caribbean Verse*; Kamau Brathwaite, *Rights of Passage* and *Odale's Choice*; Harris, *The Waiting Room*; Naipaul, *The Mimic Men* and *A Flag on the Island*; Walcott, *Dream on Monkey Mountain*
1968	Baldwin, *Tell Me How Long the Train's Been Gone* and *The Amen Corner*; Brooks, *In the Mecca*; Eldridge Cleaver, *Soul on Ice*; Gaines, *Bloodline*; Etheridge Knight, *Poems from Prison*; Audre Lorde, *The First Cities*; Haki Madhubuti, *Pride Poems*; Larry Neal and LeRoi Jones, *Black Fire: An Anthology*; Carolyn Rodgers, *Paper Soil*; Alice Walker, *Once: Poems*	Ama Ata Aidoo, *Our Sister Killjoy; or, Reflections from a Black-Eyed Squint*; Samson O. O. Amali, *Selected Poems*; Bibi Setsoafia, *Togbui Kpeglo II* (drama); Ayi Kwei Armah, *The Beautiful Ones Are Not Yet Born*	Evan Jones, *Understanding Poems*; Olive Senior, *Down the Road Again*; Brathwaite, *Masks*; Harris, *Tamatumari*; Lovelace, *The Schoolmaster*; Collymore, *Rhymed Reflections on the Flora and Fauna of Barbados*; Rudolph Kizerman, *Stand Up in the World*
1969	Amiri Baraka, *Four Black Revolutionary Plays* and *Black Magic: Poetry 1961–1967*; Ed Bullins, *Goin' a Buffalo* and *In the Wine Time*; LuCille Clifton, *Good Times*; Jayne Cortez, *Pisstained Stairs*; Charles Gordon, *No Place to*	Soyinka, *Poems from Prison* and *The Road*; Nwapa, *Idu*; Elechi Amadi, *The Slave*; Amu Djoleto, *Because of Woman*; Afolabi Olabimtan, *Aadota aforo* (poetry); Leopold Sedar Senghor, *Selected Poems*	Brathwaite, *Islands*; Walcott, *The Gulf and Other Poems*; Fanon, *The Wretched of the Earth*; Lionel Hutchinson, *Man From the People*; Dennis Scott, *Journeys and Ceremonies*; K. C. Lewis, *Weymouth Poems*; Paule

(continued)

	African American	African	Anglophone Caribbean
1969	Be Somebody; Haki Madhubuti, Think Black and Don't Cry Scream; James McPherson, Hue and Cry; Marshall, The Chosen Place, The Timeless People; Ishmael Reed, Yellow Back Radio Broke-Down; Sonia Sanchez, Homecoming; Al Young, Dancing Poems		Marshall, The Chosen Place, The Timeless People; Michael Gilkes, In Transit; Naipaul, The Middle Passage
1970	Maya Angelou, I Know Why the Caged Bird Sings; Toni Cade Bambara, The Black Woman; Brooks, Family Pictures and Riot; Bullins, Death List, It Bees Dat Way, and Night of the Beast: A Screen-Play; Henry Dumas, Ark of Bones; Mari Evans, I Am a Black Woman; Addison Gayle, Black Situation; Nikki Giovanni, Creation; Michael Harper, Dear John, Dear Coltrane; Hayden, Words in the Mourning Time: Poems; Madhubuti, We Walk the Way of the New World; Toni Morrison, The Bluest Eye; Sonia Sanchez, We a BaddDDD People; Alice Walker, The Third Life of Grange Copeland; Margaret Walker, Prophets for a New Day	Mongo Beti, King Lazarus; Samson O. O. Amali, Worlds Within and Other Poems; A. A. Opoku, Mese wo amen (poetry); Obi Egbuna, Daughters of the Sun and Other Stories; Ruth Finnegan, Oral Literature in Africa	Harris, Ascent to Omai; Walcott, Dream on Monkey Mountain and Other Plays and In a Fine Castle; Merle Hodge, Crick Crack Monkey; Trevor Rhone, Blue Socks Blues; Carew, Cry Black Power and Sons of the Flying Wing; John Hearne, The Candywine Development; Sylvia Wynter, Black Midas
1971	Angelou, Just Give Me a Cool Drink of Water 'fore I Diiie; Bambara,	Soyinka, Madmen and Specialists; Nwapa, This Is Lagos and Other	Naipaul, In a Free State; Collymore, Selected Poems; Lionel

Tales and Stories; Brooks, Aloneness; Cortez, Festivals and Funerals; Gaines, The Autobiography of Miss Jane Pittman; Gayle, The Black Aesthetic; Michael Harper, History Is Your Own Heartbeat; Jordan, His Own Where; Madhubuti, Dynamite Voices 1: Black Poets of the 1960s; Petry, Miss Muriel and Other Stories

Stories; Mongo Beti, The Poor Christ of Bomba; Aidoo, No Sweetness Here: A Collection of Short Stories

Hutchinson, One Touch of Nature; Tony McNeill, Hello Ungod; Figueroa, Caribbean Voices; Ramchand/Gray, West Indian Poetry; Tony McNeill, Hello Ungod; Trevor Rhone, The Harder They Come; Harris, The Age of the Rainmakers; John Campbell, Poems for All; E. M. Roach, A Calabash of Blood

1972   Baraka, Spirit Reach and Raise Race, Rays Raze; Bambara, Gorilla My Love; Brooks, Report from Part One; Bullins, Next Time; Clifton, Good News about the Earth; Giovanni, My House: Poems; Harper, Photographs: Negatives: History as Apple Tree and Song: I Want a Witness; Hayden, The Night-Blooming Circus; Himes, The Quality of Hurt; Etheridge Knight, A Poem for Brother/Man; Larry Neal, Hoodoo Hollerin' Bebop Ghosts; Reed, Mumbo Jumbo; Sanchez, It's a New Day: Poems for Young Brothers and Sistuhs; Quincy Troupe, Embryo Poems 1962–1971; Williams, Captain Blackman

James Matthews, Cry Rape; Nwapa, Emeka-Driver's Guard; Soyinka, The Man Died, A Shuttle in the Crypt, and Ogun Abibiman; Kofi Awoonor, This Earth, My Brother; Ayi Kwei Armah, Why Are We So Blest?; D. K. Kwarteng, My Sword Is My Life; Dennis Duerden and Cosmo Pieterse, African Women Talking

Harris, Black Marsden: A Tabula Rasa Comedy; Lamming, Water with Berries and Natives of My Person; Rex Nettleford, Desperate Silences; Elaine Herrin, Of Flesh and Blood—and God; Wayne Vincent Brown, On the Coast; Randall Butisingh, Love's Light; Naipaul, The Overcrowded Barracon; Mills, The Shell Book of Trinidad Stories; Carew, Rate the Sun; Salky, Breaklight; Seymour, New Writing in the Caribbean; Samuel Selvon, Water for Veronica; Neville Giuseppi, Selected Poems; Wayne Brown, On the Coast

(continued)

	African American	African	Anglophone Caribbean
1973	Bullins, *The Reluctant Rapist*; Cortez, *Scarifications*; Forrests, *There Is a Tree More Ancient Than Eden*; Harper, *Debridgement*; Knight, *Belly Song and Other Poems*; Morrison, *Sula*; Sanchez, *Love Poems*; Alice Walker, *In Love and Trouble: Stories of Black Revolutionary Petunias*	Armah, *Two Thousand Seasons*; Chinua Achebe, *Christmas in Biafra and Other Poems*; Bessie Head, *A Question of Power*; Awooner, *Night of My Blood and Messages: Poems from Ghana*	Walcott, *Another Life*; Undine Giuseppi, *The Shell Book of Trinidad Stories*; Mervyn Morris, *The Pond*; Wilfred Cartey, *The House of Blue Lightening*; Frederick Rawle, *Translantic Cargo*; A. M. Clarke, *Wheels within Wheels*; Sebastian Clarke, *Sun Song*; Lindsay Barrett, *The Conflicting Eye*; Mutabaruka, *Outcry*
1974	Angelou, *Gather Together in My Name*; Baldwin, *If Beale Street Could Talk*; Clifton, *An Ordinary Woman*; Giovanni, *Gemini: An Extended Autobiographical Statement on My First Twenty-Five Years of Being a Black Poet*; Charles Johnson, *Faith and the Good Thing*; E. Ethelbert Miller, *The Land of Smiles and the Land of No Smiles and Andromeda*; Albert Murray, *Train Whistle Guitar*; Sanchez, *Blues Book for Blue Black Magical Women*; Ntozake Shange, *for colored girls who have considered*	Buchi Emecheta, *Second-Class Citizen*; Armah, *Fragments*; Egbuna, *Emperor of the Sea and Other Stories*	Walcott, *The Joker of Serville and The Charlatan*; Oliver Jackman, *Saw the House in Half*; Willis Cummin, *Calypsoes, Symphonies and Incest*; John Wickham, *Casuarina Row*; Livingstone, *Caribbean Rhythms*; Michael Gilkes, *Couvade*; A. L. Hendricks, *Madonna of the Unknown Nation*; Joe Macmarie, *The Outsider*; Linton Johnson, *Voices of the Living and Dead*; A. L. Hendricks, *Madonna of the Unknown Nation*

| 1975 | *suicide/when the rainbow is enuf*
Angelou, *Oh Pray My Wings Are Gonna Fit Me Well*; David Bradley, *South Street*; Brooks, *Beakonings*; Bullins, *Taking of Miss Janie*; Harper, *Nightmare Begins Responsibility*; Hayden, *Angle of Ascent: New and Selected Poems*; Gayl Jones, *Corregidora*; Clarence Major, *Reflex and Bone Structure*; Carolyn Rodgers, *How I Got Ovah: New and Selected Poems*; Sanchez, *Selected Poems*; Williams, *Motherself and the Foxes*; Sherley Anne Williams, *Peacock Poems* | Djoleto, Amu, *Money Galore*; E. Y. Egblewogbe, *Victims of Greed*; Egbuna, *The Minister's Daughter*; Soyinka, *Death and the King's Horseman*; Nwapa, *Never Again*; Sutherland, *The Marriage at Anansewa* | Brathwaite, *Other Exiles Days and Night*; Carew, *The Third Gift*; Harris, *Companions of Day and Night*; Naipaul, *Guerrillas*; D. J. Henry, *We Are Two Sites and Yet Another*; Bob Marley, *Natty Dread* (record); Samuel Selvon, *Moses Ascending*; Mills, *The Shell Book of Trinidad Stories*; Frederick Rawle, *Translantic Cargo*; Joy Hearn-Hill, *Trinidad the Gem of the Caribbean*; Enid Kirton, *Pen Portraits*; Lasana Kwesi, *Poems of Rebellion*; Linton Johnson, *Dread Beat and Blood*; Anthony Kellman, *The Black Madonna and Other Poems*; Michael de Freitas, *Revo* |

(continued)

	African American	African	Anglophone Caribbean
The Reconstruction and Postmodernism Period (1976 to the Present)			
1976	Angelou, *Singin' and Swingin' and Getting Merry Like Christmas*; Octavia Butler, *Patternmaster*; Bullins, *I Am Lucy Terry* and *The Mystery of Phillis Wheatley*; Gayl Jones, *Eva's Man*; James McPherson, *Railroad*; Reed, *Flight to Canada*; Alice Walker, *Meridian*; Williams, *The Junior Bachelor Society*	Emecheta, *The Bride Price*; J. O. Eshun, *Adventures of the Kapapa*	McNeill/Dawes, *The Caribbean Poem*; Brathwaite, *Black and Blues*; Walcott, *Sea Grapes: Selected Verse* and *O Babylon*; W. S. Arthur, *Poesia Religiosa Internazionale*
1977		Emecheta, *The Slave Girl*; Kofi Aidoo, *Saworbeng: A Collection of Short Stories*; Yaw Boateng, *The Return*; Ngugi, *Petals of Blood*	Brathwaite, *Mother Poem*
1978		Kalu Okpi, *The Smugglers*; Agu Ogali, *Cool City and the JuJu Priest*; Afari Assan, *Christmas in the City*; Adaora Ulasi, *Who Is Jonah?* and *The Man from Sagamu*; Egbuna, *Diary of a Homeless Prodigal*; Emecheta, *Titch the Cat*; Armah, *The Healers*	Timothy Callendar, *How Music Came to the Ainchan People*; Neville Dawes, *Interim*
1979		Emecheta, *In the Ditch*; Nii Ofoli; Oyekan *The Messenger of Death*;	Brathwaite, *Barbados Poetry: A Checklist-Slavery to the Present*

Year			
		Owomoyela, *African Literatures: An Introduction*	
1980	Bambara, *The Salt Eater*; Bullins, *Steve and Velma*; Octavia Butler, *Wildseed*; Clifton, *Two-Headed Woman*; Knight, *Born of a Woman: New and Selected Poems*	James Matthews, *Images*; Nwapa, *Wives at War and Other Stories*; Ngugi, *Devil on the Cross*; Mongo Beti, *Remember Ruben*; Ben Okri, *Flowers and Shadows*; Egbuna, *The Rape of Lysistrata and Black Candle for Christmas*; Emecheta, *The Moonlight Bride and Nowhere to Play*; Olusegun Obasanjo, *My Command*; A. M. Oppong-Affi, *The Prophet of Doom*; Mariama Ba, *So Long a Letter* Emecheta, *Destination Biafra, The Wrestling Match and Double York*;	Lorna Goodison, *Tamarind Season*; Erna Brodber, *Jane and Luisa Will Soon Come Home*; Carew, *Children of the Sun*; Michelle Cliff, *Claiming an Identity They Taught Me to Dispise*; Naipaul, *A Congo Diary*; Walcott, *The Joker of Serville and O Babylon: Two Plays* and *Remembrance and Pantomine: Two Plays*
1981	Angelou, *The Heart of a Woman*; David Bradley, *The Chaneysville Incident*; Brooks, *Primer for Blacks* and *To Disembark*; Mari Evans, *Nightstar, 1973–1978*; Jordan, *Civil Wars*; Kaufman, *The Ancient Rain: Poems 1956–1978*; Morrison, *Tar Baby*; Harryette Mullen, *Tree-Tall Women*; Alice Walker, *You Can't Keep a Good Woman Down*	Mariama Ba, *Scarlet Song*; Nwapa, *One is Enough*; Ben Okri, *Landscapes Within*; Ngugi, *Detained: A Writer's Prison Diary*; Amos Tutuola, *The Witch Herbalist of the Remote Town*; Soyinka, *Aki: The Years of Childhood* and *Opera Wonyosi*	Carew, *Sea Drums in My Blood*; Caryl Phillips, *Strange Fruit*; Walcott, *The Fortunate Traveler, Selected Poetry*; Carl Jackson, *East Wind in Paradise*; Odimumba Kwamdela, *Raining Ruins and Rockstones*

(continued)

	African American	African	Anglophone Caribbean
1982	Cortez, *Firespitter and Mervaileuz Coup de Foudre: Poetry of Jayne Cortez and Ted Joans*; Charles Johnson, *Oxherding Tale*; Marshall, *Renna and Other Stories*; Audre Lorde, *Zami: A New Spelling of My Name*; E. Ethelbert Miller, *Season of Hunger/Cry of Rain*; Gloria Naylor, *The Women of Brewster Place*; Shange, *Sasafrass, Cypress and Indigo*; Walker, *The Color Purple*; Williams, *Click Song*; Sherley Anne Williams, *Some One Sweet Angel Chile*	Ifeoma Okoye, *Behind the Clouds*	Figueroa, *An Anthology of African and Caribbean Writing in English*; Brathwaite, *Sun Poem, Gods of the Middle Passage*; Harris, *The Angel at The Gate*; Walcott, *The Isle Is Full of Noises*; John Wickham, *World Without End: Memories of a Time*; Beryl Gilroy, *In for a Penny*
1983	Gaines, *A Gathering of Old Men*; Marshall, *Praisesong For the Widow*; John McCluskey, *Mr. America's Last Season Blues*	Ken Saro-Wiwa, *Basi and Company*; Nii Osundare, *Songs of the Marketplace*; Osonye TessOnwueme, *A Hen Too Soon*	Brathwaite, *Third World Poems*; Jamaica Kincaid, *At The Bottom of the River*; Walcott, *The Caribbean Poetry of Derek Walcott and the Art of Romare Beardon*
1984	Baraka, *Daggers and Javelins: Essays 1974–1979* and *The Autobiography of LeRoi Jones/Amiri Baraka*; Butler, *Clay's Ark*; J. California Cooper, *A Piece of Mine*; Jayne Cortez, *Coagulations: New and Selected*	Ifeoma Okoye, *Men Without Ears: Aklali Zaynab and The Stillborn*; Osonye Tess Onwueme, *The Broken Calabash*	Lovelace, *Jestina's Calypso and Other Plays*; Caryl Phillips, *The Shelter*; Walcott, *Midsummer, Collected Poems 1948–1984*; Claire Harris, *From the Women's Quarters*

Year			
	Poems; Forrest, *Two Wings to Veil My Face*; Charles Fuller, *A Soldier's Play*; Yusef Komunyakaa, *Copacetic*; Madhubuti, *Earthquakes*; Sanchez, *Homegirls and Handgrenades*; Shange, *See No Evil: Prefaces, Essays and Accounts*; Quincy Troupe, *Skulls Along the River*; John Edgar Wideman, *Brothers and Keepers*; August Wilson, *Ma Rainey's Black Bottom*		
1985	Baldwin, *The Price of the Ticket*; Sanchez, *I've Been A Woman: New and Selected Poems*; Shange, *Betsy Brown*; Wideman, *The Homeward Trilogy*; Williams, *Berhama Account*; Eady, *Victims*	Emecheta, *The Rape of Shavi*; Ellen Kuzwayo, *Call Me Woman*; Molara Ogundepe-Leslie, *Sew the Old Days*; Ben Okri, *Incidents at the Shrine*; Tess Onwueme, *The Desert Enroaches*; Ken Saro Wiwa, *Songs in a Time of War and Sozaboy*	Cliff, *The Land of Look Behind: Prose and Poetry*; Harris, *Carnival*; Kincaid, *Annie John*; Lovelace, *The New Hardware Store*; Phillips, *The Final Passage*; Jonathan Small, *Pigsticking Season and Death of a Pineapple Salad*; Evan Jones, *Tales from the Caribbean*
1986	Williams, *Dessa Rose*		Opal Palmer, *BakeFace and Other Guava Stories*; Michael Parchment, *My Freedom Voice*; Dance, *Fifty Caribbean Writers*; Burnett, *Caribbean Verse*; Goodison, *I Am Becoming My Mother*

(continued)

	African American	African	Anglophone Caribbean
1987	Morrison, *Beloved*		Brathwaite, *Sun Poem and X-Self*; Meryl Elaine Pile, *Aspiration*
1988	Gloria Naylor, *Mama Day*		Mark McWatt, *Interiors*; Goodison, *Hearties*; Tatanka Yotanka, *Farnum's Land*; Baugh, *A Tale from the Rainforest*
1989	Tina McElroy Ansa, *Baby of the Family*; Bebe Campbell, *Sweet Summer: Growing Up With and Without My Dad*; Henry Dumas, *Knees of a Natural Man*; Randall Kenan, *A Visitation of Spirits*; Yusef Komunyakaa, *February in Sydney*; Clarence Major, *Some Observations of a Stranger at Zani in the Latter Part of the Century*; Terry McMillan, *Disappearing Act*; Walker, *Temple of My Familiar*	Onueme, *Legacies*; Soyinka, *Mandela's Earth and Other Poems*	Caryl Phillips, *High Ground*; Naipaul, *A Turn in the South*; Olive Senior, *Arrival of the Snake Woman*; Walcott, *Omeros*; Arnold Ward, *Sandbox Knock!*; Yotanka, *Dorothea's Ambition*
1990	Ellison, *Flying Home*; Charles Johnson, *Middle Passage*; Reginald McKnight, *I Get on the Bus*; Walter Mosely, *Devil in a Blue Dress*; August Wilson, *Two Trains Running*	Adeola James, *In Their Own Voices, African Women Writers Talk*	Cliff, *Bodies of Water*; Harris, *The Four Banks of the River Space*; Kincaid, *Lucy*; Anthony Kellman, *Watercourse*; Goodison, *Baby, Mother the King of Swords*; Brown, *Caribbean New Wave*; Cudjoe, *Caribbean Women Writers*

1991	Clifton, *Quilting*; Cooper, *Family*; Cornelius Eady, *The Gathering of My Name*; Kenan, *Let the Dead Bury Their Dead*; Marshall, *Daughters*; Harryette Mullen, *Trimmings*; Alice Walker, *Everything We Know: Earthling Poems 1965–1990*; Sherley Anne Williams, *Letters from a New England Negro*	Ama Aidoo, *Change*; Ben Okri, *The Famished Road*; Onwueme, *Parables for a Season*	Phillips, *Cambridge*; Walcott, *Steel*; Cecil Foster, *No Man in the House*
1992	Bebe Campbell, *Your Blues Ain't Like Mine*; Cooper, *The Matter Is Life*; Rita Dove, *Through the Ivory Gale*; Mari Evans, *A Dark and Splendid Mass* and *I Look at Me*; Forrest, *Divine Days*; Jordan, *Technical Difficulties*; Terry McMillan, *Waiting to Exhale*; Morrison, *Jazz*; Walker, *Possessing the Secret of Joy*	Ben Okri, *An African Elegy*; Yvonne Vera, *Why Don't You Carve Other Animals*; Soyinka, *From Zia with Love*	Lamming, *Conversations: A Collection of Essays, Addresses and Interviews*; Martin DeCourcey Haynes, *A Doc In the Making*

(continued)

	African American	African	Anglophone Caribbean
1993	Angelou, *On the Pulse of Morning and Wouldn't Take Nothing for My Journey Now*; Tina McElroy Ansa, *Ugly Ways*; Butler, *Parable of the Sower*; Clifton, *The Book of Light*; Gaines, *A Lesson Before Dying*; Komunyakaa, *Neon Vernacular*		Lamming, *The Pleasures of Exile*; Kevyn Arthur, *England and Nowhere*; John Wickham, *Discoveries and Landings and Landscapes*; Cliff, *Free Enterprise*; Collymore, *The Man Who Loved Attending Funerals*; Brathwaite, *Zea Mexican Diary*, *Trenchtown Rock*, and *Roots*; Harris, *The Carnival Trilogy* and *Resurrection at Sorrow Hill*; Phillips, *Crossing the River*; Walcott, *Odyssey: A Stage Version*
1994	Connie Briscoe, *Sisters and Lovers*; Nathan McCall, *Makes Me Want to Holler: A Young Black Man In America*; Edwidge Danticat, *Breath, Eyes, Memory*; Miller, *First Light: New and Selected Poems*; Brent Staples, *Parallel Time: Growing Up in Black and White*	Onwueme, *Tell It to Women*; Yvonne Vera, *Without a Name*	Mark McWatt, *The Language of El Dorado*; Brodber, *Louisiana*; Carew, *Rape of Paradise* and *Ghosts in our Blood—With Malcolm X in Africa, England, Caribbean*; Edwidge Dantaicat, *Breath, Eyes, Memory*; Naipaul, *A Way in the World*; Senior, *Gardening in the Tropics*
1995	Cooper, *In Search of Satisfaction*; Dandicat, *Krik? Krak!*; Dove, *Mother Love*; Cornelius Eady, *You Don't Miss Your Water*; Harryette	Nwapa, *The Lake Goddess*	Kincaid, *The Autobiography of My Mother*; Leone Ross, *Born Fi Dead*; Senior, *Discerner of Hearts*

	Mullen, *Muse and Drudge*; Sanchez, *Wounded in the House of a Friend*; Dorothy West, *The Wedding* and *The Richer, The Poorer*; Alex Pate, *Losing Absalom*	Onwueme, *Riot to Heaven*	Leone Ross, *All the Blood Is Red*
1996	Tina Ansa, *The Hand I Fan With*; Connie Briscoe, *Big Girls Don't Cry*; Cooper, *Some Love Pain, Some Time Stories*; Toi Derricotte, *Tender*; Tananarive Due, *The Between*; McMillan, *How Stella Got Her Groove Back*; Walter Mosely, *A Little Yellow Dog*; August Wilson, *Seven Guitars*		
1997	Julie Dash, *Daughters of Dust*; Toi Derricotte, *Captivity*; Sandra Jackson-Opokei, *The River Where Blood is Born*; Morrison, *Paradise*	Vera, *Under the Tongue*; Onwueme, *The Missing Foe*	Phillips, *The Nature of Blood*; Kincaid, *My Brother*; Lovelace, *Salt*; Leone Ross, *Wild Ways: Stories of Women on The Road*; Walcott, *The Bounty*
1998	Cooper, *The Wake of the Wind*; Tananarive Due, *The Healing*; Miller, *Whispers, Secrets and Promises*; Elizabeth Nunez, *Beyond The Limbo Silence*		

(continued)

	African American	African	Anglophone Caribbean
1999	Ellison, *Juneteenth*		Leone Ross, *Orange Laughter*
2000	Cooper, *The Future Has a Past;* Nunez, *Bruised Hibiscus;* Kevin Young, *Giant Steps: The New Generation of African American Writers*		Margaret Gill, *Lyric You: In Honour of Kamau Brathwaite*
2001	Cornelius Eady, *Autobiography of a Juke Box and a Dollar Short;* McMillan, *A Day Late and a Dollar Short;* Sharan Strange, *Ash*		
2002	Tina Ansa, *You Know Better;* Connie Briscoe, *P. G. County;* June Jordan, *Some of Us Did Not Die: New and Selected Essays of June Jordan*		

Appendix 2

Literary Distinctions, Societies, Circles, and Associations

PULITZER PRIZE

Poetry

1950   Gwendolyn Brooks, *Annie Allen*
1987   Rita Dove, *Thomas and Beulah*
1994   Yusef Komunyakaa, *Neon Vernacular*
1998   Charles Wright, *Black Zodiac*

Fiction

1977   Alex Haley, *Roots*
1978   James Alan McPherson, *Elbow Room*
1983   Alice Walker, *The Color Purple*
1988   Toni Morrison, *Beloved*

Drama

1970   Charles Gordone, *No Place to Be Somebody*
1982   Charles Fuller, *A Soldier's Play*
1987   August Wilson, *Fences*
1990   August Wilson, *The Piano Lesson*

Nobel Prize for Literature

1986   Wole Soyinka (African)
1991   Derek Walcott (Caribbean)
1992   Toni Morrison (African American)
2001   V. S. Naipaul (Caribbean)

Societies, Circles, and Associations

1980   Middle Atlantic Writers Association
1981   The Langston Hughes Society
1984   The Zora Neale Hurston Society
1987   The Dark Room Collective
1990   The Richard Wright Circle
1992   African American Literature and Culture Society
1992   Carolina African American Writer's Collective
1993   The Toni Morrison Society
1994   Alain Locke Society
1995   Cave Canem
1997   Charles W. Chesnutt Society
1997   The George Moses Horton Society
1998   The John Edgar Wideman Society

Appendix 3

Archives and Research Centers

Amistad Research Center at Tulane University, New Orleans, La. 70118
Auburn Avenue Research Library of African American Culture and History, Atlanta, Ga. 30303
Furious Flower Poetry Center, MSC 1501, James Madison University, Harrisonburg, Va. 22807
James Weldon Johnson Memorial Collection, Beinecke Rare Book and Manuscript Library, Yale University, New Haven, Conn. 06520
Archives/Special Collections, Fisk University, Nashville, Tenn. 37208
Moorland-Spingarn Research Center, Howard University, Washington, D.C. 20059
Schomburg Center for Research in Black Culture, New York Public Library, New York, N.Y. 10037-1801
Archives and Special Collections, Woodruff Library, Atlanta University Center, Atlanta, Ga. 30314

Bibliography

Abrahams, Roger D. *Afro-American Folktales*. New York: Pantheon Books, 1985.

Abrams, M. H., and Stephen Greenblatt, eds. *The Norton Anthology of English Literature*. New York: W. W. Norton, 2000.

Adam, Alton A. "Whence Came the Calypso?" *Caribbean* 8 (May 1955): 218–20, 230, 235.

Adell, Sandra. *Double-Consciousness/Double Bind: Theoretical Issues in Twentieth-Century Black Literature*. Urbana and Chicago: Illinois University Press, 1994.

Adoff, Arnold. *The Poetry of Black America: Anthology of the Twentieth Century*. New York: Harper and Row, 1973.

African American Literature: Voices in a Tradition. Austin, Tex.: Holt, Rinehart, Winston, 1998.

Alexander, Elizabeth. *The Venus Hottentot: Poems*. Saint Paul, Minn.: Graywolf Press, 2004.

Allan, Jita Tuzyline. *Womanist and Feminist Aesthetics: A Comparative Review*. Athens: Ohio University Press, 1995.

Allen, Carol. *Black Women Intellectuals: Strategies of Nation, Family, and Neighborhoods in the Works of Pauline Hopkins, Jessie Fauset, and Marita Bonner*. New York: Garland, 1998.

The American Negro Writer and His Roots. New York: The American Society of African Culture, 1959.

Anadolu-Okur, Nilgun. *Contemporary African-American Theater: Afrocentricity in the Works of Larry Neal, Amiri Baraka, and Charles Fuller*. New York: Garland, 1997.

Andrews, William L. *African American Autobiography: A Collection of Critical Essays*. Englewood Cliffs, N.J.: Prentice Hall, 1993.

———. *To Tell a Free Story: The First Century of Afro-American Autobiography 1760–1865*. Urbana: University of Illinois Press, 1986.

———, ed. *The African-American Novel in the Age of Reaction*. New York: Mentor Books, 1992.

Andrews, William L., Frances Smith Foster, and Trudier Harris, eds. *The Oxford Companion to African American Literature*. New York: Oxford University Press, 1997.

Ani, Marimba. *Yurugu: An African-Centered Critique of European Cultural Thought and Behavior*. New York: Africa World Press, 1994.

Appiah, Kwame Anthony, and Henry Louis Gates Jr., eds. *Africana: The Encyclopedia of the African American Experience.* New York: Basic *Civitas* Books, 1999.

———. *Identities.* Chicago: University of Chicago Press, 1995.

Aptheker, Herbert. "Afro-American Superiority: A Neglected Theme in the Literature." 91 *Phylon* (1970): 336–43.

Arata, Esther. *More Black American Playwrights: A Bibliography.* Metuchen, N.J.: Scarecrow, 1978.

Arnold, A. James. *Modernism and Negritude: The Poetry and Poetics of Aime Cesaire.* Cambridge: Harvard University Press, 1981.

Asante, Molefi Kete. *The Afrocentric Idea.* Philadelphia: Temple University Press, 1987.

———. *Afrocentricity: The Theory of Social Change.* 2nd ed. Chicago: African-American Images, 2003.

Asante, Molefi Kete, and Abu S. Abarry, eds. *African Intellectual Heritage: A Book of Sources.* Philadelphia: Temple University Press, 1996.

Atkinson, Yvonne, and Philip Page. "Toni Morrison and the Southern Oral Tradition." *Studies in the Literary Imagination.* 31, 2 (1998): 97–107.

Awkward, Michael. *Inspiriting Influences: Tradition, Revision, and Afro-American Women's Novels.* New York: Columbia University Press, 1989.

Aubert, Alvin. *Against the Blues: Poems.* Detroit: Broadside Press, 1972.

Bailey, Cornelia Walker. *God, Dr. Buzzard, and the Bolito Man: A Saltwater Geechee Talks About Life on Sapelo Island.* New York: Knopf, 2001.

Baker, Houston, Jr. *Blues, Ideology, and Afro-American Literature: A Vernacular Theory.* Chicago: University of Chicago Press, 1984.

———."Hybridity, the Rap Race, and Pedagogy for the 1990s." *Black Music Research Journal* 11 (fall 1991): 217–28.

———. *The Journey Back: Issues in Black Literature and Criticism.* Chicago: University of Chicago Press, 1980.

———. *Modernism and the Harlem Renaissance.* Chicago: University of Chicago Press, 1987.

———. *Workings of the Spirit: The Poetics of Afro-American Women's Writing.* Chicago: University of Chicago Press, 1991.

Baker, Houston, Jr., and Dana D. Nelson. "Preface: Violence, the Body and 'The South.'" *American Literature* 73, 2 (2001): 231–44.

Baker, Houston, Jr., and Patricia Redmond, eds. *Afro-American Literary Study in the 1990s.* Chicago: University of Chicago Press, 1989.

Baker, Jean-Claude and Chris Chase. *Josephine: The Hungry Heart.* New York: Cooper Square Press, 2001.

Baldwin, James. "Everybody's Protest Novel" 1949. In *African American Literary Criticism, 1773 to 2000,* edited by Hazel Arnett Ervin, 91–93. New York: Twayne, 1999.

———. *The Fire Next Time.* New York: Dell Publishing Co., 1962.

———. "Many Thousand Gone," 1953. In *African American Literary Criticism, 1773 to 2000,* edited by Hazel Arnett Ervin, 99–102. New York: Twayne, 1999.

———. *Nobody Knows My Name.* New York: Dell Publishing Co., 1961.

Bambara, Toni Cade. *The Black Woman.* New York: New American Library, 1970.

Baraka, Amiri. *Blues People: Negro Music in White America* (1963). New York: William Morrow, 1999.

———. "expressive language." *Home: Social Essays,* 166–72. New York: William Morrow, 1966.

———. *The Music: Reflections on Jazz and Blues.* New York: William Morrow, 1987.

Barksdale, Richard, and Keneth Kinnamon, eds. *Black Writers of America: A Comprehensive Anthology.* New York: Macmillan, 1972.

Barlow, William. "I Been 'Buked and I Been Scorned (The Folk Roots of the Blues)." In *Looking Up at Down, The Emergence of Blues Culture,* 7–24. Philadelphia: Temple University Press, 1989.

———. *Looking Up at Down: The Emergence of Blues Culture.* Philadelphia: Temple University Press, 1989.

Barry, Peter. *Beginning Theory: An Introduction to Literary and Cultural Theory.* Manchester, U.K.: Manchester University Press, 1995.

Bell, Bernard W. *The Afro-American Novel and Its Tradition.* Amherst: Massachusetts University Press, 1987.

———. *The Folk Roots of Contemporary Afro-American Poetry.* Detroit: Broadside Press, 1974.

Bell, Bernard W., Emily Grosholz, and James B. Stewart, eds. *W.E.B. DuBois on Race and Culture: Philosophy, Politics, and Poetics.* New York: Routledge, 1996.

Bell, Roseann P., Bettye J. Parker, and Beverly Guy-Sheftall, eds. *Sturdy Black Bridges: Visions of Black Women in Literature.* New York: Doubleday, 1979.

Belton, Don, ed. *Speak My Name: Black Men on Masculinity and the American Dream.* Boston: Beacon Press, 1997.

Bennett, Michael, and Vanessa D. Dickerson, eds. *Recovering the Black Female Body: Self-Representation by African American Women.* New Brunswick, N.J.: Rutgers University Press, 2001.

Benston, Kimberly W. *Performing Blackness: Enactments of African-American Modernism.* New York: Routledge, 2000.

Berry, Faith, ed. *Good Morning Revolution: Uncollected Writings of Langston Hughes.* New York: Citadel, 1992.

Billingslea-Brown, Alma Jean. *Crossing Borders Through Folklore: African American Women's Fiction and Art.* Columbia: University of Missouri Press, 1999.

Blassingame, John W. *The Slave Community: Plantation Life in the Antebellum South.* New York: Oxford University Press, 1972.

Blount, Marcellus. "The Preacherly Text: African American Poetry and Vernacular Performance." *PMLA* 107 (1992): 582–93.

Blount, Marcellus and George P. Cunningham, eds. *Representing Black Men.* New York: Routledge, 1995.

Bobo, Jacqueline. *Black Feminist Cultural Criticism.* Malden, Mass.: Blackwell Publisher, 2001.

Bogle, Donald. *Toms, Coons, Mulattoes, Mammies, and Bucks: An Interpretative History of Blacks in American Films.* New York: Continuum, 1989.

Bone, Robert. *The Negro Novel in America.* New Haven: Yale University Press, 1972.

———. "Richard Wright and the Chicago Renaissance" *Callaloo* 9.3 (summer 1986): 446–68.

Boyd, Herb, and Robert L. Allen, eds. *Brotherman, The Odyssey of Black Men in America—An Anthology.* New York: Ballantine Books, 1995.

Boyd, Todd. *Am I Black Enough for You?: Popular Culture from the 'Hood and Beyond.* Bloomington: Indiana University Press, 1997.

Boyd, Valerie. *Wrapped in Rainbow: The Life of Zora Neale Hurston.* New York: Scribner, 2002.

Branch, Muriel Miller. *The Water Brought Us: The Story of the Gullah-Speaking People.* New York: Cobblehill Books/Dutton, 1995.

Brathwaite, Kamau. *Roots.* Ann Arbor: The University of Michigan Press, 1993.

Braxton, Joanne M. *Black Women Writing Autobiography: A Tradition Within a Tradition.* Philadelphia: Temple University Press, 1989.

Braxton, Joanne M., and Andree Nicola McLaughlin. *Wild Women in the Whirlwind: Afra-American Culture and the Contemporary Literary Renaissance.* New Brunswick, N.J.: Rutgers University Press, 1990.

Breitman, George, ed. "Message to the Grass Roots," *Malcolm X Speaks: Selected speeches and Statements.* New York: Pathfinder, 1989.

Bremen, Paul, ed. *You Better Believe It: Black Verse in English from Africa, the West Indies, and the United States.* New York: Penguin, 1973.

Brewer, John Mason. *The Word on the Brazos: Negro Preacher Tales from the Brazos Bottoms of Texas.* Austin: Texas University Press, 1958.

Brooks, Gwendolyn. *Selected Poems: Gwendolyn Brooks.* New York: Harper & Row, 1963.

———. *Poetry and the Heroic Voice,* ed. D. H. Melhem. Lexington: University of Kentucky Press, 1987.

Brown, Claude. "The Language of Soul." In *Rappin' and Stylin' Out: Communication in Urban Black America,* edited by Thomas Kochman, 136–39. Urbana: University of Illinois Press, 1972.

Brown, Fahamisha Patricia. *Performing the Word, African American Poetry as Vernacular Culture.* New Brunswick, N.J.: Rutgers University Press, 1999.

Brown, Lloyd W. "Black Entitles: Names as Symbols in Afro-American Literature." *Studies in Black Literature* I (spring 1970): 16–44.

———. "The Expatriate Consciousness in Black American Literature." In *African American Literary Criticism, 1773 to 2000,* edited by Hazel Arnett Ervin, 135–40. New York: Twayne, 1999.

Brown, Sterling A. *The American Negro: His History and Literature.* New York: Arno Press, 1969.

———. "Blues as Folk Poetry." *Folk-Say: A Regional Miscellany.* ed. Benjamin A. Botkin. Vol. 1. Norman: University of Oklahoma Press, 1930.

———. *The Collected Poems of Sterling A. Brown*. Selected by Michael S. Harper. New York: Harper & Row, 1980.

———. "Negro Characters as Seen by White Authors." In *African American Literary Criticism, 1773 to 2000*, edited by Hazel Arnett Ervin, 55–81. New York: Twayne, 1999.

———. "Negro Folk Expression: Spirituals, Seculars, Ballads, and Songs." *Phylon* 34 (1953): 45–61.

———. *Negro Poetry and Drama*. New York: Arno Press, 1969.

———. "Our Literary Audience." In *African American Literary Criticism, 1773 to 2000*, edited by Hazel Arnett Ervin, 51–54. New York: Twayne, 1999.

———. *Southern Roads*. New York: Harcourt, Brace, 1932.

Brown, William Wells. *The Black Man: His Antecedents, His Genius and His Achievements* (1863). New York: Kraus Reprint Company, 1969.

Brown-Guillory, Elizabeth, ed. *Wines in the Wilderness: Plays by African American Women from the Harlem Renaissance to the Present*. Westport, Conn.: Praeger, 1990.

———. *Their Place on the Stage: Black Women Playwrights in America*. Westport, Conn.: Praeger, 1988.

Bruce, Dickson D., Jr., "Protest Literature." In *The Oxford Companion to African American Literature*, edited by William Andrews, Frances Smith Foster, and Trudier Harris, 600–604. New York: Oxford University Press, 1997.

Bruck, Peter, ed. *The Black American Short Story in the Twentieth Century: A Collection of Critical Essays*. Amsterdam: John Benjamins Publishing Co., 1977.

Byrd, Rudolph P., and Beverly Guy-Sheftall, eds. *Traps: African American Men on Gender and Sexuality*. Bloomington: Indiana University Press, 2001.

Bullins, Ed, ed. *New Plays from the Black Theater*. New York: Bantam Books, 1969.

Busby, Margaret. Introduction, *Daughters of Africa: An International Anthology of Words and Writings by Women of African Descent from the Ancient Egyptian to the Present*, edited by Margaret Busby, xxviii–li. New York: Ballantine, 1992.

Butler-Evans, Elliot. *Race, Gender, and Desire: Narrative Strategies in the Fiction of Toni Cade Bambara, Toni Morrison, and Alice Walker*. Philadelphia: Temple University Press, 1991.

Byerman, Keith. "Epistolary Novel." In *The Oxford Companion to African American Literature*, edited by William Andrews, Frances Smith Foster, and Trudier Harris, 257. New York: Oxford University Press, 1997.

———. *Fingering the Jagged Grain: Tradition and Form in Recent Black Fiction*. Athens: University of Georgia Press, 1995.

Bynum, Edward Bruce, and Linda James Meyers, eds. *The African Unconscious: Roots of Ancient Mysticism and Modern Psychology*. New York: Teachers College Press, 1999.

Callahan, John. *In the African American Grain: The Pursuit of Voice in Twentieth-Century Black Fiction*. Urbana: University of Illinois Press, 1988.

———, ed. *The Collected Essays of Ralph Ellison*. New York: Modern Library, 2003.

Carby, Hazel. "Policing the Black Woman's Body in an Urban Content" 18.4 *Critical Inquiry* (summer 1992): 738–55.

———. *Reconstructing Womanhood: The Emergence of the Afro-American Woman Novelist*. New York: Oxford University Press, 1987.

Carlisle, Rodney. *The Roots of Black Nationalism*. Port Washington, N.Y.: Associated Kennikat Press, Inc., 1975.

Carroll, Rebecca, ed. *I Know What the Red Clay Looks Like: The Voice and Vision of Black Women Writers*. New York: Crown Publishers, 1994.

———, ed. *Swing Low: Black Men Writing*. New York: Crown Publishers, 1994.

Chapman, Abraham, ed. *New Black Voices: An Anthology of Afro-American Literature*. New York: Mentor Books, 1972.

Chapman, Dorothy. *Index to Black Poetry*. Boston: G. K. Hall, 1974.

Chesnutt, Charles. *The Conjure Woman*. Boston: Houghton, Mifflin and Company, 1899.

Christian, Barbara. "Alice Walker: The Black Woman Artist as Wayward." In *Black Women Writers: A Critical Evaluation*, edited by Mari Evans, 457–93. New York: Anchor Books/Doubleday, 1984.

———. *Black Women Novelists: The Development of a Tradition, 1892–1976*. Westport, Conn.: Greenwood Publishing Group, 1980.

———. "There It Is: The Poetry of Jayne Cortez." *Callaloo* 9.2 (winter 1986): 235–39.

Clark, Edward. *Black Writers in New England: A Bibliography with Biographical Notes*. Boston: Suffolk University, 1985.

Clark, Keith. *Black Manhood in James Baldwin, Ernest J. Gaines, and August Wilson*. Urbana: University of Illinois Press, 2002.

Clarke, John Henrik, ed. *Black American Short Stories: A Century of the Best*. New York: Hill and Wang, 1993.

Cobb-Moore, Geneva. "Diaries and Journals." In *The Oxford Companion to African American Literature*, edited by William Andrews, Frances Smith Foster, and Trudier Harris, 216–18. New York: Oxford University Press, 1997.

Collins, Patricia Hill. *Black Feminist Thought: Knowledge, Consciousness, and the Politics of Empowerment*. New York: Routledge, 1991.

Collins, Patricia Hill, and Margaret L. Andersen, eds. *Race, Class, and Gender: An Anthology*. Belmont Calif.: Wadsworth, 1992.

Conyers, James L., and Alva Barnett. *African History, Culture and Social Policy*. Lanham, Md.: International Scholars Publications, 1999.

Cook, Mercer, and Stephen Henderson. *The Militant Black Writer*. Madison: University of Wisconsin Press, 1969.

Cook, Michael G. *Afro-American Literature in the Twentieth Century: The Achievement of Intimacy*. New Haven: Yale University Press, 1990.

Cooper, J. California. *Some Soul to Keep*. New York: St. Martin's Press, 1987.

Coser, Stelamaris. *Bridging the Americas: The Literature of Toni Morrison, Paule Marshall, and Gayl Jones*. Philadelphia: Temple University Press, 1994.

Creel, Margaret W. *A Peculiar People: Slave Religion and Community Culture Among the Gullah*. New York: New York University Press, 1988.

Cripps, Thomas. *Slow Fade to Black: The Negro in American Film, 1900–1942.* New York: Oxford University Press, 1977.

Cruz, Jon. *Culture on the Margins: The Black Spiritual and the Rise of American Cultural Interpretation.* Princeton: Princeton University Press, 1999.

Courlander, Harold. *A Treasury of African Folklore.* New York: Marlowe and Company, 1996.

———. *A Treasury of Afro-American Folklore.* New York: Marlowe and Company, 1996.

Dance, Daryl. *Honey Hush! An Anthology of African American Women's Humor.* New York: W. W. Norton, 1998.

———. *Shuckin' and Jivin': Folklore from Contemporary Black America.* Bloomington: Indiana University Press, 1978.

Dandridge, Rita B. *Black Women's Blues: A Literary Anthology, 1934–1988.* New York: G. K. Hall, 1992.

Davies, Carole Boyce. *Black Women, Writing and Identity: Migrations of the Subject.* New York: Routledge, 1994.

———. *Moving Beyond Boundaries: Black Women's Diasporas, Vol 2.* New York: New York University Press, 1995.

———. *Moving Beyond Boundaries: International Dimensions of Black Women's Writing, Vol 1.* New York: New York University Press, 1995.

Davis, Arthur P. "Novels of the New Black Renaissance (1960–1977): A Thematic Survey." *CLA.* 21.4 (June 1978): 457–90.

Davis, Arthur P., Sterling A. Brown, and Ulysses Lee, eds. *The Negro Caravan.* New York: Dryden Press, 1941.

Davis, Arthur P., and Saunders Redding, eds. *Calvacade: Negro American Writing from 1760 to the Present.* Boston: Houghton Mifflin, 1971.

Davis, Charles T., and Henry Louis Gates. *Black Is the Color of the Cosmos: Essays on Afro-American Literature and Culture, 1942–1981.* Washington, D.C.: Howard University Press, 1989.

Davis, Thadious. *Nella Larsen: Novelist of the Harlem Renaissance.* Baton Rouge: Louisiana State University Press, 1994.

Davis, Thadious, and Trudier Harris, eds. *Afro-American Writers After 1955: Dramatists and Prose Writers (Dictionary of Literary Biography, Vol 38).* New York: Gale, 1985.

———, eds. *Afro-American Fiction Writers After 1955 (Dictionary of Literary Biography, Vol 33).* New York: Gale, 1984.

de Man, Paul. *Blindness and Insight: Essays in the Rhetoric of Contemporary Criticism.* Minneapolis: University of Minnesota, 1985.

Denard, Carolyn. "Blacks, Modernism, and the American South: An Interview." [Interview with Toni Morrison.] *Studies in the Literary Imagination.* 31, 2 (1998): 1–16.

Deodene, Frank, and William French. *Black American Poetry Since 1949: A Preliminary Checklist.* Chatham, N.J.: Chatham Bookseller, 1971.

Derrida, Jacques. *Writing and Difference.* Translated by Alan Bass. Chicago: University of Chicago Press, 1980.

DeSaints, Christopher. "Badman." In *The Oxford Companion to African American Literature*, edited by William Andrews, Frances Smith Foster, and Trudier Harris, 42. New York: Oxford University Press, 1997.

de Weever, Jacqueline. *Mythmaking and Metaphor in Black Women's Fiction*. New York: St. Martin's Press, 1991.

Diawara, Manthia. *Black American Cinema*. New York: Routledge, 1994.

Dick, Bruce, and Amritjit Singh, eds. *Conversations with Ishmael Reed*. Jackson: University Press of Mississippi, 1995.

Dickson-Carr, Darryl. *African American Satire: The Sacredly Profane Novel*. Columbia: University of Missouri, 2001.

Diedrich, Maria, Henry Louis Gates Jr., and Carl Pederson, eds. *Black Imagination and the Middle Passage*. New York: Oxford University Press, 1999.

Dillard, J. L. *Black English: Its History and Usage in the United States*. New York: Vintage Books, 1972.

Dixon, Melvin. "The Black Writer's Use of Memory." In *History and Memory in African-American Culture*, edited by Geneviève Fabre and Robert O'Meally, 18–27. New York: Oxford University Press, 1994.

Donalson, Melvin, ed. *Cornerstones: An Anthology of African American Literature*. New York: St. Martin's Press, 1996.

Dubey, Madhu. *Black Woman Novelists and the Nationalist Aesthetic*. Bloomington: Indiana University Press, 1994.

DuBois, W.E.B. "Criteria of Negro Art," 1926. In *African American Literary Criticism, 1773 to 2000*, edited by Hazel Arnett Ervin, 39–43. New York: Twayne, 1999.

———. "The Talented Tenth." In *The Negro Problem: A Series of Articles by Representative American Negroes of Today*, 33–75. New York: James Potts, 1903.

duCille, Ann. *The Coupling Convention: Sex, Text, and Tradition in Black Women's Fiction*. New York: Oxford University Press, 1993.

Dumas, Henry. *Ark of Bones and Other Stories,* edited by Eugene B. Redmond. New York: Random House, 1974.

Dundes, Alan, ed. *Mother Wit from the Laughing Barrel*. Englewood Cliffs, N.J.: Prentice-Hall, 1973.

Dyson, Michael Eric. *Between God and Gangsta' Rap: Bearing Witness to Black Culture*. New York: Oxford University Press, 1995.

———. *Reflecting Black: African American Cultural Criticism*. Minneapolis: Minnesota University Press, 1993.

Early, Gerald. *Speech and Power: The African-American Essay and Its Cultural Content from Polemics to Pulpit, Vol 1*. Hopewell, N.J.: The Ecco Press, 1992.

———, ed. My Soul's High Song: *The Collected Writing of Countee Cullen*. New York: Anchor Books, 1990.

Elia, Nada. *Trances, Dances and Vociferations: Agency and Resistance in Africana Women's Narratives*. New York: Garland, 2000.

Ellis, Thomas Sayers. *The Genuine Negro Hero*. Kent, Ohio: Kent State University Press, 2001.

Ellis, Trey. "The New Black Aesthetic." *Callaloo* 12 (winter 1989): 233–43.

Ellison, Ralph. "The Art of Fiction: An Interview." In *Shadow and Act* by Ralph Ellison, 169–83. New York: Signet, 1964.

———. "Change the Joke and Slip the Yoke." In *Shadow and Act* by Ralph Ellison, 61–73. New York: Signet Book, 1964.

———. "Richard Wright's Blues." In *Shadow and Act*, by Ralph Ellison, 89–104. New York: Signet, 1964.

Emanuel, James A. "America Before 1950: Black Writers' Views." *Negro Digest* 38 (August 1969): 26–34; 67–69.

Empson, William. *Seven Types of Ambiguity* (1930). New York: New Directions, 1966.

Ernest, John. *Resistance and Reformation in Nineteenth-Century African-American Literature: Brown, Wilson, Jacobs, Delany, Douglass and Harper*. Jackson: University Press of Mississippi, 1995.

Ervin, Hazel Arnett. *Ann Petry: A Bio-Bibliography*. New York: G. K. Hall, 1993.

———, ed. *African American Literary Criticism, 1773 to 2000*. New York: Twayne, 1999.

Ervin, Hazel Arnett, and Hilary Holladay, eds. *Ann Petry's Short Fiction: Critical Essays*. Westport, Conn.: Praeger, 2004.

Euba, Femi. *Archetypes, Imprecators, and Victims of Fate: Origins and Development of Satire in Black Drama*. Westport, Conn.: Greenwood Press, 1989.

Fabre, Geneviève. "The Slave Ship Dance." In *Black Imagination and the Middle Passage*, edited by Maria Diedrich, Henry Louis Gates Jr. and Carla Pedersen, 33–46. New York: Oxford University Press, 1999.

Fabre, Geneviève, and Robert O'Meally, eds. *History and Memory in African-American Culture*. New York: Oxford University Press, 1994.

Fabre, Michel, ed. *From Harlem to Paris: Black American Writers in France, 1840–1980*. Urbana: University of Illinois Press, 1993.

Fairbanks, Carol, and Eugene Engeldinger. *Black American Fiction: A Bibliography*. Lanham, Md.: Scarecrow Press, 1978.

Fanon, Frantz. "The Negro and Psychopathology." In *Black Skin, White Masks* by Frantz Fanon, 141–209. New York: Grove Press, 1967.

Farnsworth, Robert M. *Melvin B. Tolson, 1898–1966: Plain Talk and Poetic Prophecy*. Columbia: University of Missouri Press, 1984.

Ferguson, SallyAnn H. *Charles W. Chesnutt. Selected Writings*. Boston: Houghton Mifflin, 2001.

Fernando, S. H., Jr. *The New Beats: Exploring the Music, Culture, and Attitudes of Hip-Hop*. New York: Doubleday-Anchor, 1994.

Fetrow, Fred M. *Robert Hayden*. New York: Twayne, 1984.

Finney, Nikky. *Rice*. Toronto: Sister Vision Press, 1998.

Fish, Stanley. *Is There a Text in This Class? The Authority of Interpretive Communities*. Cambridge, Mass.: Harvard University Press, 1980.

Folks, Jeffrey J. *From Richard Wright to Toni Morrison: Others in Modern and Postmodern American Narrative*. New York: Peter Lang Publishers, 2001.

Fontenot, Chester, Jr. "Ishmael Reed and the Politics of Aesthetics, or Shake Hands and Come Out Conjuring." *Black American Literature Forum* 12.1 (spring 1978): 20–23.

Ford, Nick Aaron. "A Blueprint for Negro Authors." *Phylon* 31 (1950): 374–77.

Forrest, Leon, and Ralph Waldo Ellison. *There Is a Tree More Ancient than Eden.* (1973) Chicago: Another Chicago Press, 1988.

Fossett, Judith Jackson, and Jeffrey A. Tucker, eds. *Race Consciousness: African-American Studies for the New Century.* New York: New York University Press, 1997.

Foster, Frances Smith. "Diasporic Literature." In *The Oxford Companion to African American Literature*, edited by William Andrews, Frances Smith Foster, and Trudier Harris, 218–22. New York: Oxford University Press, 1997.

———. *Witnessing Slavery: The Development of Ante-bellum Slave Narratives.* Madison: University of Wisconsin Press, 1994.

———. *Written by Herself: Literary Production by African American Women, 1746–1892.* Bloomington: Indiana University Press, 1993.

Foster, Marie M. *Southern Black Creative Writers, 1829–1953.* Westport, Conn.: Greenwood Publishing Group, 1988.

Fowler, Carolyn (see also Carolyn F. Gerald). *Black Arts and Black Aesthetics, A Bibliography.* Atlanta: First World, 1976.

———. (Carolyn F. Gerald). "The Black Writer and His Role." In *African American Literary Criticism, 1773 to 2000*, edited by Hazel Arnett Ervin, 129–34. New York: Twayne, 1999.

Fox, Robert Elliot. *Conscientious Sorcerers: The Black Postmodernist Fiction of LeRoi Jones/Amiri Baraka, Ishmael Reed, and Samuel R. Delany.* Westport, Conn.: Greenwood Publishing Group, 1987.

Frank, Robert, and Henry Sayre, eds. *The Line in Postmodern Poetry.* Urbana: University of Illinois Press, 1988.

Fuller, Hoyt W., ed. "A Survey: Black Writers' Views on Literary Lions and Values." *Negro Digest* 28 (January 1968): 10–48, 81–89.

Fultz, Lucille. "Southern Ethos/Black Ethics in Morrison's Fiction." *Studies in the Literary Imagination* 31, 2 (1998): 79–95.

Gabbin, Joanne. *Furious Flower: A Video Anthology of African American Poetry, 1960–95* (1998); www.newsreel.org.

———. "Poetry." In *The Oxford Companion to African American Literature*, edited by William Andrews, Frances Smith Foster, and Trudier Harris, 584–92. New York: Oxford University Press, 1997.

———. *Sterling A. Brown: Building the Black Aesthetic Tradition.* Charlottesville: Virginia University Press, 1985.

Gates, Henry Louis Jr. *Figures in Black: Words, Signs, and the Racial Self.* New York: Oxford University Press, 1987.

———, *The Signifying Monkey: A Theory of Afro-American Literary Criticism.* New York: Oxford University Press, 1988.

———, ed. *"Race," Writing, and Difference.* Chicago: University of Chicago Press, 1985.

————, ed. *Reading Black, Reading Feminist: A Critical Anthology.* New York: Meridian, 1990.

————, ed. *The Schomburg Library of Nineteenth-Century Women Writers.* New York: Oxford University Press, 1988.

Gates, Henry Louis, Jr., and Nellie Y. McKay, eds. *The Norton Anthology of African American Literature.* New York: W. W. Norton, 1997.

Gates, Nathaniel, ed. *Cultural and Literary Critiques of the Concepts of "Race."* New York: Garland, 1997.

Gatewood, Willard B. *Aristocrats of Color: The Black Elite, 1880–1920.* Bloomington: Indiana University Press, 1990.

Gayle, Addison, ed. *The Black Aesthetic.* Garden City, N.Y.: Doubleday, 1971.

————. *Black Expression, Essays By and About Black Americans in the Creative Arts.* New York: Weybright and Talley, 1969.

————. "Cultural Nationalism: The Black Novel and the City." *Liberator* 45 (July 1969): 14–17.

————. *The Way of the World: The Black Novel in America.* Garden City, N.Y.: Doubleday, 1975.

Gerald, Carolyn F. (see also Carolyn Fowler). "The Black Writer and His Role." In *African American Literary Criticism, 1773 to 2000,* edited by Hazel Arnett Ervin, 129–34. New York: Twayne, 1999.

George, Nelson. *Hip Hop America.* New York: Viking, 1998.

Georgia Writers' Project. *Drums and Shadows: Survival Studies Among the Georgia Coastal Negroes.* Athens: University of Georgia Press, 1986.

Gibson, Donald B. *Five Black Writers: Essays on Wright, Ellison, Baldwin, Hughes, and LeRoi Jones.* New York: New York University Press, 1970.

Giddings, Paula. *When and Where I Enter: The Impact of Black Women on Race and Sex in America.* New York: Bantam Books, 1984.

Gikandi, Simon. *Encyclopedia of African Literature.* New York: Routledge, 2002.

————. *Reading the African Novel.* Portsmouth, N.H.: Heinemann, 1987.

Gilroy, Paul. *The Black Atlantic: Modernity and Double Consciousness.* Cambridge: Harvard University Press, 1995.

Giovanni, Nikki. *Black Feeling, Black Talk/Black Judgement.* New York: William Morrow, 1970.

Gladney, Marvin. "The Black Arts Movement and Hip Hop." *African American Review* 29.2 (summer 1995): 291–301.

Glaysher, Frederick, ed. *Collected Poems: Robert Hayden.* New York: Liveright, 1985.

Glen, Robert. *Black Rhetoric: A Guide to Afro-American Communication.* Metuchen, N.J.: Scarecrow Press, 1976.

Golden, Thelma, ed. *Black Male: Representations of Masculinity in Contemporary American Art.* New York: Whitney Museum of Art, 1994.

Gordon, Lewis, ed. *Existence in Black: An Anthology of Black Existential Philosophy.* New York: Routledge, 1997.

Gordon, Lewis, and Renee T. White, eds. *Black Texts and Textuality: Constructing and Deconstructing Blackness.* Lanham, Md.: Rowman and Littlefield, 1999.

Govan, Sandra. "Speculative Fiction." In *The Oxford Companion to African American Literature*, edited by William Andrews, Frances Smith Foster, and Trudier Harris, 683–87. New York: Oxford University Press, 1997.

Graham, Maryemma. "Novel." In *The Oxford Companion to African American Literature*, edited by William Andrews, Frances Smith Foster, and Trudier Harris, 541–48. New York: Oxford University Press, 1997.

———, ed. *The Cambridge Companion to the African American Novel*. New York: Cambridge University Press, 2003.

Greene, Lee. *Blacks in Eden: The African American Novel's First Century*. Charlottesville: Virginia University Press, 1996.

———. "The Pain and the Beauty: The South, the Black Writer, and the Conventions of the Picaresque." In *The American South*, edited by Louis D. Rubin Jr., 264–88. Baton Rouge: Louisiana State University Press, 1980.

Griffin, Farah Jasmine. *"Who Set You Flowin'?": The African-American Migration Narrative*. New York: Oxford University Press, 1995.

Griffin, Farah Jasmine, and Cheryl J. Fish, eds. *A Stranger in The Village, Two Centuries of African-American Travel Writing*. Boston: Beacon Press, 1998.

Griffin, John Howard. *Black Like Me*. New York: Signet, 1961.

Gross, Seymour L. "Stereotype to Archetype: The Negro in American Literary Criticism." In *Images of the Negro in American Literature*, edited by Seymour L. Gross and John Edward Hardy, 1–26. Chicago: University of Chicago Press, 1966.

Guerin, Wilfred L., Earle G. Labor, Lee Morgan, and John R. Willingham. *A Handbook of Critical Approaches to Literature*. New York: Harper and Row, 1979.

Guerrero, Ed. *Framing Blackness: The African American Image in Film*. Philadelphia: Temple University Press, 1993.

Guy-Sheftall, Beverly, ed. *Words of Fire: An Anthology of African American Feminist Thought*. New York: New Press, 1995.

Gwaltney, John Langston. *Drylongso: A Self-Portrait of Black America*. New York: New Press, 1993.

Hakutani, Yoshinobu, and Robert Butler, eds. *The City in African-American Literature*. Madison, N.J.: Fairleigh Dickinson University Press, 1995.

Hall, Perry A. *In the Vineyard: Working in African American Studies*. Knoxville: University of Tennessee Press, 1999.

Hall, Stuart, ed. *Representation: Cultural Representations and Signifying Practices*. London: Sage, 1997.

Hamalian, Leo, and James V. Hatch. *The Roots of African American Drama*. Detroit: Wayne State University Press, 1992.

Hamer, Judith A., and Martin J., eds. *Centers of the Self, Short Stories by Black American Women from the Nineteenth Century to the Present*. New York: Hill and Wang, 1994.

Handley, George B. *Post Slavery Literature in the Americas: Family Portraits in Black and White*. Charlottesville: University of Virginia Press, 2000.

Harasym, Sarah. *The Post-Colonial Critic: Gayatri Chakravorty Spivak*. New York: Routledge, 1990.

Harper, Brian Phillip. *Are We Not Men?: Masculine Anxiety and the Problem of African Identity*. New York: Oxford University Press, 1996.

Harper, Michael S. "Don't They Speak Jazz?" *MELUS* 10 (spring 1983): 3–6.

———. "Remembering Robert Hayden" *Michigan Quarterly Review* 21 (winter 1982): 182–86.

Harper, Michael S., and Robert B. Stepto, eds. *Chant of Saints: A Gathering of Afro-American Literature, Art, and Scholarship*. Urbana: University of Illinois Press, 1979.

Harris, Leonard. *Philosophy Born of Struggle: An Anthology of Afro-American Philosophy from 1017*. Dubuque, Ia.: Kendall/Hunt, 1983.

———. *Philosophy of Alain Locke: Harlem Renaissance and Beyond*. Philadelphia: Temple University Press, 1991.

Harris, Trudier. "Bad Woman." In *The Oxford Companion to African American Literature*, edited by William Andrews, Frances Smith Foster, and Trudier Harris, 42–43. New York: Oxford University Press, 1997.

———. "Healing." In *The Oxford Companion to African American Literature*, edited by William Andrews, Frances Smith Foster, and Trudier Harris, 349–50. New York: Oxford University Press, 1997.

———. "The Meaning of a Tradition." In *The New Calvacade: Afro-American Writing from 1760 to the Present, Vol II*, edited by Arthur P. Davis, J. Saunders Redding, and Joyce Ann Joyce, 832–44. Washington, D.C.: Howard University Press, 1991.

Harris, William J. "Black Aesthetic." In *The Oxford Companion to African American Literature*, edited by William Andrews, Frances Smith Foster, and Trudier Harris, 67–70. New York: Oxford University Press, 1997.

Hatch, James, and Omani Adbullah. *Black Playwrights, 1823–1977: An Annotated Bibliography*. New York: Bowker, 1977.

Hatcher, John. *From the Auroral Darkness: The Life and Poetry of Robert Hayden*. New York: Oxford University Press, 1984.

Hawthorn, Jeremy. *A Glossary of Contemporary Literary Theory*. New York: Arnold, 1998.

Hemphill, Essex. *Brother to Brother: New Writings by Black Gay Men*. Los Angeles: Alyson Publications, 1991.

Henderson, Mae. *Borders, Boundaries, and Frames: Essays in Cultural Criticism and Cultural Studies*. New York: Routledge, 1994.

———. "Speaking in Tongues: Dialogics, Dialectics, and the Black Woman Writer's Literary Tradition." In *African American Literary Theory: A Reader*, edited by Winston Napier, 348–68. New York: New York University Press, 2000.

———. "Toni Morrison's Beloved: Re-membering the Body as Historical Text." In *Comparative American Identities: Race, Sex, and Nationality in the Modern Text*, edited by Hortense J. Spillers, 62–86. New York: Routledge, 1991.

Henderson, Stephen E. "Cliché, Monotony, and Touchstone: Folk Song Composition and the New Black Poetry." In *Black Southern Voices: An Anthology of Fiction, Poetry, Drama, Nonfiction, and Critical Essays*, edited by John Oliver Killens and Jerry W. Ward Jr., 529–49. New York: Meridian, 1992.

————. "The Heavy Blues of Sterling Brown: A Study of Craft and Tradition." *Black American Literature Forum* 14 (spring 1980): 32–44.

————. "Inside the Funk Shop, A Word on Black Words." In *African American Literary Theory: A Reader*, edited by Winston Napier, 97–101. New York: New York University Press, 2000.

————. "Progress Report on a Theory of Black Poetry" (1975). In *African American Literary Theory: A Reader*, edited by Winston Napier, 102–22. New York: New York University, 2000.

————. "The Question of Form and Judgment in Contemporary Black American Poetry, 1962–1977." In *A Dark and Sudden Beauty: Two Essays on Black American Poetry by George Kent and Stephen Henderson*, edited by Houston A. Baker Jr., 19–36. Philadelphia: Afro-American Studies Program of the University of Pennsylvania, 1977.

————.*Understanding the New Black Poetry: Black Speech and Black Music as Poetic References.* New York: William Morrow, 1973.

————. "Worrying the Line: Notes on Black American Poetry." In *The Line in Postmodern Poetry*, edited by Robert Frank and Henry Sayre. Urbana: University of Illinois Press, 1988.

Henry, Joseph. "A MELUS Interview: Ishmael Reed." In *African American Literary Criticism, 1773 to 2000*, edited by Hazel Arnett Ervin, 235–41. New York: Twayne, 1999.

Hernton, Calvin. *The Sexual Mountain and Black Women Writers.* New York: Doubleday, 1987.

Higginson, William J., and Meagan Calogeras. *Haiku World: An International Poetry Almanac.* Otowa Bunkyo-ku, Japan: Kodansha International, 1997.

Hill, Patricia Liggins, ed. *Call and Response: The Riverside Anthology of the African American Literary Tradition.* Boston: Houghton Mifflin, 1997.

Hill, Patricia Liggins, and Margaret L. Andersen, eds. *Race, Class, and Gender: An Anthology.* Belmont, Calif.: Wadsworth, 1992.

Hogue, Lawrence. *The African American Male, Writing, and Difference: A Polycentric Approach to African American Literature, Criticism, and History.* Albany, N.Y.: State University of New York Press, 2003.

————. *Race, Modernity, Postmodernity: A Look at the History and the Literatures of People of Color Since the 1960s.* New York: State University of New York Press, 1996.

Holloway, Joseph E. *Africanisms in American Culture.* Bloomington: Indiana University Press, 1990.

Holloway, Joseph E., and Winifred Vass. *The African Heritage of American English.* Bloomington: Indiana University Press, 1993.

Holloway, John S. *Confronting the Veil: New Deal African American Intellectuals and the Evolution of a Radical Voice.* New York: Routledge, 1998.

Holloway, Karla F. C. *Moorings and Metaphors: Figures of Culture and Gender in Black Women's Literature.* New Brunswick, N.J.: Rutgers University Press, 1992.

————. *Passed On: African American Mourning Stories.* Durham: Duke University Press, 2002.

hooks, bell. "'Homeplace': A Site of Resistance." In *Yearning: Race, Gender, and Cultural Politics*, 41–50. Boston: South End Press, 1990.

———. *Reel to Real: Race, Sex, and Class at the Movies*. New York: Routledge, 1996.

———. "Revolutionary Attitudes." In *Black Looks, Race and Representation*, 1–7. Boston: South End Press, 1992.

Hord, Fred Lee. *Reconstructing Memory: Black Literary Criticism*. Chicago: Third World Press, 1991.

Houston, Helen. *The Afro-American Novel, 1965–1975: A Descriptive Bibliography of Primary and Secondary Materials*. Troy, N.Y.: Whitson Publishers Company, 1977.

Hubbard, Dolan. *The Sermon and the African American Literary Imagination*. Columbia: University of Missouri, 1994.

———, ed. *The Souls of Black Folk One Hundred Years Later*. Columbia: University of Missouri Press, 2003.

Hudson, Theodore. *From LeRoi Jones to Baraka: The Literary Works*. Durham, N.C.: Duke University Press, 1973.

Hudson-Weems, Clenora, "Africana Womanism: An Overview." *The Western Journal of Black Studies*, 24, no. 3(fall 2000).

———. *Africana Womanism: Reclaiming Ourselves*. Troy, Mich.: Bedford Publishers, 1993.

Hughes, Carl Milton. *The Negro Novelist: A Discussion of the Writings of American Negro Novelists, 1940–1950*. New York: Citadel, 1970.

Hughes, Langston. "The Negro Artist and the Racial Mountain." *The Nation*, June 23, 1926. Reprinted in *African American Literary Criticism, 1773 to 2000* ed. Ervin (1999:48).

———. *Selected Poems of Langston Hughes*. New York: Vintage Books, 1974.

———, ed. *The Book of Negro Humor*. Santa Cruz, Calif.: Apollo, 2000.

Hughes, Langston, and Arna Bontemps, eds. *The Book of Negro Folklore*. New York: Dodd, Mead and Company, 1958.

Hull, Gloria T. *Color, Sex, and Poetry: Three Women Writers of the Harlem Renaissance*. Bloomington: Indiana University Press, 1987.

Hull, Gloria T., Patricia Bell Scott, and Barbara Smith, eds. *All the Women Are White, All the Blacks Are Men, But Some of Us Are Brave*. New York: The Feminist Press of CUNY, 1986.

Hurston, Zora Neale. *Mules and Men*. New York: Harper, 1935.

———. *Tell My Horse: Voodoo and Life in Haiti and Jamaica*. New York: Perennial, 1990.

Inge, M. Thomas, Maurice Duke, and Jackson Bryer. *Black American Writing, Bibliographical Essays*. New York: St. Martin's Press, 1978.

Irele, F. Abiola. *The African Imagination: Literature in Africa and the Black Diaspora*. New York: Oxford University Press, 2001.

Irle, F. Abiola, and Simon Gikandi, eds. *The Cambridge History of African and Caribbean Literature*. Cambridge: Cambridge University Press, 2004.

Jablon, Madelyn. *Black Metafiction: Self-Consciousness in African American Literature*. Iowa City: Iowa University Press, 1998.

Jack, Belinda Elizabeth. *Negritude and Literary Criticism: The History and Theory of 'Negro African' Literature in French*. Westport, Conn.: Greenwood Press, 1996.

Jackson, Blydon. "A Survey Course in Negro Literature." *College English* 35 (March 1973): 631–36.

———. *The Waiting Years*. Baton Rouge: Louisiana State University Press, 1976.

Jackson, Bruce, ed. *"Get Your Ass in the Water and Swim Like Me": Narrative Poetry from Black Oral Tradition*. Cambridge: Harvard University Press, 1974.

———, ed. *Wake Up Dead Man: Afro-American Worksongs from Texas*. Cambridge: Harvard University Press, 1972.

Jackson, Gale. "The Way We Do: A Preliminary Investigation of the African Roots of African American Performance." In *African American Literary Criticism, 1773 to 2000*, edited by Hazel Arnett Ervin, 312–20. New York: Twayne, 1999.

Jackson, Major, and Al Young. *Leaving Saturn: Poems*. Athens: University of Georgia Press, 2002.

Jacques-Garvey, Amy, ed. *The Philosophy and Opinions of Marcus Garvey, 1923–25*. New York: Atheneum, 1969.

———. *The Philosophy and Opinions of Marcus Garvey, Or Africa for the Africans*. Dover, Mass.: Majority Press, 1986.

James, Darius. *That Blaxploitation: Roots of the Badasssss'Tude (Rated X by an All Whyte Jury)*. New York: St. Martin's Press, 1995.

James, Joy, and Lewis Gordon. *Transcending the Talented Tenth: Black Leaders and American Intellectuals*. New York: Routledge, 1996.

James, Joy, and T. Denean Sharpley-Whiting. *The Black Feminist Reader*. Malden, Mass.: Blackwell Publisher, 2000.

James, Stanlie M., and Abena P.A. Busia, eds. *Theorizing Feminisms: The Visionary Pragmatism of Black Women*. New York: Routledge, 1993.

James, Willis Laurence. "The Romance of the Negro Folk Cry in America." 16 *Phylon* (1950): 15–30.

Jahn, Janheinz. *Neo-African Literature: A History of Black Writing*. New York: Grove, 1968.

Janken, Kenneth R. "Expatriatism." In *The Oxford Companion to African American Literature*, edited by William Andrews, Frances Smith Foster, and Trudier Harris, 262–64. New York: Oxford University Press, 1997.

Jeffers, Lance. "On Listening to the Spirituals." *When I Know the Power of My Hand*. Detroit: Broadside Press, 1974.

Jekyll, Walter, ed. *Jamaican Song and Story: Annancy Stories, Digging Singer, Ring Tunes and Dancing Tunes*. New York: Dover Publications, 1966.

Jimoh, A. Yemisi. *Spirituals, Blues, and Jazz People in African American Fiction: Living in Paradox*. Knoxville: University of Tennessee Press, 2002.

Johnson, Abby A., and Ronald Johnson. *Propaganda and Aesthetics: The Literary Politics of Afro-American Magazines in the Twentieth Century*. Amherst: Massachusetts University Press, 1991.

Johnson, Barbara. "The Critical Difference: BartheS/BalZac." *The Critical Difference:*

Essays in the Contemporary Rhetoric of Reading by Barbara Johnson, 3–12. Baltimore: The John Hopkins University Press, 1980.

Johnson, Charles R. *Being and Race: Black Writing Since 1970.* Bloomington: Indiana University Press, 1990.

Johnson, Charles S. "The Significance of the Negro Renaissance." In *The Portable Harlem Renaissance Reader,* edited by David Levering Lewis, 206–18. New York: Penguin, 1995.

Johnson, Guy B. *John Henry: Tracking Down a Negro Legend.* Chapel Hill: University of North Carolina Press, 1929.

Johnson, James Weldon. Preface, *God's Trombones: Seven Negro Sermons in Verse.* 1927. New York: Penguin, 1976, 1–11.

———, ed. *The Book of American Negro Poetry.* New York: Harcourt, Brace, 1922. Rev ed. San Diego: Harvest Books, 1969.

Jones, Charles C. *Negro Myths from the Georgia Coast.* New York: Gale Group, 1969.

Jones, Gayl. *Liberating Voices: Oral Tradition in African American Literature.* Cambridge: Harvard University Press, 1991.

Jones, Leroi (Amiri Baraka). "In Search of the Revolutionary Black Theatre." *Negro Digest* 35 (April 1966): 20–24.

———. "What the Arts Need Now." *Negro Digest* 36 (April 1967): 5–6.

Jones, Leroi, and Larry Neal, eds. *Black Fire: An Anthology of Afro-American Writings.* New York: William Morrow, 1968.

Jones-Jackson, Patricia. *When Roots Die.* Athens: University of Georgia Press, 1987.

Jordan, Jennifer. "Cultural Nationalism in the 1960s: Politics and Poetry." In *Race, Politics and Culture: Critical Essays on Radicalism of the 1960s,* edited by Adolph Reed, 29–60. New York: Greenwood Press, 1987.

Joyce, Joyce Ann. *Warriors, Conjurers and Priests: Defining African-Centered Literary Criticism.* Chicago: Third World Press, 1994.

Joyner, Charles. *Down by the Riverside: A South Carolina Slave Community.* Urbana: University of Illinois Press, 1986.

Kafka, Phillipa. *The Great White Way: African American Women Writers and American Success Mythologies.* New York: Garland, 1993.

Karrer, Wolfgang, and Barbara Pushmann-Nolenz, eds. *The African American Short Story, 1970 to 1990: A Collection of Critical Essays.* Trier, Germany: Wissenschaftlicher Verlag, 1995.

Keizer, Arlene R. "Poetry, Religious and Didactic." In *The Oxford Companion to African American Literature,* edited by William Andrews, Frances Smith Foster, and Trudier Harris, 592–94. New York: Oxford University Press, 1997.

Kelly, Robin D. G. *Race Rebels: Culture, Politics, and the Black Working Class.* New York: Macmillan, 1994.

Kent, George. *Blackness and the Adventure of Western Culture.* Chicago: Third World Press, 1973.

Kerlin, Robert T. *Negro Poets and Their Poems.* Washington, D.C.: The Associated Publishers, 1935.

Kester, Gunilla T. *Writing the Subject: Bildung and the African American Text.* New York: Peter Lang, 1997.

Killens, John, and Jerry Ward, eds. *Black Southern Voices, An Anthology.* New York: Meridian, 1992.

King, Debra Walker. *Deep Talk: Reading African-American Literary Names.* Charlottesville: University of Virginia Press, 1998.

Kochman, Thomas, ed. *Rappin' and Stylin' Out: Communication in Urban Black America.* Urbana: University of Illinois Press, 1962.

Kostelanctz, Richard. *Politics in the African-American Novel: James Weldon Johnson, W.E.B. DuBois, Richard Wright, and Ralph Ellison.* Westport, Conn.: Greenwood Publishing Group, 1991.

Krasner, David. *Resistance, Parody, and Double Consciousness in African American Theatre 1895–1910.* New York: St. Martin's Press, 1997.

Lee, A. Robert. *Designs of Blackness: Mappings in the Literature and Culture of Afro-America.* London: Pluto Press, 1998.

Leech, Geoffrey. *Semantics.* New York: Penguin, 1975.

Leitch, Vincent, *American Literary Criticism from the Thirties to the Eighties.* New York: Columbia University Press, 1988.

Leitch, Vincent, William Cain, Laurie A. Finke, Barbara E. Johnson, John McGowan, and Jeffrey J. Williams, eds. *The Norton Anthology of Theory and Criticism.* New York: W. W. Norton, 2001.

Lester, Cheryl. "Letters." In *The Oxford Companion to African American Literature,* edited by William Andrews, Frances Smith Foster, and Trudier Harris, 435–37. New York: Oxford University Press, 1997.

Lester, Julius. *Black Folktales.* New York: Grove Press, 1991.

Levin, Amy K. *Africanism and Authenticity in African American Women's Novels.* Gainesville: University Press of Florida, 2003.

Levine, Lawrence W. *Black Culture and Black Consciousness: Afro-American Folk Thought from Slavery to Freedom.* New York: Oxford University Press, 1977.

Lewis, David Levering, ed. *The Portable Harlem Renaissance Reader.* New York: Penguin, 1995.

———. *W.E.B. DuBois: A Reader.* New York: Henry Holt, 1995.

———. *W.E.B. DuBois: The Biography of a Race, 1868–1919.* New York: Henry Holt, 1993.

Liddell, Janice Lee, and Yakini Belinda Kemp. *Arms Akimbo: Africana Women in Contemporary Literature.* Gainesville: University Press of Florida, 1999.

Little, Jonathan D. "Miscegenation." In *The Oxford Companion to African American Literature,* edited by William Andrews, Frances Smith Foster, and Trudier Harris, 503–5. New York: Oxford University Press, 1997.

Locke, Alain. "Art or Propaganda?" In *African American Literary Criticism, 1773 to 2000,* edited by Hazel Arnett Ervin, 49–50. New York: Twayne, 1999.

———. "Black Watch on the Rhine." *Opportunity* (January 1924): 6–9.

———, ed. *The New Negro: An Interpretation.* New York: Antheneum, 1925.

Logan, Shirley Wilson. *"We Are Coming": The Persuasive Discourse of Nineteenth-Century Black Women.* Carbondale: Southern Illinois University Press, 1999.

———, ed. *With Pen and Voice: A Critical Anthology of Nineteenth-Century African-American Women.* Carbondale: Southern Illinois University Press, 1995.

Long, Richard A., and Eugenia W. Collier, eds. *Afro-American Writing: An Anthology of Prose and Poetry, Vols. 1–2.* New York: New York University Press, 1972.

———. *Afro-American Writing: An Anthology of Prose and Poetry, Vol II.* New York: New York University Press, 1972.

Lott, Eric. *Love and Theft: Blackface Minstrelsy and the American Working Class.* New York: Oxford University Press, 1995.

Lott, Tommy L. *The Invention of Race: Black Culture and the Politics of Representation.* Malden, Mass.: Blackwell, 1999.

———. "A No Theory Theory of Contemporary Black Cinema." In *African American Literary Criticism, 1773 to 2000,* edited by Hazel Arnett Ervin, 339–48. New York: Twayne, 1999.

Lovell, John. "Reflections on the Origins of the Negro Spirituals." *Negro American Literature Forum* 3 (1969): 91–97.

Lowe, John. "Humor." In *The Oxford Companion to African American Literature,* edited by William Andrews, Frances Smith Foster, and Trudier Harris, 370–75. New York: Oxford University Press, 1997.

Lubiano, Wahneema, ed. *The House that Race Built.* New York: Vintage Books, 1998.

Lyotard, Jean-Francois. *The Postmodern Conditions: A Report on Knowledge.* Minneapolis: University of Minnesota Press, 1979.

Madgett, Naomi Long. *Remembrances of Spring: Collected Early Poems (Lotus Poetry).* East Lansing: Michigan State University Press, 1993.

Madhubuti, Haki R. *Black Men: Obsolete, Single, Dangerous?* Chicago: Third World Press, 1990.

———. *Earthquakes and Sunrise Missions.* Chicago: Third World Press, 1984.

Major, Clarence. *Calling the Wind, Twentieth-Century African-American Short Stories.* New York: Harper Perennial, 1993.

———. *Juba to Jive: A Dictionary of African-American Slang.* New York: Penguin, 1970.

Malone, Jacqui. *Steppin' on the Blues: The Visible Rhythms of African American Dance.* Urbana: University of Illinois Press, 1996.

Mama, Amina. *Beyond the Masks: Race, Gender, and Subjectivity.* New York: Routledge, 1995.

Man, Paul De. *Blindness and Insight: Essays in the Rhetoric of Contemporary Criticism.* Minneapolis: University of Minnesota Press, 1985.

Margolies, Edward, and David Bakish. *Afro-American Fiction 1853–1976: A Guide to Information Sources.* New York: Gale Group, 1979.

Marsh-Lockett, Carol P. *Black Women Playwrights: Visions on the American Stage.* New York: Garland, 1998.

———. "Womanism." In *The Oxford Companion to African American Literature,* edited by William Andrews, Frances Smith Foster, and Trudier Harris, 784–85. New York: Oxford University Press, 1997.

Martin, Reginald. *Ishmael Reed and the New Black Aesthetic*. New York: St. Martin's Press, 1988.

Martinez, Gerald, Diana Martinez, and Andres Chavez. *What It Is . . . What It Was!; The Black Film Explosion of the 70s in Words and Pictures*. New York: Hyperion, 1998.

Matthews, Geraldine. *Black American Writers, 1773 to 1949: A Bibliography and Union List*. Boston: G. K. Hall, 1976.

Matthews Victoria Earl. "The Value of Race Literature: An Address." In *With Pen and Voice: A Critical Anthology of Nineteenth-Century African-American Women*, edited by Shirley Wilson Logan. Carbondale: Southern Illinois University Press, 1995.

Mbiti, John. *African Religions and Philosophy*. 2nd ed. Westport, Conn.: Heinemann, 1992.

———. *Introduction to African Religion*. Jordan Hill, Oxford: Heinemann, 1975.

McCall, Nathan. *Makes Me Wanna Holler: A Young Black Man in America*. New York: Vintage Books, 1995.

McDowell, Deborah. "Afterword: Recovery Missions: Imaging the Body Ideals." In *Recovering the Black Female Body, Self-Representation by African American Women*, edited by Michael Bennett and Vanessa D. Dickerson, 296–317. New Brunswick, N.J.: Rutgers University Press, 2001.

———. *"Changing Same": Black Women's Literature, Criticism, and Theory*. Bloomington: Indiana University Press, 1995.

McDowell, Deborah, and Arnold Rampersad, eds. *Slavery and the Literary Imagination*. Baltimore: John Hopkins University Press, 1990.

McKay, Nellie Y., and Frances Smith Foster, eds. *Incidents in the Life of a Slave Girl* by Harriet Jacobs. New York: W. W. Norton, 2001.

McLendon, Jacquelyn Y. *The Politics of Color in the Fiction of Jesse Fauset and Nella Larsen*. Charlottesville: University of Virginia Press, 1995.

McMillan, Terry. Introduction, *Breaking Ice: An Anthology of Contemporary African-American Fiction*, edited by Terry McMillan, xv–xxiv. New York: Penguin, 1990. Reprinted in *African American Literary Criticism, 1773 to 2000*, edited by Hazel Arnett Ervin, 309–11. New York: Twayne, 1999.

McPherson, James Alan. *Hue and Cry: Short Stories by James Alan McPherson*. Boston: Little, Brown, 1969.

Melhem, D. H., ed. *Poetry and the Heroic Voice*. Lexington: University Press of Kentucky, 1987.

Miller, E. Ethelbert. *First Light: New and Selected Poems*. Baltimore: Black Classic Press, 1994.

Miller, R. Baxter. *Black American Literature and Humanism*. Lexington: Kentucky University Press, 1981.

———. *Langston Hughes and Gwendolyn Brooks: A Reference Guide*. New York: G. K. Hall, 1979.

Mishkin, Tracy, ed. *Literary Influence and African-American Writers: Collected Essays.* New York: Garland, 1995.

Mitchell, Angelyn. *Within the Circle: An Anthology of African American Literary Criticism from the Harlem Renaissance to the Present.* Durham, N.C.: Duke University Press, 1994.

Mitchell, Henry. *Black Preaching.* Philadelphia: Lippincott, 1970.

Moore, Gerald, and Ulli Beier. *The Penguin Book of Modern African Poetry.* New York: Penguin Books, 1963.

Moore, Lenard. *Forever Home.* Laurinburg, N.C.: Saint Andrews Press, 1992.

Moore, Opal. *Lot's Daughters.* Chicago: Third World Press, 2004

Mori, Aoi. *Toni Morrison and Womanist Discourse.* New York: Peter Lang, 1999.

Morrison, Toni. *Playing in the Dark: Whiteness and the Literary Imagination.* Cambridge: Harvard University Press, 1992.

———. "Rootedness: The Ancestor as Foundation" (1980). In *African American Literary Criticism, 1773 to 2000*, edited by Hazel Arnett Ervin, 198–202. New York: Twayne, 1999.

Moses, Wilson Jeremiah. *The Golden Age of Black Nationalism, 1850–1925.* New York: Oxford University Press, 1988.

Mosley, Albert G. *African Philosophy: Selected Readings.* Englewood Cliffs, N.J.: Prentice Hall, 1995.

Mufwene, Saltkoko S., and Nancy Condon, eds. *Africanisms in Afro-American Language Variations.* Athens: Georgia University Press, 1993.

Mullen, Harryette. "African Signs and Spirit Writing." In *African American Literary Theory: A Reader*, edited by Winston Napier, 623–42. New York: New York University Press, 2000.

Murray, Albert. *The Hero and the Blues.* New York: Vintage Books, 1996.

———. "Something Different, Something More." In *Anger and Beyond: The Negro Writer in the United States*, edited by Herbert Hill, 112–37. New York: Harper and Row, 1966.

———. *Stompin' the Blues* (1976) 25th anniv ed. Bt Bound, 2000.

Nadel, Alan. "Reading the Body: Meridian and the Archeology of Self." In *Alice Walker: Critical Perspectives Past and Present*, 155–67, edited by Henry Louis Gates, Jr., and K. A. Appiah. New York: Amistad, 1993.

Napier, Winston, ed. *African American Literary Theory: A Reader.* New York: New York University Press, 2000.

Neal, Larry. "The Black Arts Movement." In *African American Literary Criticism, 1773 to 2000*, edited by Hazel Arnett Ervin, 122–28. New York: Twayne, 1999.

———. "The Black Contribution to American Letters: Part II, The Writer as Activist—1960 and After." In *The Black American Reference Book*, edited by Mable M. Smythe, 785–88. Englewood Cliffs, N.J.: Prentice Hall, 1976.

Nelson, Emmanuel S., ed. *Critical Essays: Gay and Lesbian Writers of Color.* New York: Haworth Press, 1993.

Nero, Charles I. "Toward A Black Gay Aesthetic: Signifying in Contemporary Black

Gay Literature." In *African American Literary Criticism, 1773 to 2000*, edited by Hazel Arnett Ervin, 321–27. New York: Twayne, 1999.

Nielsen, Aldon Lynn. *Black Chant: Languages of African-American Postmodernism.* Cambridge: Cambridge University Press, 1997.

———. *Writing Between the Lines: Race and Intertextuality.* Athens: Georgia University Press, 1994.

O'Brien, John. *Interviews with Black Writers.* New York: Liveright, 1973.

Ogunyemi, Chikwenzi Okongo. "Womanism: The Dynamics of the Black Female Novel in English." *Signs* 11.1 (autumn 1985): 63–80.

Okpewho, Isidore. *African Oral Literature: Backgrounds, Character, and Continuity.* Bloomington: Indiana University Press, 1992.

———. *The Epic of Africa.* New York: Oxford University Press, 1979.

———. "The Resources of the Oral Epic." In *African Intellectual Heritage: A Book of Sources*, edited by Molefi Kete Asante and Abu S. Abarry, 119–30. Philadelphia: Temple University Press, 1996.

Olaniyan, Tejumola. *Scars of Conquest/Masks of Resistance: The Invention of Cultural Identities in African-American and Caribbean Drama.* New York: Oxford University Press, 1995.

O'Meally, Robert G., ed. *The Jazz Cadence of American Culture.* New York: Columbia University Press, 1998.

O'Meally, Robert G., and Geneviève E. Fabre, eds. *History and Memory in African American Culture.* New York: Oxford University Press, 1994.

O'Neale, Sondra A. *Jupiter Hammon and the Biblical Beginnings of African American Literature.* Lanham, Md.: Scarecrow Press, 1993.

Onyewuenyi, Innocent C. "Traditional African Aesthetics: A Philosophical Perspective." In *African Philosophy: Select Readings*, edited by Albert G. Mosley, 421–27. Englewood Cliffs, N.J.: Prentice Hall, 1995.

Outlaw, Lucius T. *On Race and Philosophy.* New York: Routledge, 1996.

Owomoyela, Oyekan. *A History of Twentieth-Century African Literature.* Lincoln: University of Nebraska Press, 1993.

Pate, Alex. "Making Home in the New Millennium: Reflections." In *African American Literary Criticism, 1773 to 2000*, edited by Hazel Arnett Ervin, 487–91. New York: Twayne, 1999.

Patterson, Massie, and Lionel Belasco. *Calypso Songs of the West Indies.* New York: M. Baron, 1943.

Perkins, Annie. "'To Cultivate a Space': The Sonnets of Gwendolyn Brooks in Light of the English Sonnet Tradition." Unpublished dissertation. Washington, D.C.: Howard University, 1989.

Perkins, William Eric. *Droppin' Science: Critical Essays on Rap Music and Hip Hop Culture.* Philadelphia: Temple University Press, 1995.

Peters, Erskine. "The Poetics of the Afro-American Spiritual." *Black American Literature Forum* 22.3 (fall 1989): 559–78.

Peterson, Bernard L. "Drama." In *The Oxford Companion to African American Litera-*

ture, edited by William Andrews, Frances Smith Foster, and Trudier Harris, 228–34. New York: Oxford University Press, 1997.

Peterson, Carla. *"Doers of the Word": African-American Women Writers and Speakers in the North, 1830–1900*. New York: Oxford University Press, 1995.

Petry, Ann. "New England's John Henry." *Negro Digest* 3.5 (March 1945): 71–73.

———. "The Novel as Social Criticism." In *African American Literary Criticism, 1773 to 2000*, edited by Hazel Arnett Ervin, 94–98. New York: Twayne, 1999.

Pettis, Joyce. *Toward Wholeness in Paule Marshall's Fiction*. Charlottesville: University Press of Virginia, 1995.

Pitts, Walter. "West Africa Poetics in the Black Preaching Style." *American Speech* 64 (1989): 137–49.

Plumpp, Sterling. *Black Rituals*. Chicago: Third World Press, 1987.

Porter, Dorothy [Wesley]. *Early Negro Writing: 1760–1837*. Baltimore: Black Classic Press, 1971.

———. *North American Negro Poets: A Bibliographical Checklist of Their Writings, 1760–1944*. New York: Martino Publishers, 2002.

Posnock, Ross. *Color and Culture: Black Writers and the Making of the Modern Intellectual*. Cambridge: Harvard University Press, 2000.

Potter, Russell. *Spectacular Vernaculars: Hip-Hop and the Politics of Postmodernism*. Albany: SUNY Press, 1995.

Powell, Richard J. "The Blues Aesthetic: Black Culture and Modernism" (1997). In *African American Literary Criticism, 1773 to 2000*, edited by Hazel Arnett Ervin, 289–302. New York: Twayne, 1999.

Pryse, Marjorie, and Hortense Spiller, eds. *Conjuring: Black Women Fiction, and Literary Tradition*. Bloomington: Indiana University Press, 1985.

Quashie, Kevin Everod, Joyce Lausch, and Keith D. Miller. *New Bones, Contemporary Black Writers in America*. Upper Saddle River, N.J.: Prentice Hall, 2001.

Rampersad, Arnold. "Biography, Autobiography, and Afro-American Culture." *Yale Review* 73 (autumn 1983): 1–16.

———. "Langston Hughes and Approaches to Modernism in the Harlem Renaissance." In *The Harlem Renaissance: Revaluations*, edited by Amrijit Singh, William S. Shriver, and Stanley Brodwin, 49–71. New York: Garland, 1989.

———. "Langston Hughes' *Fine Clothes to the Jew*." *Callaloo* 9.1 (winter 1986): 144–57.

———. *The Life of Langston Hughes, Vol 1: 1902–1941 (I, Too, Sing America)*. New York: Oxford University Press, 1986.

———. *The Life of Langston Hughes, Vol 2: 1941–1967 (I Dream a World)*. New York: Oxford University Press, 1988.

———, ed. *The Collected Poems of Langston Hughes*. New York: Knopf, 1995.

Randall, Dudley, ed. *The Black Poets*. New York: Bantam Books, 1971.

Redmond, Eugene B. *Drumvoices: The Mission of Afro-American Poetry*. Garden City, N.Y.: Anchor, 1976.

Redmond, Eugene B., ed. *Ark of Bones and Other Stories by Henry Dumas*. New York: Random House, 1974.

Redmond, Eugene B., ed. "The Black American Epic: Its Roots, Its Writers." *The Black Scholar* 11 (January 1971): 15–22.

———, ed. *Break Word with the World IV and V: A Commemorative Collection.* Edwardsville, Ill.: Department of English Language and Literature at Southern Illinois University, 1994–95.

Rivera, Louis Reyes, and Tony Medina. *Bum Rush the Page: A Def Poetry Jam.* New York: Three Rivers Press, 2001.

Roberts, John W. *From Trickster to Badman: The Black Folk Hero to Slavery and Freedom.* University Park: Pennsylvania State University Press, 1990.

Rodgers, Carolyn. "Black Poetry Where It's At." *Black World* 18.11 (September 1969): 7–16.

———. "Uh Nat'chal Thang—The WHOLE TRUTH—US." *Black World* 60 (September 1971): 4–14.

Ropo, Sekoni. *Folk Poetics: A Sociosemiotic Study of Yoruba Trickster Tales.* Westport, Conn.: Greenwood Press, 1994.

Rose, Tricia. *Black Noise: Rap Music and Black Culture in Contemporary American Music/Culture.* Hanover, N.H.: Wesleyan University Press, 1994.

Rosenthal, David H. *Hard Bop: Jazz and Black Music 1955–1965.* New York: Oxford University Press, 1992.

Rotenberg, Robert, and Gary McDonogh, eds. *The Cultural Meaning of Urban Space.* Westport, Conn.: Bergin and Garvey, 1993.

Rowell, Charles. *Afro-American Literary Bibliographies: An Annotated List of Bibliographical Guides for the Study of Afro-American Literature, Folklore and Related Areas.* Ann Arbor: University of Michigan Press, 1976.

———, ed. *Ancestral House, The Black Short Story in The Americas and Europe.* Boulder, Colo.: Westview Press, 1995.

Rushdy, Ashrah. "Reading Black, White and Gray in 1968: The Origins of the Contemporary Narrativity of Slavery." In *Criticism and the Color Line: Desegregating American Literary Studies,* edited by Henry Wonham, 63–94. New Brunswick, N.J.: Rutgers University Press, 1996.

Salaam, Kalamu ya. "Black Arts Movement." In *The Oxford Companion to Africa American Literature,* edited by William Andrews, Frances Smith Foster, and Trudier Harris, 70–74. New York: Oxford University Press, 1997.

Salaam, Mtume ya. "The Aesthetics of Rap." In *African American Literary Criticism, 1773 to 2000,* edited by Hazel Arnett Ervin, 445–52. New York: Twayne, 1999.

Samuels, Wilfred D. "Soothsayer and Interpreter: Darwin T. Turner and African American Literary Criticism." *Langston Hughes Review* 11.2 (fall 1992): 15–27.

Sanders, Kimberly. *Skin Deep, Spirit Strong: The Black Female Body in American Culture.* Ann Arbor: University of Michigan Press, 2003.

Sanders, Mark A. *Afro-Modernist Aesthetics and the Poetry of Sterling A. Brown.* Athens: Georgia University Press, 1999.

Schafer, William John, and Johannes Reidel. *The Art of Ragtime: Form and Meaning of an Original Black American Art.* Baton Rouge: Louisiana State University Press, 1973.

Schatt, Stanley. "You Must Go Home Again: Today's Afro-American Expatriate Writers." *Negro American Literature Forum* 7.3 (fall 1973): 80–82.

Schuyler, George. "Instructions for Contributors." *The Saturday Evening Quill* (April 1929): 20.

Sekora, John, and Darwin T. Turner, eds. *The Art of Slave Narrative: Original Essays in Criticism and Theory*. Macomb: Western Illinois University Press, 1982.

Sexton, Adam, ed. *Rap on Rap: Straight-up Talk on Hip Hop Culture*. New York: Delta, 1995.

Shapiro R. Norman, ed. *Negritude, Black Poetry from Africa and the Caribbean*. New York: October House, 1970.

Sherman, Joan Rita, ed. *Invisible Poets: Afro-Americans of the Nineteenth Century*. Urbana: University of Illinois Press, 1989.

Shields, John C. *Collected Works of Phillis Wheatley*. New York: Oxford University Press, 1989.

———. "Colonial and Early National Era." In *The Oxford Companion to African American Literature*, edited by William Andrews, Frances Smith Foster, and Trudier Harris, 445–48. New York: Oxford University Press, 1997.

———. "The Short Story." In *The Oxford Companion to African American Literature*, edited by William Andrews, Frances Smith Foster, and Trudier Harris, 660–65. New York: Oxford University Press, 1997.

Shockley, Ann. *Afro-American Women Writers, 1746–1933: An Anthology and Critical Guide*. New York: G. K. Hall, 1988.

Singh, Amrijit, William S. Shriver, and Stanley Brodwin, eds. *The Harlem Renaissance: Revaluations*. New York: Garland, 1989.

Smith, Barbara. *Home Girls: A Black Feminist Anthology*. New York: Kitchen Table: Women of Color Press, 1983.

———. "Toward a Black Feminist Criticism." In *African American Literary Criticism, 1773 to 2000*, edited by Hazel Arnett Ervin, 162–17. New York: Twayne, 1999.

———. *The Truth That Never Hurts: Writings on Race, Gender, and Freedom*. New Brunswick, N.J.: Rutgers University Press, 1998.

Smith, Gary. "The Literary Ballads of Sterling A. Brown." *CLA Journal* 32 (1989): 393–409.

Smith, Valerie. "Form and Ideology in Three Slave Narratives" (1987). *Self-Discovery and Authority in Afro-African Novels* by Valerie Smith, 9–41. Cambridge: Harvard University Press, 1991.

———. *Not Just Race, Not Just Gender: Black Feminist Readings*. New York: Routledge, 1998.

———. *Representing Blackness: Issues in Film and Video*. New Brunswick, N.J.: Rutgers University Press, 1997.

Smitherman, Geneva. *Black Talk: Words and Phrases from the Hood to the Amen Corner*. Boston: Houghton Mifflin, 1994.

———. *Talkin and Testifyin: The Language of Black America*. Boston: Houghton Mifflin, 1977.

Snead, James A. "Repetition as a figure of black culture" (1984). In *African American*

Literary Criticism, 1773 to 2000, edited by Hazel Arnett Ervin, 206–22. New York: Twayne, 1999.

Sollors, Werner, and Maria Diedrich, eds. *The Black Columbiad: Defining Moments in African American Literature and Culture.* Cambridge: Harvard University Press, 1994.

Southern, Eileen. *The Music of Black America: A History.* New York: W. W. Norton, 1997.

Southern, Eileen, and Josephine Wright. *African-American Traditions in Song, Sermons, Tales, and Dance, 1600–1920: An Annotated Bibliography of Literature, Collections and Artworks.* Westport, Conn.: Greenwood Publishing Group, 1990.

Spencer, Jon Michael, ed. *Sacred Music of the Secular City: From Blues to Rap.* Durham, N.C.: Duke University Press, 1992.

Spillers, Hortense. "All the Things You Could Be By Now If Sigmund Freud's Wife Was Your Mother." In *African American Literary Theory: A Reader,* edited by Winston Napier, 580–97. New York: New York University Press, 2000.

———. ed. *Comparative American Identities: Race, Sex, and Nationality in the Modern Text.* New York: Routledge, 1991.

Standley, Fred L., and Louis H. Pratt. *Conversations with James Baldwin.* Jackson: University Press of Mississippi, 1989.

Stepto, Robert B. *From Behind the Veil: A Study of Afro-American Narrative.* Urbana: University of Illinois Press, 1991.

Stepto, Robert B., and Dexter Fisher, eds. *African American Literature: The Reconstruction of Instruction.* New York: Modern Language Association, 1979.

Stewart, Jeffrey C., ed. *The Critical Temper of Alain Locke: A Selection of His Essays on Art and Culture.* New York: Garland, 1983.

Stuckey, Sterling. *Slave Culture.* New York: Oxford University Press, 1987.

Sundquist, Eric J. *To Wake the Nations: Race in the Making of American Literature.* Cambridge: Harvard University Press, 1993.

———, ed. *The Oxford W.E.B. Du Bois Reader.* New York: Oxford University Press, 1996.

Tate, Claudia. *Black Women Writers at Work.* New York: Continuum, 1988.

———. *Domestic Allegories of Political Desire: The Black Heroine's Text at the Turn of the Century.* New York: Oxford University Press, 1992.

———. *Psychoanalysis and Black Novels: Desire and the Protocols of Race.* New York: Oxford University Press, 1998.

Tate, Greg. "Cult-Nats Meet Freaky Deke." *Voices Literary Supplement* (December 1986): 5–8.

Taylor, Clyde. "Salt Peanuts." *Callaloo* 5 (1982): 1–11.

Thelwell, Michael. "Toward a Collective Vision: Issues in International Literary Criticism." In *Cornerstones: An Anthology of African American Literature,* edited by Melvin Donalson, 913–25. New York: St. Martin's Press, 1996.

Thomas, H. Nigel. *From Folklore to Fiction: A Study of Folk Heroes and Rituals in the Black American Novel.* Westport, Conn.: Greenwood Publishing Group, 1988.

Thomas, Lorenzo. "The Blues Aesthetic." In *The Oxford Companion to African Ameri-*

can Literature, edited by William Andrews, Frances Smith Foster, and Trudier Harris, 87–89. New York: Oxford University Press, 1997.

———. *Extraordinary Measures: Afrocentric Modernism and Twentieth-Century American Poetry*. Tuscaloosa: University of Alabama Press, 2000.

Thompson, Robert Farris. *Black Gods and Kings: Yoruba Art at UCLA*. Bloomington: Indiana University Press, 1976.

———. *Flash of the Spirit, African and Afro-American Art and Philosophy*. New York: Random House, 1984.

Thompson, Ronald. *Africa and Unity: The Evolution of Pan Africanism*. London: Longman, 1969.

Tracy, Stephen C. *Langston Hughes and the Blues*. Urbana and Chicago: University of Illinois Press, 1988.

Traylor, Eleanor W. "A Blues View of Life (Literature and The Blues Vision)." In *African American Literary Criticism, 1773 to 2000*, edited by Hazel Arnett Ervin, 285–88. New York: Twayne, 1999.

Troupe, Quincy, and Rainer Schulte. *Giant Talk: An Anthology of Third World Writers*. New York: Random House, 1975.

Turner, Darwin T. "Afro-American Literary Critics: An Introduction." *Black World* (July 1970): 54–57.

———. "The Negro Novelist and the South." *Southern Humanities Review* 1(1967): 21–29.

Turner, Lorenzo D., and Kathera Wyly Mills. *Africanisms in the Gullah Dialect*. Columbia: University of South Carolina Press, 2000.

Twining, Mary A., and Keith Baird. *Sea Island Roots: African Presence in the Carolinas and Georgia*. Lawrenceville, N.J.: Africa World Press, 1991.

Valade, Roger M. *The Essential Black Literature Guide*. New York: Visible Ink Press, 1996.

Van Deburg, William L. *Black Camelot: African-American Culture Heroes in Their Times, 1960–1980*. Chicago: University of Chicago Press, 1997.

Wade-Gayles, Gloria. *No Crystal Stair: Visions of Race and Gender in Black Women's Fiction*. New York: Pilgrim Press, 1997.

Walker, Alice. "The Black Writer and the Southern Experience." In *In Search of Our Mothers' Gardens: Womanist Prose*, by Alice Walker. New York: Harcourt Brace Jovanovich, 1983, 15–21.

———. *In Search of Our Mothers' Gardens: Womanist Prose*. New York: Harcourt Brace Jovanovich, 1983.

Walker, Margaret. *Richard Wright, Daemonic Genius: A Portrait of the Man, A Critical Look at His Work*. New York: Amistad, 1988.

Wall, Cheryl A. *Changing Our Own Words, Essays on Criticism, Theory, and Writing by Black Women*. New Brunswick, N.J.: Rutgers University Press, 1989.

Wallace, Michelle. *Invisibility Blues: From Pop to Theory*. London: Verso, 1990.

Walters, Ronald. *Pan-Africanism in the African Diaspora: An Analysis of Modern Afrocentric Political Movements*. Detroit: Wayne State University Press, 1993.

Ward, Douglas Turner. "Needed: A Theater for Black Themes." *Negro Digest* 37 (December 1967): 34–39.

Ward, Jerry W., Jr. "Alvin Aubert: The Levee, the Blues, the Mighty Mississippi." In *African American Literary Criticism, 1773 to 2000*, edited by Hazel Arnett Ervin, 278–84. New York: Twayne, 1999.

———. Foreword, *Black Southern Voices: An Anthology*, 5–9. New York: Meridian, 1992.

———, ed. *Trouble the Waters: 250 Years of African-American Poetry*. New York: Mentor, 1997.

Wardi, Anissa Janine. *Death and the Arc of Mourning in African American Literature*. Gainesville: University Press of Florida, 2003.

Warren, Kenneth W. *Black and White Strangers: Race and American Literary Realism*. Chicago: University of Chicago Press, 1995.

Washington, James Melvin, ed. *A Testament of Hope: The Essential Writings and Speeches of Martin Luther King, Jr.* San Francisco: Harper Collins, 1986.

Washington, Mary Helen. *Black-Eyed Susans and Midnight Birds: Stories by and About Black Women*. New York: Anchor, 1989.

———. *Invented Lives: Narratives of Black Women, 1860–1960*. New York: Anchor Books/Doubleday, 1987.

———. Introduction, *A Voice from the South* by Anna Julia Cooper, xxvii–liv. New York: Oxford University Press, 1988.

Washington, Robert E. *The Ideologies of African American Literature: From the Harlem Renaissance to the Black Nationalist Revolt*. Lanham, Md.: Rowman and Littlefield, 2001.

Watkins, Mel. *On the Real Side: Laughing, Lying and Signifying—the Underground Tradition of African-American Humor that Transformed American Culture from Slavery to Richard Pryor*. New York: Simon and Schuster, 1994.

Watta, Oumarou. *Allegory for Real: A Theory of the Afro-American Novel: Essays*. Washington, D.C.: Pyramid Papyrus, 1992.

Watts, Jerry Gafio. *Heroism and the Black Intellectual: Ralph Ellison, Politics, and Afro-American Intellectual Life*. Chapel Hill: North Carolina University Press, 1994.

Weixlmann, Joe, and Chester J. Fontenot, eds. *Black American Prose Theory: Studies in Black American Literature*, vol 1. Greenwood, Fla.: Penkeville, 1984.

———, eds. *Belief Versus Theory in Black American Literary Criticism: Studies in Black American Literature*, vol. 2. Greenwood, Fla.: Penkeville, 1986.

———, eds. *Black Feminist Criticism and Critical Theory*, vol 3. Greenwood, Fla.: Penkeville, 1988.

Welsh-Asante, Kariamu, ed. *The African Aesthetic: Keeper of the Traditions*. Westport, Conn.: Greenwood, 1993.

Werner, Craig H. "Chicago Renaissance." In *The Oxford Companion to African American Literature*, edited by William Andrews, Frances Smith Foster, and Trudier Harris, 132–33. New York: Oxford University Press, 1997.

———. "Early Twentieth Century." In *The Oxford Companion to African American*

Literature, edited by William Andrews, Frances Smith Foster, and Trudier Harris, 453–56. New York: Oxford University Press, 1997.

———. *Playing the Changes: From Afro-Modernism to the Jazz Impulse*. Urbana: University of Illinois Press, 1994.

West, Cornel. *Race Matters*. Boston: Beacon Press, 1993.

West, Elizabeth J. "Black Nationalism." In *The Oxford Companion to African American Literature*, edited by William Andrews, Frances Smith Foster, and Trudier Harris, 75–79. New York: Oxford University Press, 1997.

Whitlow, Roger. *Black American Literature: A Critical History*. Chicago: Burnham, Inc., 1973.

Wideman, John Edgar. Preface, *Breaking Ice: An Anthology of Contemporary African-American Fiction*, edited by Terry McMillan, v–x. New York: Penguin, 1990. Reprinted in *African American Literary Criticism, 1773 to 2000*, edited by Hazel Arnett Ervin, 303–8. New York: Twayne, 1999.

Williams, Emily Allen. *Anglophone Caribbean Poetry, 1970–2001: An Annotated Bibliography*. Westport, Conn.: Greenwood Publishing Group, 2002.

Williams, John A., and Charles F. Harris. *Amistad 1*. New York: Random House, 1970.

———. *Amistad 2*. New York: Random House, 1971.

Williams, Pontheola T. *Robert Hayden: A Critical Analysis of His Poetry*. Urbana: University of Illinois Press, 1987.

Williams, Sherley Anne. "The Blues Roots of Contemporary Afro-American Poetry" (1979). In *African American Literary Criticism, 1773 to 2000*, edited by Hazel Arnett Ervin, 179–91. New York: Twayne, 1999.

———. *Dessa Rose*. New York: William Morrow, 1986.

———. *Give Birth to Brightness: A Thematic Study in Neo-Black Literature*. New York: Dial Press, 1972.

———. "Some Implication of Womanist Theory." In *African American Literary Theory: A Reader*, edited by Winston Napier, 348–68. New York: New York University Press, 2000.

Williams, Susan Miller, and Charles Colcock Jones. *Gullah Folktales from the Georgia Coast*. Athens: University of Georgia Press, 2000.

Willis, Susan. *Specifying: Black Women Writing the American Experience*. Madison: University of Wisconsin Press, 1990.

Wintz, Cary D. *Black Culture and the Harlem Renaissance*. Houston, Tex.: Rice University Press, 1995.

Woll, Allen L. *Black Musical Theatre: From Coontown to Dreamgirls*. Baton Rouge: Louisiana State University Press, 1989.

Wonham, Henry B., ed. *Criticism on the Color Line: Desegregating American Literary Studies*. New Brunswick, N.J.: Rutgers University Press, 1996.

Wright, Richard. "A Blueprint for Negro Writing" (1937). In *The Portable Harlem Renaissance Reader*, ed. David L. Lewis. New York: Viking Press, 1994.

———. "How Bigger Was Born." In *Native Son* by Richard Wright, 433–62. New York: Perennial Classics, 1998.

Yancy, George, ed. *African American Philosophers: 17 Conversations*. New York: Routledge, 1998.

Yancy, Preston. *The Afro-American Short Story: A Comprehensive Annotated Index with Selected Commentaries*. Westport, Conn.: Greenwood Publishing Group, 1986.

Yarborough, Richard. "The Quest for the American Dream in Three Afro-American Novels: If He Hollers, Let Him Go, The Street, and Invisible Man," *MELUS* 8.4 (1981): 33–59.

Yearwood, Gladstone. *Black Film as a Signifying Practice: Cinema, Narration and the African American Aesthetic Tradition*. Lawrenceville, N.J.: Africa World Press, 1998.

Young, Kevin, ed. *Giant Steps, The New Generation of African American Writers*. New York: Perennial, 2000.

Young, S. Glenell, and Janet L. Sims-Wood. *The Psychology and Mental Health of Afro-American Women: A Selected Bibliography*. Toudle Hills, Md.: Afro Resources, 1984.

Index of Terms

realism, 111

Reconstruction and postmodernism period, 112

Reconstruction, reaction, and realism period, 113

Renaissances and radicalism period, 114

repetition, 115

representation, 115

resolution, 115

rhetorical question, 116

rhyme, 116

rhyme scheme, 116

rhythm and blues, the, 117

riff, 117

ring shout, 117

rites de passage, 118

ritual, 118

roman à clef, 118

romance, 118

rootlessness, 118

"safe space," 118

satire/satirical, 118

saturation, 118

scansion, 119

scat, 119

science fiction, 119

secret societies, 119

semiotics, 120

sermon, 120

sermonic rhetoric, 121

setting, 121

sexuality, 121

shadow, 121

Shakespearean sonnet, 121

short story, 121

shouts, 122

"shucking and jiving," 122

sign, 122

signification, 122

signifying/signification, 122

simile, 122

skaz, 123

slang, 123

slave narrative, 124

sociological novel, 124

soliloquy, 124

sonnet, 124

"sorrow songs," 124

soul, 124

sounding, 124

sounds, 125

South, the, 125

South Side Writers, the, 125

speakerly text, 125

"speaking in tongues," 125

specifying, 126

speculative fiction, 126

"spirit possession," 126

"spirit-writing," 126

spirituals, 127

spirituality, 127

"spoken word, the," 127

stanza, 128

stereotypes, 128

storytelling, 128

stranger, 128

stream of consciousness, 128

structuralism, 128

style, 128

subjective correlative, 129

subversive, 130

symbols/symbolism, 130

synchronicity, 130

syncopation, 130

synecdoche, 130

tale, 130

"tale-within-a-tale," 130

"talented tenth, the," 130

talking book, the, 130

testifyin/testifying, 131

theater/theatre, 131

"theatre of the absurd," 131

theme, 131

Third World, 131

toasts, 131

tone, 132

tradition, 132

tragedy, 132

trickster, 133

"two-ness," 133

ubi sunt, 133

Hazel Arnett Ervin is currently an associate professor of English at Morehouse College, where she teaches courses in African American literature such as the Harlem Renaissance, the contemporary novel, and major authors. The UNCF/Mellon Fellow and a Fulbright scholar of 2001, she is also the recipient of several NEH awards. Her literary interests include Ann Petry and African American literary criticism. In addition to articles that have appeared in the *CLA Journal* and the *Langston Hughes Review,* Ervin's publications include *Ann Petry: A Bio-Bibliography* (1993); *African American Literary Criticism, 1773–2000* (1999); and the coedited *Ann Petry's Short Fiction: Critical Essays* (2004). Forthcoming works include *The Critical Response to Ann Petry, An Ann Petry Encyclopedia,* and a book on Gullah literary culture.